P9-DHN-000

EVERYBODY'S NORMAL TILL YOU GET TO KNOW THEM

Other Resources by John Ortberg

If You Want to Walk On Water, You've Got to Get Out of the Boat

If You Want to Walk On Water, You've Got to Get Out of the Boat audio

The Life You've Always Wanted

The Life You've Always Wanted audio

Love Beyond Reason

JOHN ORTBERG

EVERYBODY'S NORMAL TILL YOU GET TO KNOW THEM

GRAND RAPIDS, MICHIGAN 49530 USA

We want to hear from you. Please send your comments about this book to us in care of the address below. Thank you.

ZONDERVAN™

Everybody's Normal Till You Get to Know Them

This title is also available as a Zondervan audio product.
Visit www. zondervan.com/audiopages for more information.

Requests for information should be addressed to:

Zondervan, *Grand Rapids, Michigan 49530*

Library of Congress Cataloging-in-Publication Data

Ortberg, John.
Everybody's normal till you get to know them / John Ortberg.
p. cm.
Includes bibliographical references.
ISBN 0-310-22864-6
1. Community—Religious aspects—Christianity. I. Title.
BV625.O78 2003
248.4—dc21
2002154461

This edition printed on acid-free paper.

Other translations used are *Today's New International Version* (TNIV), the *New Revised Standard Version* (NRSV), the King James Version (KJV), the *New American Standard Bible* (NASB), the *New King James Version* (NKJV), and the *Good News Bible* (GNB). Emphasis is added by the author in some verses.

Printed in the United States of America

06 07 08 09 10 /❖DCI/ 20 19 18 17 16

To Rick Blackmon,
who knows all about me
and loves me anyway

CONTENTS

PART 3: THE SECRETS OF STRONG RELATIONSHIPS

ACKNOWLEDGMENTS

If it's true that all books are in some sense the product of community, then it is especially so when the book is *about* community.

I am grateful to those who read parts or all of the manuscript and offered suggestions to improve it: Becky Brauer, Mindy Caliguire, Bill Donahue, and John Ortberg Sr. Tiffany Staman is a joy to have both as an administrative assistant and as a cousin; she added to the value of this manuscript in more ways than I can count. Jack Kuhatschek is everything an author could hope for in an editor: encourager, wisdom figure, critic, and friend.

As always, Nancy has been a patient sounding board and a ceaselessly energetic partner in the project of life.

Laura, Mallory, and Johnny give me a treasured gift I had never anticipated—not just someone to write about (an occupational hazard for all children whose parents write), but someone to write *for*.

PART 1

"NORMAL: THERE'S NO SUCH THING, DEAR"

CHAPTER 1

THE PORCUPINE'S DILEMMA

To make a start where we are, we must recognize that our world is not normal, but only usual at present.

DALLAS WILLARD

Community is the place where the person you least want to live with always lives.

HENRI NOUWEN

In certain stores you will find a section of merchandise available at greatly reduced prices. The tip-off is a particular tag you will see on all the items in that area. Each tag carries the same words: *as is*.

This is a euphemistic way of saying, "These are damaged goods." Sometimes they're called *slightly irregular.* The store is issuing you fair warning: "This is the department of Something's-Gone-Wrong. You're going to find a flaw here: a stain that won't come out; a zipper that won't zip; a button that won't butt—there will be a problem. These items are *not normal*.

"We're not going to tell you where the flaw is. You'll have to look for it.

"But we know it's there. So when you find it—and you will find it—don't come whining and sniveling to us. Because there is a fundamental rule when dealing with merchandise in this corner of the store: No returns. No refunds. No exchanges. If you were looking for perfection, you walked down the wrong aisle. You have received fair warning. If you want this item, there is only one way to obtain it. You must take it *as is*."

When you deal with human beings, you have come to the "as-is" corner of the universe. Think for a moment about someone in your life. Maybe the person you know best, love most. That person is *slightly irregular*.

That person comes with a little tag: *There's a flaw here. A streak of deception, a cruel tongue, a passive spirit, an out-of-control temper. I'm not going to tell you where it is, but it's there. So when you find it—and you will find it—don't be surprised. If you want to enter a relationship with this model, there is only one way. "As is."*

If you were looking for perfection, you've walked down the wrong aisle.

We are tempted to live under the illusion that somewhere out there are people who are normal. In the movie *As Good As It Gets*, Helen Hunt is wracked by ambivalence toward Jack Nicholson. He is kind and generous to her and her sick son, but he is also agoraphobic, obsessive-compulsive, and terminally offensive: If rudeness were measured in square miles, he'd be Texas. In desperation, Helen finally cries to her mother: *I just want a normal boyfriend.*

Oh, her mother responds in empathy, *everybody wants one of those. There's no such thing, dear.*

When we enter relationships with the illusion that people are normal, we resist the truth that they are not. We enter an endless attempt to fix them, control them, or pretend that they are what they're not. One of the great marks of maturity is to accept the fact that everybody comes "as is."

Dietrich Bonhoeffer said people enter relationships with their own particular ideals and dreams of what community should look like. He wrote surprising words:

> But God's grace quickly frustrates all such dreams. A great disillusionment with others, with Christians in general, and, if we

> are fortunate, with ourselves, is bound to overwhelm us as surely as God desires to lead us to an understanding of genuine Christian community.... The sooner this moment of disillusionment comes over the individual and the community, the better for both.... Those who love their dream of a Christian community more than the Christian community itself become destroyers of that Christian community even though their personal intentions may be ever so honest, earnest, and sacrificial.

Everybody's Weird

Of course, the most painful part of this is realizing that I am in the "as-is" department as well. Throughout history human beings have resisted owning up to that little tag. We try to separate the world into normal, healthy people (like us) and difficult people. Sometime ago the title of a magazine article caught my eye: "Totally Normal Women Who Stalk Their Ex-Boyfriends."

The phrase that struck me was "totally normal women." What would one of these look like (or a totally normal man, for that matter)? And if the obsessive stalking of a past lover is not just normal but *totally* normal, how far would you have to go to be a little strange?

We all want to look normal, to think of ourselves as normal, but the writers of Scripture insist that no one is "totally normal"—at least not as God defines normal. "*All* we like sheep have gone astray," they tell us. "*All* have sinned and fall short of the glory of God."

This explains a very important aspect of the opening pages of Scripture.

One of the most ironic remarks about the Bible I hear from time to time is when someone says that it's a book about pious, stained-glass characters who do not reflect the real world.

I always know that means they haven't read it. Have you ever noticed how many messed-up families there are in Genesis?

Here's a quick summary:

Cain is jealous of Abel and kills him. Lamech introduces polygamy to the world. Noah—the most righteous man of his generation—gets drunk and curses his own grandson.

Lot, when his home is surrounded by residents of Sodom who want to violate his visitors, offers instead that they can have sex with his daughters. Later on, his daughters get him drunk and get impregnated by him—and Lot is the most righteous man in Sodom!

Abraham plays favorites between his sons Isaac and Ishmael; they're estranged.

Isaac plays favorites between his sons Jacob and Esau; they're bitter enemies for twenty years. Jacob plays favorites between Joseph and his other eleven sons; the brothers want to kill Joseph and end up selling him into slavery.

Their marriages are disasters:

Abraham has sex with his wife's servant, then sends her and their son off to the wilderness at his wife's request. Isaac and Rebekah fight over which boy gets the blessing. Jacob marries two wives and ends up with both of their maids as his concubines as well when they get into a fertility contest.

Jacob's firstborn son, Reuben, sleeps with his father's concubine.

Another son, Judah, sleeps with his daughter-in-law when she disguises herself as a prostitute. She does this because she is childless since her first two husbands—both sons of Judah—were so wicked that God killed them both; and Judah reneged on his obligations to her.

These people need a therapist.

These are not the Waltons. They need Dr. Phil, Dr. Laura, Dr. Ruth, Dr. Spock, Dr. Seuss—they need somebody. (Feel any better about your family?)

Why does the writer of Genesis include all this stuff?

There's a very important reason. The writer of Scripture is trying to establish a deep theological truth: *Everybody's weird.*

Every one of us—*all we like sheep*—have habits we can't control, past deeds we can't undo, flaws we can't correct. This is the cast of characters God has to work with. In the way that glass is predisposed to shatter and nitroglycerin is predisposed to explode, we are predisposed to do wrong when conditions are right. That predisposition is what theologians call "depravity." We lie and sacrifice integrity for the sake of a few dollars ("I don't understand, Officer—my speedometer must be broken"). We gossip for the sake of a few moments' feeling of superiority. We try to create false impressions of productivity at work to advance more rapidly. (A new software package allows you to surf the net at work, then with one click switch to a fake screen that makes it look as if you're working on a project; it's called "boss screen.") We seek to intimidate employees or children to gain control, or simply to enjoy the feeling of power.

Everybody's weird. This is such a fundamental insight, you may want to close the book for a moment and share this thought with the person closest to you. Or the person it most reminds you of. Or perhaps these are the same person.

Because we know in our hearts that this is not the way we're supposed to be, we try to hide our weirdness. *Every one of us* pretends to be healthier and kinder than we really are; we all engage in what might be called "depravity management."

Every once in a while somebody's "as-is" tag becomes high profile. A Pulitzer Prize-winning historian is guilty of plagiarism; a politician's career explodes in sexual scandal; a powerful CEO resigns in disgrace over illegal document shredding. What's surprising is not that such things happen; it's that the general public response is, "Can you believe it? And they seemed so *normal.*" As if you and I, of course, would be incapable of such behavior.

***Every one of us* pretends to be healthier and kinder than we really are; we all engage in what might be called "depravity management."**

The problem with the human race is not that we have just a few bad apples in our midst. Writers in the field known as abnormal psychology work hard to distinguish the abnormal from the normal among us. One of the dangers in studying the topic, sometimes called the "intern syndrome," is that students start to see themselves in every diagnosis. "There is almost no one who has not harbored secret doubts about his or her normality," a recent textbook says. But writers in Scripture say that when it comes to the most important form of pathology, we are all in the same diagnostic category: "All we like sheep have gone astray. . . ." From a spiritual perspective, our "secret doubts about our normality" have something important to tell us. As Neil Plantinga puts it, "In a biblical view of the world, sin is a familiar, even predictable part of life, but *it is not normal*. And the fact that 'everybody does it' doesn't make it normal."

From the time of Adam in the Garden of Eden, sin and hiding have been as inevitable as death and taxes. Some people are pretty good at hiding. But the weirdness is still there. Get close enough to anyone, and you will see it. *Everybody's normal till you get to know them*.

The Longing to Connect

And yet . . .

The yearning to attach and connect, to love and be loved, is the fiercest longing of the soul. Our need for community with people and the God who made us is to the human spirit what food and air and water are to the human body. That need will not go away even in the face of all the weirdness. It marks us from the nursery to the convalescent home. An infant lifts up her face hopefully, she holds out two stubby little arms in her desire to be held, she beams a smile of delight when she is picked up and rocked—what heart can keep from melting?

At the other end of the spectrum, the widowed father of a man I know falls in love with a woman at his church. He proposes, she accepts. They walk down the aisle. He is eighty-four, a retired doctor; she is eighty-one, a retired missionary. It is her first marriage. She kissed dating good-bye during the Truman administration. You would think she might have given up on the whole marriage deal by now; yet she finds not only Mr. Right, but *Dr.* Right. They throw off the age curve of the Newly Married class by six decades.

Our need for community with people and the God who made us is to the human spirit what food and air and water are to the human body.

As frustrating as people can be, it's hard to find a good substitute. A friend of mine was ordering breakfast during a recent trip in the South. He saw grits on the menu, and being a Dutchman who spent most of his life in Michigan, he had never been very clear on the nature of this item. So he asked the waitress, "What exactly is a grit?"

Her response was a classic. "Honey," she said (in the South, waitresses are required by law to address all customers as "honey"), "Honey, they don't come by themselves."

Grits don't exist in isolation. No grit is an island, entire unto itself. Every grit is a part of the mainland, a piece of the whole. You can't order a single grit. They're a package deal.

"Call it a clan, call it a tribe, call it a network, call it a family," says Jane Howard. "Whatever you call it, whoever you are, you need one." It is not good for man to be alone. Dallas Willard says, "The natural condition of life for human beings is reciprocal rootedness in others." Honey, you don't come by yourself.

Edward Hallowell, a senior lecturer at Harvard Medical School, speaks of the basic human need for community. He uses the term *connection:* the sense of being part of something that matters, something larger than ourselves. We need face-to-face interactions; we need to be seen and known and served and do these same things for others. We need to bind ourselves to each other with promises of love and loyalty made and kept. These connections involve other people, of course (and especially God); but Hallowell observes that people draw life even from connecting to pets, to music, or to nature.

There is a reason for this. Neil Plantinga notes that the Hebrew prophets had a word for just this kind of connectedness of all things: *shalom*—"the webbing together of God, humans, and all creation in justice, fulfillment, and delight." *Try to imagine*, the old prophets told people then, and tell us still, *what such a state of affairs would look like*.

In a world where *shalom* prevailed, all marriages would be healthy and all children would be safe. Those who have too much would give to those who have too little. Israeli and Palestinian children would play together on the West Bank; their parents would build homes for one another. In offices and corporate boardrooms, executives would secretly scheme to help their colleagues succeed; they would compliment them behind their backs. Tabloids would be filled with accounts of courage and moral beauty. Talk shows would feature mothers and daughters who love each other deeply, wives who give birth to their husbands' children, and men who secretly enjoy dressing as men.

Disagreements would be settled with grace and civility. There would still be lawyers, perhaps, but they would have really useful jobs like delivering pizza, which would be non-fat and low in cholesterol. Doors would have no locks; cars would have no alarms. Schools would no longer need police presence or even hall monitors; students and teachers and janitors would honor and value one another's work. At recess, every kid would get picked for a team.

Churches would never split.

People would be neither bored nor hurried. No father would ever again say, "I'm too busy," to a disappointed child. Our national sleep deficit would be paid off. Starbucks would still exist but would sell only decaf.

This is what we would look like if we lived up to the norms God set for human life—if our world were truly *normal*. One day it will be.

Divorce courts and battered-women shelters would be turned into community recreation centers. Every time one human being touched another, it would be to express encouragement, affection, and delight.

No one would be lonely or afraid. People of different races would join hands; they would honor and be enriched by their differences and be united in their common humanity.

And in the center of the entire community would be its magnificent architect and most glorious resident: the God whose presence fills each person with unceasing splendor and ever-increasing delight.

The writers of Scripture tell us that this vision is the way things are supposed to be. This is what we would look like if we lived up to the norms God set for human life—if our world were truly *normal*. One day it will be.

A Matter of Life or Death

Dietrich Boenhoeffer wrote, "Whoever cannot stand being in community should beware of being alone." Some people fear being hurt or losing their freedom if they get too close to others, so they withdraw into work or hobbies or watching TV. But isolation does not work either. I didn't get here on my own, and my identity and purpose are tied inextricably to relationships: I am the son of John Sr. and Kathy, the brother of Barbie and Bart, the husband of Nancy, the father of Laura, Mallory, and Johnny. I am a pastor, friend, neighbor. I was not put on this earth merely to please or amuse myself. And people who seek to live for themselves alone, says Bonhoeffer, "plunge into the bottomless pit of vanity, self-infatuation, and despair." We are all part of the grits. And, honey, we don't come by ourselves.

This connectedness has also been called "reciprocal rootedness." We were created to draw life and nourishment from one another the way the roots of an oak tree draw life from the soil. Community—living in vital connectedness with others—is essential to human life. Researcher Rene Spitz showed that infants who are not held and hugged and touched, even if they have parents who give them food and clothes, suffer from retarded neurological development. Also, the earliest studies of suicide showed the major risk factor to be social isolation.

But the most important reason to pursue deep community is not for the physical or emotional benefits it brings, great as those may be. Community is the place God made us for. Community is the place where God meets us.

How to Get Close without Getting Hurt

Here's the rub: How do you pursue this beautiful dream of community with actual, real-life people? Weird, not-normal, as-is, dysfunctional people? Your friends, your colleagues, your spouse, your children, your parents, your small group, your church, your coworkers? Can it really happen?

The North American Common Porcupine is a member of the rodent family that has around 30,000 quills attached to his body. Each quill can be driven into an enemy, and the enemy's body heat will cause the microscopic barb to expand and become more firmly embedded. The wounds can fester; the more dangerous ones, affecting vital organs, can be fatal.

The porcupine is not generally regarded as a lovable animal. The Latin name *(erethizon dorsatum)* means "the irritable back," and they all have one. Books and movies celebrate almost every conceivable animal—not just dogs and cats and horses, but also pigs (*Babe*; Arnold Ziffel from the old TV show *Green Acres*), spiders *(Charlotte's Web)*, dolphins (*Flipper*), bears (*Gentle Ben*), and killer whales *(Free Willy)*.

Even skunks have Pepe Le Pew. I don't know of any famous porcupines. I don't know any child who has one for a pet.

As a general rule, porcupines have two methods for handling relationships: withdrawal and attack. They either head for a tree or stick out their quills. They are generally solitary animals. Wolves run in packs; sheep huddle in flocks; we speak of herds of elephants and gaggles of geese and even a murder of crows. But there is no special name for a group of porcupines. They travel alone.

Porcupines don't always want to be alone. In the late autumn, a young porcupine's thoughts turn to love. But love turns out to be a risky business when you're a porcupine. Females are open to dinner and a movie only once a year; the window of opportunity closes quickly. And a girl porcupine's "no" is the most widely respected turndown in all the animal kingdom. Fear and anger make them dangerous little creatures to be around.

This is the Porcupine's Dilemma: How do you get close without getting hurt?

This is our dilemma, too. Every one of us carries our own little arsenal. Our barbs have names like rejection, condemnation, resentment, arrogance, selfishness, envy, contempt. Some people hide them better than others, but get close enough and you will find out they're there. They burrow under the skin of our enemies; they can wound and fester and even kill. We, too, learn to survive through a combination of withdrawal and attack. We, too, find ourselves hurting (and being hurt by) those we long to be closest to.

This is the Porcupine's Dilemma: How do you get close without getting hurt? This is our dilemma, too.

Yet we, too, want to get close. We meet neighbors, go on dates, join churches, form friendships, get married, have children. We try to figure out how to get close without getting hurt. We wonder if there isn't a softer, less-barbed creature out there—a mink or an otter, perhaps.

And of course, we can usually think of a number of particularly prickly porcupines in our lives. But the problem is not just them. I'm somebody's porcupine. So are you.

Attack and Withdraw

On a Sunday afternoon as I write these words, the conflict in the Middle East is boiling again. It is striking to me that in the newspapers this morning two words from that region are becoming familiar to the West. These words express the only two ways that many of the people involved currently see for dealing with each other. The first word is an Arabic word: *jihad*, attack. This is a story from a survivor of the 1990s war in Yugoslavia, as told by Miroslav Volf:

> I am a Muslim, and I am thirty-five years old. To my second son, I gave the name "Jihad." So he would not forget the testament of his mother—revenge. The first time I put my baby at my breast, I told him, "May this milk choke you if you forget." So be it. The Serbs taught me to hate. . . . My student, Zoran, the only son of my neighbor, urinated into my mouth. As the bearded hooligans standing around laughed, he told me: "You are good for nothing else, you stinking Muslim woman". . . Jihad—war. This is the only way.

What we see in drive-by shootings and suicide bombings is only the ultimate outworking of anger that is in all of our hearts. We get hurt, and we want to hurt back. Little *jihads* get fought every day between people who work together in the same office, between people who lead small groups in the same church; between husband and wife, between parent and child. *Jihads* go back as far as Cain and Abel: "While they were in the field, Cain attacked his brother Abel and killed him."

The second word is a Hebrew word, *hafrada*. *Hafrada* is a word for separation and withdrawal. A newspaper account explains the policy: "Wall of the West Bank. Keep all but a few Palestinians out of Israel. Shut off most . . . dealings with the other side. And enforce it all with overwhelming military might."

We know about walls, too. The Berlin Wall and the Iron Curtain are expressions of the same impulse that causes all of us to withdraw and withhold ourselves. Sometimes the wall is a newspaper at a breakfast table that expresses an emotional distance that cannot be bridged. Separation is as old as Adam and Eve: "I heard you in the garden, and I was afraid, . . . so I hid."

It's early in my marriage. My wife brings our three small children to my office. I have an argument with her along the general lines of *my life is harder than your life so you should serve me more*. My side doesn't do so well. I don't verbally attack her; I just create distance. I pay a little less attention to her, a little more attention to the kids. I give them a little more energy than usual. I don't look at her or touch her as I normally would, though I am civil and polite. When you know someone well, you can calibrate this behavior precisely. I am cold enough so she can feel my displeasure. But it's subtle enough so that if she asks, "What's wrong?" I can say, "Nothing. Why—what's wrong with you?" I understand about withdrawal.

Jihad and *hafrada*. Attack and withdrawal. It is an ironic thing that the Middle East—home of many of the world's great religions—should bequeath these two words to the art of human relationships.

But these are not just problems faced by strife-torn populations in a distant part of the world. Dallas Willard writes that assault and withdrawal are the two essential forms of relational sin. We assault others when we act against what is good for them. This is true even if it happens with their consent—to give a whiskey to an alcoholic, for example. We withdraw from someone when we regard their well-being as a matter of indifference to us. Attack and withdrawal are practiced by every human being on earth, and they damage every marriage and family and workplace and church.

At root, they are the two expressions of the one great sin, which is a lack of love, the violation of the one great commandment. All of our relational mismanagement is really a variation on these two tendencies of the fallen human heart. When we feel threatened, we want to hurt others or hide from them. We, too, head for a tree or stick out our quills.

But there is a better way.

Things don't have to be that way.

The Dance of the Porcupines

Miracle of miracles: Relationship does happen—even for porcupines. On rare occasions, one porcupine will share space with another, and they become friends. Once in a great while, one gets raised in captivity and will eat directly from a human hand. Porcupines learn to keep their barbs to themselves. Not only that, they figure out how to get together at least long enough to make sure that another generation will come along. In an image too wonderful to be made up, naturalist David Costello writes, "Males and females may remain together for some days before mating. They may touch paws and even walk on their hind feet in the so-called 'dance of the porcupines.'"

Miracle of miracles: Relationship does happen—even for porcupines.

Only God could have thought up two porcupines fox-trotting paw-to-paw, where no one but they and he will ever see. It turns out there really is an answer to the ancient question, how do porcupines make love? They pull in their quills and learn to dance.

Porcupines learn that they and their fellow porcupines come "as is." Like people. So this is not a book for normal people to learn how to handle difficult people. It is not for normal people at all. *There is no such thing, dear.* Not since the Fall.

This is a book about how imperfect people like you and me can pursue community with other imperfect people. This is a book about how porcupines learn to dance. So you will have to start with the actual porcupines right there in your life.

The writers of Scripture speak about God's dream for community primarily in terms of the church. This includes local congregations, with their services and programs. But God's dream for community encompasses the redemption of all spheres of life, so this also includes the way you relate to your family, friends, neighbors, and coworkers; the people you golf with or go shopping with; the man behind the counter where you stop to fill up the gas tank and grab a cup of coffee. Therefore I hope that you won't read this book alone. I hope you'll read it with people in your small group. I hope you'll read it with a friend or your spouse or someone in your family, so that together you can think about how to build the kind of community God made you for.

God has not given up on his dream. And you and I have a role to play in it. Our task is to create little islands of shalom in a sea of isolation.

It's time to pull in your quills and start dancing.

Learning to Dance:

1. What is one relationship in your life that you need to accept "as is" and stop trying to control or change?

2. Where is it hard for you to acknowledge your "as-is" tag? In what ways do you try to hide your "weirdness" by engaging in "depravity management"?

3. Dietrich Bonhoeffer spoke of the necessity of being disillusioned if we are to accept the reality of good and bad in community. When was a time you were disillusioned in a relationship? How did you respond?

4. Of the two forms of relational problems—attack and withdrawal—which are you most likely to employ? Why? What is the usual outcome?

5. The Porcupine's Dilemma is getting close without getting hurt. How do you tend to respond when you feel someone has hurt you?

6. God's ultimate desire for the world is *shalom*—"the webbing together of God, humans, and all creation in justice, fulfillment and delight." What is one step you could take to contribute to *shalom* in your little world?

7. Think of a porcupine or two you would like to get closer to—a friend, a coworker, someone in your small group, or a family member. How could you begin to deepen the relationship?

CHAPTER 2

THE WONDER OF ONENESS

God's aim in human history is the creation of an inclusive community of loving persons, with himself included as its primary sustainer and most glorious inhabitant.

DALLAS WILLARD

All life is meeting.

MARTIN BUBER

There is a little volume called *The All Better Book* in which elementary school children try to solve some of the world's knottiest problems: what to do about the ozone layer, and how to help people stop smoking. Here's the toughest:

"With billions of people in the world, someone should be able to figure out a system where no one is lonely. What do you suggest?"

> People should find lonely people and ask their name and address. Then ask people who aren't lonely their name and address. When you have an even amount of each, assign lonely and not lonely people together in the newspaper.
>
> KALANI, AGE 8 (OBVIOUSLY THIS IS A GIRL WITH THE GIFT OF ADMINISTRATION.)

> Make food that talks to you when you eat. For instance, it would say, "How are you doing?" and "What happened to you today?"
>
> MAX, AGE 9

> We could get people a pet or a husband or a wife and take them places.
>
> MATT, AGE 8 (THIS MAKES YOU WONDER ABOUT MATT'S UNDERSTANDING OF MARRIAGE.)

But the most touching response, the one that can break your heart, comes last:

> Sing a song. Stomp your feet. Read a book. (Sometimes I think no one loves me, so I do one of these.)
>
> BRIAN, AGE 8

"With billions of people in the world, someone should figure out a system where no one is lonely." For centuries, some of the smartest grown-ups who ever lived have devoted themselves to this problem. This God-designed hunger for community is why Plato wrote *The Republic* and Augustine wrote *The City of God*. It's why so many of our stories are about our longing to reach community—from *The Odyssey* to Walton's mountain, from Camelot to Lake Wobegon, from Mayberry to *Boyz in the Hood*. It's why we attend churches, join bowling leagues, go on blind dates.

It's why the single-most-remembered American speech of the twentieth century was a plea for all human beings one day being able to eat together at the table of fellowship, join hands, and sing a common song. Social scientist Jean Elshtain notes that Martin Luther King Jr. captured the conscience of a society because he was articulating, not just his dream, but the human dream—God's dream. "His speech would never have seized the nation if he had stood before the Lincoln Memorial and stated, 'I have a preference. I have a personal preference today.'"

The Pain of Loneliness

"With billions of people in the world, someone should figure out a system where no one is lonely."

There is no pain like the pain of loneliness. Lee Strobel wrote about the time *Chicago Tribune* columnist Marla Paul confessed in print a few years ago: *I am lonely*. "This loneliness saddens me," she wrote. "How did it happen I could be forty-two years old and not have enough friends?" She asked her husband if there was something wrong with her. She wondered if people were just too busy for friends. It seemed as though "every woman's friendship quota has been filled and she's no longer accepting new applicants." She wondered if perhaps "there are women out there who don't know how lonely they are. It's easy enough to fill up the day with work . . . [but it's] not enough."

Paul concluded her column:

> I recently read my daughter Han Christian Andersen's *The Ugly Duckling*. I felt an immediate kinship with this bird who flies from place to place looking for creatures with whom he belongs. He eventually finds them. I hope I do too.

She subsequently wrote about the unexpected nerve this column struck. People stopped her at work, while shopping, at her daughter's school: "You too? I thought I was the only one." Letters came in from homemakers and CEOs. This column elicited seven times her usual amount of mail, and the letters all had the same theme: *Why do I feel so lonely? Why is it so hard to make good friends?*

If loneliness is common for women, it is epidemic among men. One survey indicated that 90 percent of the male population in America lack a true friend. But we prefer not to talk about it. "No one wants to admit that they're lonely," writes psychiatrist Jacqueline Olds. "Loneliness is something people associate with losers." Loneliness has such a sting, in fact, that people will admit to being lonely in anonymous polls, but when asked to give their names they will say they are independent and self-sufficient.

Loneliness, said Mother Teresa, is the leprosy of modern society. And no one wants anybody to know they're a leper.

Jean Vanier is the founder of the world famous L'Arche community for the mentally handicapped and their helpers. It was there that one of the brilliant writers of our time, Henri Nouwen, found what had eluded him when he taught at places like Harvard and Yale: belonging, acceptance, home. Vanier wrote, "We all carry our own deep wound, which is the wound of our loneliness. We find it hard to be alone, and we try to flee from this in hyperactivity, through television and in a million other ways." Albert Schweitzer said, "We are all so much together, but we are all dying of loneliness."

What Really Matters

"With billions of people in the world, someone should figure out a system where no one is lonely."

Edward Hallowell writes that for most people the two most powerful experiences in life are *achieving* and *connecting*. Most of what grabs our attention and commands our energy falls under these two categories.

Connecting has to do with our relational world—things like falling in love, forming great friendships, being cared for when we are sick, or receiving words of deep affection from parents.

Achieving has to do with our accomplishments—winning contests, pursuing career success, or realizing a difficult goal.

Hallowell points out that our society is increasingly devoted to, obsessed with, and enslaved by achieving, and increasingly bankrupt and impoverished when it comes to connecting.

Achieving is not a bad thing—when it's done in the right way and for the right reasons. But it is no substitute for connecting. In fact, if it is to be done right, it must honor community. The only really significant achievements are those that enrich the life of community.

Achieving is not a bad thing—when it's done in the right way and for the right reasons. But it is no substitute for connecting.

So it is ironic that achievement for its own sake has become a kind of idol in our society. I have never known anyone who failed at relationships—who was isolated, lonely, unconnected, had no deep friendships—yet had a meaningful and joy-filled life. Not a single person. The twentieth century was littered with people who achieved great things but never connected. People who accumulated vast amounts of wealth, fame, or power but never acquired an open heart. People who had a Rolodex of contacts but not a single friend. Every one of them died with bitter regrets. Every one.

Conversely, I have never known anyone who succeeded at relationships—who cultivated great friendships, who was devoted to their family, who mastered the art of giving and receiving love—yet had a bad life.

No matter how little money we have, no matter what rung we occupy on anybody's corporate ladder of success, in the end what everybody discovers is that what matters is other people. Human beings who give themselves to relational greatness—who have friends they laugh with, cry with, learn with, fight with, dance with, live and love and grow old and die with—these are the human beings who lead magnificent lives.

When they die, not one of them regrets having devoted themselves to people: their friends, their neighbors, their children, their family. Not one.

The "Human-shaped Void"

We were made to know oneness. That is why loneliness is so painful.

In the story of the Creation in the book of Genesis, a little refrain keeps recurring:

"And God said . . . and it was so . . . and God saw that it was good."

The writer is emphasizing that everything that exists is the effortless activity of an unimaginably powerful God, and all of it is unspeakably delightful:

This is the song of Creation: "*And God said . . . and it was so . . . and God saw that it was good.*"

Until the final act—when the song comes screeching to a halt.

God creates a man in his own image. God looks at this man, who bears his likeness, and he says, "Not good." Why does God look at man and say "Not good"? Because he likes women better?

Not quite. This is a radical comment about the fundamental importance of human relationships.

What is striking is that the Fall has not yet occurred. There is no sin, no disobedience, nothing, to mar the relationship between God and man.

The human being is in a state of perfect intimacy with God. Each word he and God speak with each other is filled with closeness and joy; he walks with God in the garden in the cool of the day. He is known and loved to the core of his being by his omniscient, love-filled Creator. Yet the word God uses to describe him is "alone." And God says that this aloneness is "not good."

Community is what you were created for. It is God's desire for your life. It is the one indispensable condition for human flourishing.

Sometimes in church circles when people feel lonely, we will tell them not to expect too much from human relationships, that there is inside every human being a God-shaped void that no other person can fill. That is true. But apparently, according to the writer of Genesis, God creates inside this man a kind of "human-shaped void" that God himself will not fill.

No substitute will fill this need in you for human relationship:

Not money
Not achievement
Not busyness
Not books
Not even God himself

Even though this man was in a state of sinless perfection, he was "alone." And it was not good.

Community is what you were created for. It is God's desire for your life. It is the one indispensable condition for human flourishing. According to Jean Vanier, "A community is not simply a group of people who live together and love each other. It is a place of resurrection."

Life-giving Relationships

"With billions of people in the world, someone should figure out a system where no one is lonely."

Being in meaningful relationships is life-giving in the most literal sense.

One of the most thorough research projects on relationships is called the Alameda County Study. Headed by a Harvard social scientist, it tracked the lives of 7,000 people over nine years. Researchers found that the most isolated people were *three times more likely to die* than those with strong relational connections.

People who had bad health habits (such as smoking, poor eating habits, obesity, or alcohol use) but strong social ties lived *significantly longer* than people who had great health habits but were isolated. In other words, it is better to eat Twinkies with good friends than to eat broccoli alone. Harvard researcher Robert Putnam notes that if you belong to no groups but decide to join one, "you cut your risk of dying over the next year *in half*."

For another study, as reported in the *Journal of the American Medical Association*, 276 volunteers were infected with a virus that produces the common cold. The study found that people with strong emotional connections did four times better fighting off illness than those who were more isolated. These people were less susceptible to colds, had less virus, and produced significantly less mucous than relationally isolated subjects. (I'm not making this up. They produced less mucous. This means it is literally true: Unfriendly people are snottier than friendly people.)

Yet, we are becoming increasingly disconnected from each other. This is the thesis of the most in-depth study of contemporary society done in a few decades. Robert Putnam took the title of his book, *Bowling Alone*, from the fact that while more people than ever are bowling these days, fewer are doing it in leagues. He and a team of researchers documented that for twenty-five years American society has experienced a steady decline of what sociologists call *social capital*—a sense of connectedness and community. (This was illustrated by, among other things, the T-shirt slogan that the Volunteer Fire Department in Gold Beach, Oregon, used to promote their annual fund-raising event: "Come to our breakfast, we'll come to your fire.") Whether it's measured by civic involvement, volunteer organizations, neighborhood relationships, or religious participation, Putnam found, the level of community in America is at its lowest point in our lifetimes, and this loss of social capital results in lower educational performance, more teen pregnancy, greater depression, and higher crime rates.

The Divine Community

"With billions of people in the world, someone should figure out a system where no one is lonely."

Someone did.

That Someone is God. That system is called community. I believe that if you had to sum up in a single word what God is up to, what his goal is in creating the universe and the persons who inhabit it, that word would be *community*. This business of community turns out to be something far deeper than just building a successful network of emotional support. It is not simply about loneliness avoidance. It is the reason why the universe exists, and why you and I do as well.

Dallas Willard puts it like this: "God's aim in human history is the creation of an inclusive community of loving persons, with himself included as its primary sustainer and most glorious inhabitant."

Difficult or not, the idea of the Trinity turns out to be vitally important because it tells us that God himself has been experiencing community throughout eternity.

To see why community matters so much to God, we have to go far back in time, back before even the first human beings were created, and try to think what life was like for God before anything else existed. This is where the doctrine of the Trinity becomes very important. As I was growing up, most of what I heard about the Trinity was very confusing to me. I can remember hearing all kinds of metaphors used to try to explain this idea of God as Trinity: The Trinity is like an egg that has a shell, white, and yolk; the Trinity is like water that can be steam, liquid, or ice. But none of these analogies helped very much.

The earliest attempts of the church to describe the Trinity don't talk about eggs or water. They tell us that the Father, Son, and Holy Spirit exist as three *persons*. One God—perfect oneness—yet three persons.

Difficult or not, the idea of the Trinity turns out to be vitally important because it tells us that God himself has been experiencing community throughout eternity. Community is rooted in the being of God.

Did you ever wonder what life is like inside the Trinity? The writers of Scripture are most interested in talking about God's relationship to us, so we don't know a lot about this. But it is worth considering.

Do you think there was a lot of bickering about who is the most omniscient or the most omnipotent or which member is the oldest? My wife and I will occasionally argue about division-of-labor issues—whose turn it is to take out the dog or empty the dishwasher. Can you imagine that kind of discussion going on within the Trinity?

Not quite. "The life of God is a life of self-giving and other-receiving love," writes Miroslav Volf. Father, Son, and Spirit are so close that Jesus could say, "The Father is *in me* and I am *in the Father*." The ancient Greek word for this "mutual indwelling" of the Trinity is *perichoresis*, which is related to our word *choreography*. The Trinity exists as a kind of eternal dance of joyful love among Father, Son, and Spirit. This can get a little abstract, so let me try painting a (human and inadequate) picture of what "mutual indwelling" involves.

"Hold You Me?"

When our first daughter, Laura, needed comforting during infancy, Nancy and I would usually use one of two phrases. When Laura was crying and we didn't know why, when we had tried all the obvious solutions like feeding her and taking care of hygiene issues and she was still distressed, we would hold her and repeat over and over in the most empathic tones we were capable of—"Honey, honey, honey," or "I know, I know"—nodding our heads as if we really did know. We generally didn't know, but it seemed reassuring to say we did.

After a while, Laura internalized this. By the time she was approaching her first birthday, she would sometimes wake up in the morning and begin to cry; but instead of just making crying sounds like other babies, she would cry words to herself over and over, "Honey, honey, honey . . . I know, I know."

Laura would cry them to herself with great compassion, nodding her little head just as she had seen us do. She was the world's first self-comforting baby. Sometimes Nancy and I would lie in bed and crack up over the sound of a one-year-old reassuring herself: "Honey, honey, honey."

But never for very long. When we would go into her room, Laura would switch to another phrase. She would poke her head up off her pillow (at that age she had just a strip of red hair that ran down the center of her scalp—it looked like a Mohawk haircut), raise her stubby little arms into the air, curl her fingers daintily toward us, and ask plaintively, "Hold you me?" The grammar was a little confused, but the meaning was clear and the request was impossible to refuse. Who could say no? The irresistible invitation. The universal cry of the human heart. *Hold you me?*

The connection that takes place between a mother and a child is perhaps the clearest picture in our world of what has been called the "human moment." It creates a little circle of life: A mother ceases to think about herself and focuses on her child; she gives love and warmth and blessing and the child receives life. At the same moment, the act of giving doesn't empty the mother; she receives the joy of pouring herself out in service and love, and she, too, is given life. The human moment reflects a kind of relational ecosystem in which life becomes greater and richer as it flows back and forth from one person to another.

Larry Crabb calls this process "connecting."

> When two people connect, when their beings intersect as closely as two bodies during intercourse, something is poured out of one and into the other that has the power to heal the soul of its deepest wounds and restore it to health. The one who receives experiences the joy of being healed. The one who gives knows the even greater joy of being used to heal. Something good is in the heart of each of God's children that is more powerful than everything bad. It's there, waiting to be released, work its magic.

Even an infant being held knows, with an understanding deeper than words, that what is being expressed with the body is in fact the decision of the soul: to hold another person in one's heart. *I will seek your good; I will share your joy and hurt; we will know a kind of oneness, you and I.* It is the brief enactment of a covenant. It is a promise of self-giving love.

The work of building community is the noblest work a person can do. The desire for community is the deepest hunger a human being can have. It was the desire of Marilyn Monroe and Kurt Cobain; the desire of Brian, age eight; the deepest longing of old Howard Hughes, if only he'd known it.

But no merely human circle of life is truly sufficient. Every circle requires another larger circle to support it. The well-being of families depends in part on schools and neighborhoods and workplaces and cities and nations and economies. Every merely human circle is broken, just as those of us who make them up are broken.

Dallas Willard states, "Ultimately, every human circle is doomed to dissolution if it is not caught up in the life of the only genuinely self-sufficient circle of sufficiency, that of the Father, Son, and Holy Spirit. For that circle is the only one that is truly and totally self-sufficient. And all the broken circles must ultimately find their healing there, if anywhere."

The life of the Trinity is an unceasing offering and receiving of self-giving love. The Father holds the Son in his heart, and the Son does the same with the Father. "The Father is in me and I am in the Father," Jesus says, and the Spirit holds and is held as well. "Hold you me"—offering themselves to one another in ceaseless, joy-filled, mutually submissive, generous, creative, self-giving love—is what the Trinity has been doing from before the beginning of time.

Life within the Trinity

Frederick Bruner, in a wonderful essay on the Trinity, begins with the person of the Holy Spirit:

> One of the most surprising discoveries in my own study of the doctrine and experience of the Spirit in the New Testament is what I can only call the shyness of the Spirit. . . .
>
> What I mean here is not the shyness of timidity (cf. II Timothy 1:7) but the shyness of deference, the shyness of a concentrated attention on another; it is not the shyness (which we often experience) of self-centeredness; but the shyness of an other-centeredness.

It is, in a word, the shyness of love. Bruner points out the ministry of the Spirit in the Johannine passages, which is constantly to draw attention not to himself but to the Son. The Spirit comes in the Son's name, bears witness to the Son, and glorifies the Son.

When he teaches, Bruner sometimes represents the ministry of the Spirit by drawing a stick figure on a chalkboard to represent Jesus. Then, to express what the Spirit does, he stands behind the chalkboard, reaches around with one hand, and points with a single finger to the image of Jesus: "Look at him; listen to him; learn from him, follow him, worship him, be devoted to him, serve him, love him, be preoccupied with him."

This is the shyness of the Holy Spirit.

But when we look at the Son, oddly enough we see that he didn't walk around saying, "I'm the greatest!" Rather, he said, "If I glorify myself, my glory means nothing." He said he came not to be served but to serve. He submitted to the Spirit, who, according to Mark, drove him into the wilderness. He told the Father during his climactic struggle, "Not my will, but yours be done." Jesus, too, has this shyness.

Then there is the Father. Twice in the synoptic gospels we hear the voice of the Father: once at Jesus' baptism, and again at the Transfiguration. Both times his words are a variation of this message: "This is my priceless Son; I am deeply pleased with him. Listen to *him*!"

It is noteworthy, Bruner writes, that this voice does not say, "Listen to me, too, after listening to him; don't forget that I'm here, too; don't be taken up with my Son."

God created human beings because he was so in love with community that he wanted a world full of people to share it with.

This is because "God the Father is shy, too. The whole blessed Trinity is shy. Each member of the Trinity points faithfully and selflessly to the other in a gracious circle."

Growing up, I remember hearing teachers speak about God as a proud, almost arrogant being who could get away with his pride because he is God. The doctrine of the Trinity tells me this is not so. The whole blessed Trinity is shy—but not with the shyness of timidity. Rather, God exists as Father, Son, and Spirit in a community of greater humility, servanthood, mutual submission, and delight than you and I can imagine. The Trinity is "a self-sufficing community of unspeakably magnificent personal beings of boundless love, knowledge, and power," as Dallas Willard puts it.

This tells us something about how deep our hunger for community is. God did not create human beings because he was lonely or bored. The religions surrounding Judaism in the Ancient Near East suggested that the gods made human beings to be their lackeys because they needed someone to provide them with food. But the God of the Israelites did not create because he was needy.

God created human beings because he was so in love with community that he wanted a world full of people to share it with. He wanted to invite them all to the dance. And life within the Trinity was to be the pattern for our lives. Neil Plantinga writes, "At the center of the universe, self-giving love is the dynamic currency of the trinitarian life of God. The persons within God exalt each other, commune with each other, defer to one another. Each person, so to speak, makes room for the other two."

So God made human beings in his own image. People have speculated for a long time about exactly what that image consists of. Theologians have noted that Genesis itself seems to tie this image to the fact that we, like God, have the capacity for relationships: "In the image of God he created them; male and female he created them." He makes them two, and yet the two are capable of achieving a kind of oneness. God, who is three and yet one, creates human beings in his image and says the two shall become one.

When Nancy and I were dating, I read her a poem by Shakespeare about two lovers:

> They so loved that love in twain
> Had the essence but of one.
> Two distincts, division none;
> Number there in love was slain.

When I finished reading it, I was in tears, but Nancy had a kind of glazed look in her eyes. This is generally the response I get when I read it to people, so let me say a word about what it means.

Shakespeare is saying that even though they were two separate people ("two distincts"; "love in twain"), their love had the effect of removing the barriers that normally divide people ("division none"), so that they were united in heart and soul. Two and yet one. "Number there in love was slain." The logic of mathematics—where two is always two and can never be one—was transcended by the logic of love.

In the Trinity, God is three and yet one.

God creates human beings male and female—and the two are one.

Jesus prays for his followers, for the church, for all redeemed humanity to become one.

This is the "new math" of God: Everything equals one.

The Great Invitation

What is most amazing is that God invites us into the Fellowship of the Trinity.

> "My prayer is not for them alone. I pray also for those who will believe in me through their message, that all of them may be one, Father, just as you are in me and I am in you. *May they also be in us* so that the world may believe that you have sent me."

We have been invited into this fellowship of love. This is why Jesus says, "Where two or three are gathered together in my name, there am I in the midst of them." To gather "in his name" is not restricted to church services. In the Bible, a person's name generally stands for his or her character and identity. To gather in Jesus' name means to relate to other people with the same spirit of servanthood, submission, and delight that characterizes Jesus in the Trinity. Whenever that happens, Jesus says, he can't just stand idly by. He is always a part of it, basking in it, cheering it on. A community of loving people is God's signature.

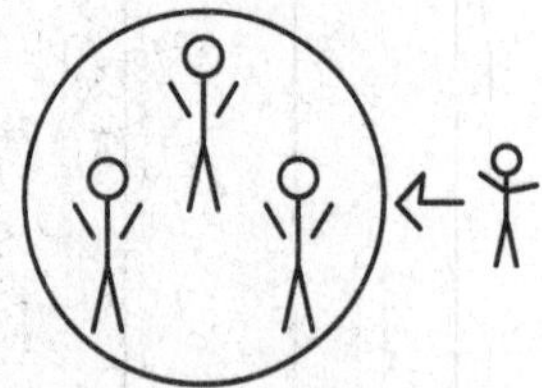

This is why the experience of authentic community is so life-giving. We are taking our place in fellowship with Life himself. When I am in isolation, I feel lonely. When I am in community, I experience what might be called "fullness of heart." The human heart is forever empty if it is closed in upon itself. In community—the divine community especially—a heart comes alive. To experience community is to know the joy of belonging, the delight at being known and loved, the opportunity for giving and growing, the safety of finding a true home.

What does a full heart look like? Brennan Manning tells the story of a man named Ed Farrell, who traveled from his home in Detroit to spend a two-week vacation in Ireland to celebrate his uncle's eightieth birthday. When the great day dawned, Ed and his uncle rose early to greet the sun. They walked along the shores of Lake Killarney, loving the emerald green grass and crystal blue waters. For twenty minutes they watched the scene together in silence. Then the uncle began to do an unusual thing for an eighty-year-old man: He began to skip along the shore of the lake, smiling like a schoolboy in love. Ed was puffing hard as he tried to catch up to him.

To experience community is to know the joy of belonging, the delight at being known and loved, the opportunity for giving and growing, the safety of finding a true home.

"Uncle Seamus, you look very happy. Do you want to tell me why?"

"Yes," said the old man, tears running down his face. "You see, the Father is very fond of me. Ah, me Father is so very fond of me."

So it is in the Fellowship of the Trinity: "The Father is very fond of me." This is the fellowship into which we are invited—one that can make eighty-year-old hearts laugh and cry and dance for the sheer joy of being loved. We were not made for loneliness; we were made for this joy.

When Jesus prays for us to be invited into the divine circle, it is not a casual request. There is an enormous price to be paid for our admittance. The Son will go to the cross. The Father—who had known nothing from all eternity but perfect intimacy with his Son—will now see his Beloved suffer the anguish and alienation of sin. The Spirit will come to earth and allow himself to be quenched and grieved by human beings.

At enormous cost to every member of the Trinity, you and I have been welcomed to the eternal circle, to be held in the heart of Father, Son, Spirit.

Therefore, to fail to prize community; to tolerate disunity with the people God loves—particularly disunity in the body of Christ; or to do things that could lead to disunity is utterly unthinkable.

To allow or contribute to disunity in this fellowship is to be fundamentally at odds with the purpose of God in human history. It may be common in our world, but it is not normal in God's eyes.

The apostle Paul says, "Make every effort to keep the unity of the Spirit." Paul doesn't say create unity. This is not a human project. This oneness existed long before us. Paul uses a rare verb of intense urgency. Markus Barth writes that the sense of this command is, "Yours is the initiative! Do it now! Pay any price! Spare no pain! You are to do it! I mean it!"

In light of the beauty of community and the staggering cost the Trinity paid to invite us into it, Paul says, human beings dare not take it lightly.

The doctrine of the Trinity is honored when the oneness that characterizes it—the "unity of the Spirit"—is prized and guarded and revered by the one true church. Whenever human beings tolerate unresolved conflict in friendships or families or churches, whenever gossip and slander go unchallenged, whenever ministry leaders attack other Christians in a spirit of arrogance or want to believe and spread bad things about those who disagree with them—wherever the unity of the Spirit is treated cavalierly, the Trinity is dishonored.

All day, in a million different ways, in our homes, our neighborhoods, our churches, our families, our friendships, and our cities, you and I are either moving the world a little closer to God's picture of *shalom*—peace—or moving it a little farther away. There is a line from the musical *Les Miserables* that gets very close to what John wrote: "To love another person is to see the face of God."

You now are invited to take your place in the eternal circle of self-giving love. Every person you see, every moment of your life, is an opportunity to live in and extend the Fellowship of the Trinity. We have scores of opportunities each day. This is what each "human moment" can be about. Every time you forgive someone who hurt you, encourage someone who feels defeated, extend compassion to someone who stands alone, confront someone in love, open your heart to a friend, reconcile with an enemy, devote time to a child, you align yourself with God's central purpose in this world. Anne Lamott wrote, "The Gulf Stream will pass through a straw, provided that the straw is aligned with the Gulf Stream, and not at cross-purpose with the Gulf Stream."

To live in and contribute to God's dream of community is the reason you were born. It is what you were created for. Neglect this, and it doesn't matter what else you do—how many pyramids you build, how impressive your resumé—you are at cross-purposes with the Gulf Stream. Neglect this, and you will die a failure. Devote yourself to this one task, to loving "as-is people," and no matter what else you may not achieve, you will lead a magnificent life.

"With billions of people in the world, someone should create a system where no one is lonely."

Someone did. You see, the Father is very fond of you.

Learning to Dance

1. What are the greatest barriers to a greater sense of community and intimacy in our society? For you personally?

2. "There is no pain like the pain of loneliness." What was a lonely era in your life? What was a time when you had a great sense of belonging? In both cases, what factors contributed to this?

3. What people have taught you the most—for better or worse—about how to engage in relationships?

4. To what extent do you substitute *achieving* for *connecting?* Which one are you succeeding at the most?

5. How does the description of the Trinity as a community of humility, servanthood, and delight differ from your previous ideas about God or the Trinity? How does it affect your life to think that you have been invited into this fellowship?

6. "The Father is very fond of me." Take a few minutes this week to meditate on this story. Say this line out loud.

7. The "human moment" occurs every time we interact with another person. Look for "human moments" throughout your day today. How well do you seize them? How would you like to handle them differently?

CHAPTER 3

THE FELLOWSHIP OF THE MAT: TRUE FRIENDSHIP

Without friendships no one would choose to live,
even if they had all other good things in life.

ARISTOTLE

If you don't go to somebody's funeral,
they won't go to yours.

YOGI BERRA

One of the great stories in the Bible about community involves a paralyzed man and the friends who brought him to Jesus.

Imagine what life was like for this man—what it would mean to be a paralytic in the ancient world.

His whole life is lived on a mat three feet wide and six feet long. Someone has to feed him, carry him, clothe him, move him to keep him from being covered with bedsores, clean him when he soils himself. He will never know the sense of independence we prize so fiercely.

Nothing can be done medically—no surgeries, no rehab programs, no treatment centers.

There is no way to contribute to society. Anyone in this man's condition has to go through life as a beggar—be laid by the side of road, be dependent on people dropping coins beside him to live another day.

He dreams. Sometimes in his dreams he has a healthy body. He walks and runs, does good work, is married maybe, and plays with his children.

Then he wakes up and looks at the ceiling of a room he can never walk out of, looks at the body that holds him prisoner, looks at the mat that comprises his world—and knows he will never be free.

He has no money, no job, no influence, no family, and seemingly not much of a future. His "as-is" tag is three feet wide and six feet long.

What's he got going for him? He has friends. He has amazing friends.

He is in one of the killer small groups of all time.

In one sense, this whole story takes place because of his friends. Without his friends he never makes it to Jesus, never gets healed, never gets forgiven. All these things flow out of some very wise decisions made years ago—to have great friends.

Choosing Community

You should know that for the man in this story the development of these friendships did not happen accidentally. Because of his physical condition, the deck was stacked against friendships emerging here at all. His "as-is" tag was very visible.

Even in our day, people who wrestle with physical challenges often say that the most difficult obstacles they face are the attitudes of so-called normal people, who are sometimes anxious about how to respond, sometimes are unkind, sometimes look away and avoid meeting eye to eye. This is a fast-paced world, and it is not a very gracious place for those who can't run as fast as others.

But the ancient world could be even harsher. The Greeks regularly disposed of newborn infants with physical anomalies. Aristotle wrote, "Let there be a law that no deformed child shall be raised." In Rome, during the fifth century B.C., there was actually a statute on the books: Quickly kill a deformed child.

In Israel, this man would have suffered from another stigma. There was a common assumption that if people were suffering physically, they had brought it on themselves. In another New Testament story, the disciples see a man blind from birth and ask Jesus, "Rabbi, who sinned, this man or his parents, that he was born blind?"

Yet, here is a little band of men who refuse to let any obstacle stop them. And this is a key point for us: Their little group clearly did not come about by accident. In the face of formidable obstacles—social stigma, inconvenience, financial pressure, a high cost of time and energy—they choose to become friends.

People rarely drift into deep community. Psychologist Alan McGinnis notes that rule number one for entering into deep friendships sounds deceptively simple: Assign top priority to your relationships. Ironically, we tend to devote massive amounts of time to making money, running errands, and succeeding at our jobs, but we neglect giving our most valuable possession—time—to the experience for which we were created: community.

If you think you can fit deep community into the cracks of an overloaded schedule—think again. Wise people do not try to microwave friendship, parenting, or marriage.

One of the most countercultural statements in Scripture is a description of the early church. In speaking of the people's oneness of heart and mind, the writer notes, "They met together *daily*." They worshiped together, ate together, talked together, prayed together—on a daily basis. No wonder they grew so close.

We try to create first-century community on a twenty-first-century timetable—and it doesn't work. Maybe the biggest single barrier to deep connectedness for most of us is simply the pace of our lives. How often do you hear (or say) things like, "We've got to get together soon" or "Let's do lunch in a few weeks when things settle down"?

The requirement for true intimacy is chunks of unhurried time. If you think you can fit deep community into the cracks of an overloaded schedule—think again. Wise people do not try to microwave friendship, parenting, or marriage. You can't do community in a hurry:

You can't listen in a hurry.

You can't mourn in a hurry with those who mourn, or rejoice in a hurry with those who rejoice.

Many people lack great friends for the simple reason that they have never made pursuing community a high priority. You can't carry somebody's mat in a hurry. And everyone comes with a mat.

Everybody Has a Mat

Think about what the paralyzed man goes through in order to be friends with this group of men.

He must have wrestled with his sense of dependence sometimes. I suspect at times he became jealous of their independence, since after they had been together, everyone could walk home but him. Sometimes he must have wished in the secret places of his heart that he could trade places with one of them. He must have struggled with how they saw him in his neediness.

It is a very vulnerable thing to have someone carry your mat. When somebody's carrying your mat, they see you in your weakness. They might hurt you if they drop you.

There is this gift between these friends: trusting vulnerability and dependable faithfulness. This mat, which according to society should have created a great gulf between him and them, instead became an opportunity for servanthood and acceptance. This group becomes the Fellowship of the Mat. Wherever human beings love and accept and serve each other in the face of weakness and need, there is the Fellowship of the Mat.

Here is the truth about us: Everybody has a mat. Let the mat stand as a picture of human brokenness and imperfection. It is what is "not normal" about me. It is the little "as-is" tag that I most desire to hide. But it is only when we allow others to see our mat, when we give and receive help with each other, that healing becomes possible. Every effective Alcoholics Anonymous meeting is a Fellowship of the Mat. So are healthy families and churches.

Because everybody has a mat.

Maybe your mat is a temper you can't seem to control. You lash out at the people you most want to love. Hot words spew out of your mouth that you know you will regret with bitter tears. Your children sometimes look at you with frightened eyes. You hate the way the molten anger flows out of you, but you feel you can no more keep it in than a volcano can contain its lava.

Maybe your mat is fear. You love to hear stories of courage and boldness. In your mind you picture a hundred scenarios in which you take daring risks and tell off the bullies in your life with cool aplomb. But the reality is that you still get sweaty palms when you have to confront your mother.

Maybe your mat is an inability to trust, or the need to be in control, or an inability to speak the language of the heart. Maybe your mat involves a terrible secret of some awful thing you did that you still feel guilty about. Maybe it is a crushing sense of failure, or inadequacy, or plainness, or loneliness.

Sometimes people spend their whole lives doing "mat management." They pretend they don't have a mat. They appear to be so healthy and strong that the people around them assume they could walk anywhere they want to. They can see other peoples' mats—maybe even have a spiritual gift of "mat identification" for others—but never reveal their own. Their primary goal is to hide their brokenness from others' eyes. If this is you, you may get quite good at hiding your mat. You may convince everybody of your strength and competence. But you will not live in community.

So let me ask you a personal question: Who carries your mat for you sometimes?

—Who do you show your weakness and struggles to?

—Who do you ask to pray for you?

—Who do you let see your brokenness?

Jean Vanier writes,

> There is no ideal community. Community is made up of people with all their richness, but also with their weakness and poverty, of people who accept and forgive each other, who are vulnerable with each other. Humility and trust are more at the foundation of community than perfection.

If you want a deep friendship, you can't always be the strong one. You will sometimes have to let somebody else carry your mat.

That is what happens in the Bible story. This group of people become friends. It requires formidable character and intentionality. Perhaps because one man's vulnerability is so visible, they all become more honest about their mats. Against all odds, they form a little community: the Fellowship of the Mat.

A Community of Roof-Crashers

Then one day Jesus comes to their town. These four men find out about it, and naturally they want to hear this famous rabbi.

One of them says, "We can't just go ourselves. We've got to get our friend there. This could really encourage him. And maybe these things they're saying about Jesus are true. Maybe Jesus really can heal our friend—wouldn't that be something! We gotta get him there!"

To do that is going to make things harder logistically, but they're not thinking about themselves. They are thinking of him. Friends do that. Friends serve each other.

They tell their friend he's going to see Jesus. They will pick him up at nine o'clock. He doesn't have much choice, because when his friends pick him up, they really pick him up.

They get to the home where Jesus is teaching, and it is packed. Standing room only. "There was no room left, not even outside the door," the Bible says.

Jesus is so close, but they can't get through to him.

This story took place before that verse was written in the Bible that is so important to attenders of American suburban churches: "Thou shalt place a program on a chair to reserve thy seat; and anyone who sitteth thereupon shall be cast into the outer darkness."

The men hadn't counted on this. They had been so excited, and now they're shut out. They just watch for a while.

Then one of them—the management guy, the one with an MBA—says, "How can we get him to Jesus? Let's have a brainstorming session, and remember—when brainstorming, there's no such thing as a dumb idea."

One of them gets an idea—probably the youngest guy, the tattooed and pierced guy, because he's an outside-the-box thinker.

"Dudes! What if we make a hole and lower him through the roof! Whoaaa!"

Silence.

"Okay," asks the MBA, "any other ideas?"

There aren't any. The hole in the roof idea is the only thing they can come up with. They realize it's an unorthodox way to get into a room.

But they are desperate to get to Jesus. They had decided they wouldn't let anything get in their way, so strong is their trust in Jesus, so great their love for their friend.

So the men get some ropes for lowering the mat and head upstairs. It was common in houses to have an outside staircase leading to the roof, which was often used as a kind of patio. The friends go up and start remodeling this guy's house. (If you're worried that this story is soft on vandalism, you should know that roofs back then consisted of wooden crossbeams with a matting of reeds, branches, and dried mud in between. These guys didn't need a wrecking ball to break through. This was easily repaired.)

Imagine this:

Jesus is teaching, and because he is an excellent teacher, people are paying close attention. But suddenly the distraction level begins to rise. There is a strange noise that sounds as if it's coming from the roof. Dirt and dust and bits of reed begin to descend from the ceiling, getting in people's eyes and landing in their hair—just a few flakes at first, and then a hail of large chunks of first-century plaster. Eventually all conversation ceases and Jesus himself stops talking. Everyone is looking up now, and there's a hole in the ceiling. Four pairs of hands are rooting around, making the hole bigger.

Imagine being the guy who owns the house.

You agree to host a meeting, and suddenly you're having a spontaneous skylight installed. The owner calls his State Farm agent to see if this is covered.

"Jesus is here—can we call it an act of God?"

These men are devoted to their friend, so they decide a little roofing is not going to stand in their way. They serve him with determination, boldness, and a certain right-brained creativity. They become roof-crashers for their friend. And I have a feeling they will remember that moment for a long time.

Community gets built by servants. Great community gets built by roof-crashers.

Ironically, many of the barriers that keep us isolated are surprisingly fragile, much like the roof that stood in the way of this little community. Perhaps the dominant community-busting device in our time is a little box with a plug on the end. Most time studies show that the average American now watches four hours of television a day. Time diaries show that husbands and wives spend three or four times as much time watching television as they spend talking together; and six to seven times as much as they spend in community activities outside the home.

Dolores Curren writes that as a communication exercise she will sometimes ask family members to jot down the most often-used phrases in their home. One parent was aghast to find that the top two were, "What's on?" and "Move."

Robert Putnam, in his exhaustive research on the loss of community, writes, "Dependence on television for entertainment is not merely *a* significant predictor of civic disengagement. It is *the single most consistent* predictor that I have discovered." He adds this chilling sentence: "A major commitment to television viewing—such as most of us have come to have—is incompatible with a major commitment to community life."

There is a world of difference between being friendly to someone because they're useful to you and being someone's friend.

Friends are people who have made a major, roof-crashing commitment to other human beings. But in our society, as Lewis Smedes puts it, we have confused friends with "friendly people."

I am writing these words after just having hung up the phone. The man on the other end of the line called me by my first name; he asked how my day was going; he spoke in warm and caring tones; he was concerned for me that my long-distance carrier might not be providing the kind of service that a busy person such as I might need.

But when I told him I did not want to spend money with him, I got the clear sense that our relationship was suddenly over. He was a friendly person. But he was not my friend.

We live in a world of networking, contacts, Rolodex files, quid pro quos. But when the relationship isn't strategic anymore, when the sales dry up, when the plane lands—the relationship is over.

The relationship may be with a colleague. It may be a cordial, mutually beneficial acquaintance. It's not necessarily a bad thing. But it's not a friendship. A friend is committed to you in a way that a paid service-provider is not.

There is a world of difference between being friendly to someone because they're useful to you and being someone's friend. I love psychologist Urie Bronfenbrenner's definition of a family, which I think applies to the Fellowship of the Mat: "A group which possesses and implements an irrational commitment to the well-being of its members." The key word is *irrational.* In great communities, people carry mats and crash through roofs without asking the question, "What's in it for me?"

How often do you do a little roof-crashing? It doesn't have to involve destruction of property. Mostly it involves just two tasks: *noticing* and *doing.* When you see a friend is discouraged, you can write a note or make a phone call. When you know someone really needs to talk, take the time to listen even though you're busy. When you see a gift that you know would bring delight to someone in your family, buy it for the person for no reason at all.

When Nancy and I were first married and I was in grad school and we had a deficit cash flow, a coworker saw us in a restaurant and secretly paid our bill. Nearly twenty years later, we still remember what a gift it was.

This leads us to what might be called the irony of the mat. Our mats are usually what we are least proud of and most likely to hide. We are often convinced that if other people knew about our mats, they would stay away from us. But in reality it is precisely our mats that form the connecting points for a deeper relationship.

Psychologist Henry Cloud tells about one fellowship of the mat. Henry led a group for inpatients at a hospital who were struggling with life issues. One of the members of the group was a pastor we'll call Joe. His mat was a sexual addiction he had wrestled with for years. He had confessed and prayed over and over through the years, but he wasn't able to break it. Finally his desperation and guilt were so great he checked himself into the hospital for help. Going to this group was a part of his program.

One morning a nurse told Henry that Joe wasn't coming to the group that day. Henry went to talk with him and discovered that Joe had suffered a relapse the night before. Henry talked him into coming.

Members of the group asked Joe if he was okay. He said yes, but it was not too convincing. During previous sessions, Joe had mostly listened to other group members. He was comfortable helping to carry mats for other people; he still didn't want to show much about his own. This morning, though, Henry left him no choice.

Slowly, painfully, Joe began to allow others to see his sense of shame and failure. He spoke to them about years of guilt: standing in the pulpit and being terrified that someone might have seen him where he shouldn't have been the night before; claiming to speak for God when he was the biggest hypocrite in the congregation. And yet, for all the pain his behavior caused him, he couldn't stop.

Joe could barely choke out the words. As he told his story, he stared at the floor; he could not bring himself to look anyone in the face.

"'Look up at the group," Henry told him.

"I can't. I'm too ashamed."

"Look up at the group. I want you to look into the eyes of the people listening to you. You must do this."

Fearfully, this broken man raised his head. He looked around the circle, and every pair of eyes looking back at him was filled with tears. Every heart ached with pain for his anguish. There was no imputing shame, no condemnation, just compassion.

More than anything else, God uses people to heal people.

For the first time in his life, Joe was not alone with the brokenness that had paralyzed and crippled his soul for so long. Finally, a few people saw his deformity, yet still chose to be his friends. For the first time in his life, he had a few mat-carriers to help take him to the place of healing where he could never go on his own.

In that moment, a man who had taught on grace for so long finally tasted it, and it broke him. He wept like a child. He began to hear the words that were spoken to another crippled soul so long ago: "Child, your sins are forgiven."

Henry writes that Joe's addiction was broken that day. He still had much work to do, a long way to go. There were confessions to be made, new habits to be developed. He wasn't finished yet. But the cruel force of addiction was broken in that moment. Such is the power of the Fellowship of the Mat.

Harry Stack Sullivan was a pioneer in what is called interpersonal psychology. He used to tell his students, "It takes people to make people sick, and it takes people to make people well." Theologically, this is not strictly true: Every one of us has our own quotient of sin and brokenness that we are quite responsible for on our own without help from anyone. But for better or worse we are shaped more by people than any other force in life. In the same way, more than anything else, God uses people to heal people.

Jean Vanier writes, "A community is never there just for itself or for its own glory. It comes from and belongs to something much greater and deeper: the heart of God to bring humanity to fulfillment. A community is never an end in itself; it is but a sign pointing further and deeper, calling people to love."

Community Requires Trust

Now for a moment imagine that you are the man on the mat. You are about to go through the roof. This is the biggest risk you have ever taken in your life. You wonder if you can trust your friends to keep you safe. After all, when they carry you around at ground level, a drop would be unpleasant but not irredeemable. When you're on the roof, the stakes get raised a little higher. Has anybody tested the ropes?

You wonder if you can trust the crowd to be civil. After all, they arrived early enough to get seats. Many of them have their own list of requests. You think this may be viewed as a form of butting ahead of other people in line. If things get physical, you have no protection.

You wonder if you can trust Jesus. What if it turns out that he can't help you after all? Worse yet, what if he's in the middle of a really important point and doesn't like to be interrupted?

You lie there on your mat on the roof, thinking about all these dangers. You have a decision to make. If you go through the roof, you could get dropped, you could get ridiculed, you could get rejected. On the other hand, if you don't go through the roof, it's certain you will never be healed. This is your one shot at wholeness.

The man nods his head. He decides to roll the dice. He becomes a roof-crasher, too. And nothing will ever be the same.

Authentic Community *Always* Involves Spiritual Growth

The man's friends must wonder also how Jesus will respond. I know from personal experience that teachers can get a little touchy about being interrupted. You'll notice Jesus made sure he came to earth before there were beepers and pagers and cell phones ("in the fullness of time" is the biblical phrase for it).

Jesus looks up and sees the faces of four friends staring down at him.

They have nothing to ask for themselves. Their only thought is, "If we can just get our friend close to Jesus. . . ."

That's what great friends want to do for each other.

Then the text says an amazing thing: "When Jesus saw their faith. . . ."

Usually healing stories speak of Jesus seeing the faith of the one asking for healing for themselves or their child. Here it's the faith, not primarily of the man, but of his friends.

Do you have any idea what the faith of one person can do for a friend?

They dug a hole through a roof and sent in their friend. There is no record of their saying anything. It is not what he heard that moved Jesus; we are told that he *saw* their faith. What did he see?

A big hole in the ceiling, four faces in it—sweaty, dusty, anxious, hopeful faces thinking only of their friend and trusting somehow that Jesus has the kind of heart that will respond. Jesus sees a group who possess and act on an irrational commitment to the well-being of one of its members.

Jesus sees a little of what God intended when he made human beings. He sees a little island of *shalom* in a sea of brokenness. He sees people who love even in the face of a giant "as-is" tag. He thinks to himself that this is humanity at its finest.

He sees their faith.

Jesus turns and looks down at this twisted, motionless body on a mat. He sees not only a broken body but—as in every one of us—a broken, fallen soul.

He speaks tenderly: "Son, your sins are forgiven."

I wonder what the man on the mat thinks at this point. He hadn't really signed up to have his sins talked about.

But it's one of the things that happen when you get neck deep into community and Jesus is there in the middle of it. Being in community has a way of surfacing the sin issue.

—When I'm all alone, I can convince myself I'm quite a humble person. Then when I'm with other people and I hear someone else receiving all the praise, a voice that is decidedly not humble at all starts protesting inside me. Loudly.

—When I'm all alone, I can convince myself that I'm quite a compassionate person. I can watch a Hallmark commercial and feel very moved. Then when I'm with real human beings and I realize that I would have to expend energy and sacrifice time and be uncomfortable to practice compassion, it turns out I'm not nearly as altruistic as I thought I was.

A Dostoyevsky character said, "In my dreams, I am very often passionately determined to serve humanity . . . yet I'm quite incapable of living with anyone in one room for two days together, and I know that from experience."

I think it is reflective of what happens in deep community: Sooner or later, you get to the sin issues. "Community is the place where our limitations, our fears and our egoism are revealed to us," writes Jean Vanier. "While we are alone, we could believe we loved everyone. Now that we are with others, living with them all the time, we realize how incapable we are of loving, how much we deny to others, how closed in on ourselves we are." In deep community with Jesus, in the Fellowship of the Mat, we find our sin being talked about and forgiven.

Jesus is filling the desires of this man's friends, perhaps even deeper than they realize. When someone is your friend, your greatest desire for them—deeper than external well-being or even physical health—is that things are right between them and God. If someone is truly my friend, their deepest concern is the well-being of my character, my soul.

Paul Wadell writes, "In spiritual friendship the principal good is a mutual love for Christ and a desire to grow together in Christ. This is what distinguishes spiritual friendships from other relationships."

Count on it: In community with Jesus and with those who love you, most of what happened to this man will happen with you: Sin will get named and dealt with. And although this sounds frightening, it may be the best gift of all.

This man—who has been mocked and judged by people who assumed that his damaged body indicated that he was spiritually inferior—this man is told by Jesus, "You're clean. You're forgiven. You are right with God."

It is striking that Jesus knew the man needed forgiveness as well as healing. A friend of mine asked recently, "What sins can a paralytic do, anyway?" Jesus understood, of course, that the deadliest sins—resentment, arrogance, judgmentalism, lovelessness—are ones we can commit without lifting a finger.

A key part of this story is that there are others present in the room—teachers of the law, people who were thought of (and thought of themselves) as spiritual giants. They apparently arrived on time and got good seats. But you will notice that they had no friends to bring to Jesus. They were supposed to be the most spiritual ones—but apparently no one they knew was hurting or confused or needed Jesus.

It is worth pausing a moment to ask: Who do you think was greater in God's eyes? The experts who were specialists in the law, knew a lot about the Bible, regarded as teachers and leaders—but did not have a single person they cared for enough to bring to Jesus? Or four uncouth, etiquette-challenged roof-crashers who would do anything for their friend? This brings us to a topic that is absolutely fundamental: The connection between loving God and loving people.

The "Unity of Spiritual Orientation"

Let's start with a question: What preoccupies you? Or, where does your mind drift when you're not doing anything? What do you daydream about?

You can tell a lot about a person if you know what they think about when they're just sitting around. The King James Version translates

Proverbs 23:7 "As he thinketh in his heart, so is he." And it's really true:

An entrepreneur eats and sleeps her business start-up.

A great coach is always scribbling plays on a napkin.

A young mother worries about her children. When our children were first born, on the rare occasion when Nancy and I would spend a night in a hotel apart from them, the first thing she would do is check to see if the message light was on to inform us that the baby had been kidnapped.

The truth is, the more spiritually mature you grow, the more you will find your heart being drawn to people. You want to reach out to people, especially those neglected by society or far from God.

The average eighteen-year-old, hormone-filled adolescent male—what's he thinking about?

The average newly married husband on his wedding night—what's he thinking about?

How about the average eighty-year-old guy? (There's a theme here.)

A follow-up question: What does God think about all day? Of course, being omniscient, he can think of everything at once, but you understand the gist of the question. What preoccupies him? Where does his mind drift?

We can know—because of Jesus. He is the Word—the mind of God—made flesh. And Jesus insisted that God is constantly thinking about the people he loves so much. Jesus said the mind of the Father is moved toward people the way the mind of a shepherd keeps coming back to his lost sheep, the way the thoughts of a poor woman are obsessed with finding her lost coin. God could no more forget about people than a nursing mother could forget about her baby. The God whom Jesus revealed is a God who is ceaselessly preoccupied with finding and redeeming and loving people.

There is a very important implication to this. It is simply impossible to love the Father without sharing his heart for people.

It is critical for followers of Jesus to understand this. I grew up in circles where many people *thought* they were becoming more spiritual because they attended many church services or watched many preachers on television or memorized many Bible verses. But their *hearts* for people—especially for people far from God, for the lost, for the searching, for people with bad habits—in the tradition I grew up in that was smokers and drinkers and swearers and Democrats—their hearts toward these people got a little harder and colder and more judgmental year after year. What is bad is not just that this happened but that these people thought they were growing spiritually.

The truth is, the more spiritually mature you grow, the more you will find your heart being drawn to people. You want to reach out to people, especially those neglected by society or far from God. This comes under a critical point that Dallas Willard calls "the unity of spiritual orientation":

> To understand Jesus' teachings, we must realize that deep in our orientations of our spirit we cannot have one posture toward God and a different one toward other people. We are a whole being, and our true character pervades everything we do. We cannot, for example, love God and hate human beings.

This explains *many* of Jesus' teachings.

> "Do not judge, or you too will be judged."
>
> "If you forgive others when they sin against you, your heavenly Father will also forgive you. But if you do not forgive others their sins, your Father will not forgive your sins."
>
> Those who do not love their brother who is visible cannot love God who is invisible.

Why is this so?

It is not that God is withholding forgiveness to get back at you. Jesus' point runs much deeper. He is making a profound observation about the nature of human character. It is simply *psychologically impossible* for us to understand and desire to live in the stream of forgiveness and reconciliation and mercy with God and *not* want that with human beings.

People who don't love people *can't* love God, just as people who don't know the multiplication table can't do algebra. They may know a lot about the Bible, they may be quite churchy, and they may carefully avoid scandalous sins and be thought of as spiritually advanced. But this is an error, and one that deeply damages both those inside and outside the church. Just as love is the ultimate expression of the law, so lovelessness is the ultimate expression of sin.

This was the condition of the "teachers of the law" who sat listening to Jesus. They had no one to bring to him. And they had no love for the paralyzed man who needed Jesus' touch.

Such people did not cease to exist with the end of the first century. Churches are full of people who think they love God when in reality they have little love for the people who mean so much to him. I understand about such people because too often I fall victim to the same syndrome. I struggle with the same self-righteousness that plagued the teachers of the law. I far too often sit where they sat, disapprove as they disapproved, and forget to pick up mats and break through ceilings.

Jesus is concerned for his critics. He loves them, just as he loves the men coming through the ceiling. So he acts as if to say, "Just so you see I have authority. . . ." He turns to the man on the mat: "Get up, take your mat, go home."

Silence. Everyone watches.

Obviously, if the man had been paralyzed, all his muscles would have atrophied. Jesus not only cures paralysis but throws in muscle tone as well—

The man stands up. He lifts his mat off the ground. He folds it up. He has spent his whole life on that thing. And suddenly—never again.

His world has enlarged from three by six to as far as his feet can carry him.

Not just his body has been healed. His heart has also. His soul. Every sin has been forgiven.

Physically, relationally, spiritually, he is the healthiest guy in the room.

Imagine when he becomes an old man and hits eighty. The other members of his small group are using walkers and canes. His legs are still running strong. He got a nice warranty.

One by one the man's friends begin to pass away. Every time he looks at that mat, he remembers the little community he was part of, that crashed through a roof for him. His greatest gift, humanly speaking, wasn't his legs. It was his friends. There's no gift like the gift of community.

The Fellowship of the Mat still exists. You find it here and there, in a friendship or a marriage or a church, wherever a group possesses and implements an irrational commitment to the well-being of its members. It is not an easy fellowship to be a part of—people's mats are sometimes heavy and awkward, and there's always a roof of busyness or fear or conflict that needs to be crashed through. But those who find their way to it would never live without it again. It is the place where healing and wholeness happens. It is the fellowship where Jesus shows up: "Where two or three are gathered together in my name, there am I in the midst of them."

Learning to Dance

1. What's your mat?

2. Are you more likely to carry someone else's mat for them or to allow someone else to help carry yours? Why?

3. "The requirement for true intimacy is chunks of unhurried time." How does your schedule help or hinder you from entering into deeper community? How can you realistically pursue greater relational depth today?

4. Do a little "community self-assessment": If you're in a crisis, who do you call at three o'clock in the morning? Who prays for you on a regular basis? Who can you drop in on unannounced without any embarrassment? Who can you call to celebrate a victory in some aspect of your life? To what extent are you part of a fellowship of the mat these days?

5. Whose faith has had a deep impact on your life? How? Spend a few moments thanking God for the "roof-crashers" in your life.

6. Have you ever known someone who had a reputation for loving God but was not truly loving toward people? How do you account for this? How can you avoid this?

7. Think of the closest relationships in your life these days, one at a time. Ask yourself, "Is this relationship moving me closer to God, or farther away? Is it helping me grow spiritually and morally, or is it producing habits and attitudes that are cause for concern?"

PART 2

HOW TO GET CLOSE WITHOUT GETTING HURT

CHAPTER 4

UNVEILED FACES: AUTHENTICITY

In confession the break-through to community takes place.... If a Christian is in the fellowship of confession with a brother, he will never be alone again, anywhere.

DIETRICH BONHOEFFER

I am thinking of a game. There's a good chance it is the first game you ever played in your life. Nobody has ever written down the rules to this game, although everyone knows how to play. It has no leagues or television exposure, but it is played in some form by human beings in every culture on every continent in every century of our existence.

The game is called peek-a-boo. The rules are very simple: First you peek. Then you boo.

It is a strange thing that people don't usually play this game with other adults. It is quite rare for one couple to say to another, "Why don't you come over Friday night—we'll play peek-a-boo for a while?" Yet an adult will play it with a child day after day, week after week.

Something's going on in that child. It's as if the infant is learning: *First, I hide myself. I conceal my eyes. The hiding part of the game is crucial because during it I learn I exist even when you can't see me. I am independent. I have the capacity for aloneness. Then presto! I reveal myself! I disclose my person to you. You may see me, and I see you. We are connected, you and I. We're together. I know and am known.*

You're watching a human being begin to learn that they are an independent person—but one that can reveal themselves, can know and be known.

There is a kind of tension: *I hide myself—are you still there? I don't know. I hope so. I'm trusting you. The game depends on it. But I like having to trust you.*

This apparently silly game turns out to be crucial for the development of human beings. Psychologists like Robert Karen who study what's come to be known as "attachment theory" have spent countless hours observing parents—usually mothers—and infants engaged in this activity.

If the parent stares too much, the baby will be unhappy and turn away and try to break eye contact. If he or she feels watched all the time, the baby will get uncomfortable and begin to cry.

If the parent quits looking altogether and withholds all eye contact, the baby will initially get quite alarmed. He or she will cry, frantically try to get back the eye contact. Eventually, if this happens enough, the young child will give up, sink into a kind of depression, and not even seek contact any more.

A wise parent knows there has to be a kind of rhythm of independence and togetherness for the child to grow up right.

The Swiss psychiatrist Paul Tournier writes that this is why "a child's secrets must be respected. Something vitally important is at stake: nothing less than the formation of a person." This is one reason that, according to researchers such as Jan Yager, children who have the strongest mother-child bonds go on to build the best friendships.

The Bible says you and I were created as independent persons made in the image of God, yet with the capacity to reveal ourselves and connect with others. There is a fascinating little detail about God's relationship with the human beings he has made in Genesis. The text says the man and woman heard God when he came to walk in the garden with them "in the cool of the day." Apparently, even before the Fall, Adam and Eve didn't spend every moment of the day walking in the garden with God. We can imagine that some time was spent working, some focusing on and delighting in each other, and some walking in intimate fellowship with God. God himself set up a kind of rhythm of independence and intimacy with his human creatures. Like a wise parent, he offered them space to grow, so they could have full and rich lives which in turn they would freely choose to share with him.

The First "Human Moment"

Think back to the first face-to-face "human moment" in history—the encounter of Adam and Eve. Imagine what that was like. Tim Alan Gardner notes that Adam has just watched

> a long parade of wart hogs, hippos, orangutans, and every other type of creature all coming before him in pairs of twos—they all had dates. Now, feeling very much alone, he awakes to find not another furry, four-footed mammal, but a woman—a ravishing, delightful, completely naked woman. How do you think he reacted? As the old joke says, I think Adam's response was a full fledged, top of the lungs "YeeHaa" where he said, "Whoaaaa! Mannnnn!!!" which is where we get the word "woman."

Now Adam was no longer alone.

The first fact the writer of Genesis records about the man and the woman after their creation is that "they were both naked, and were not ashamed." I never heard that verse taught in the church where I grew up. Why does the writer say that? I don't think it was because they worked out a lot and had a really low percentage of body fat.

The writer is talking about perhaps the deepest of human longings: the longing to know and be known. Watch preschool children at recess: "Lookit me!" they will yell—at their teacher, at their parents, at a stranger walking across the playground. To be seen, affirmed, and celebrated is to know that life is good. Watch the students a few years later in junior high, sending each other notes:

> Do you like me? (check one):
>
> ☐ Yes
> ☐ No
> ☐ Maybe

To be known and liked is as close to heaven as you get in junior high.

Watch the teenagers a few years later, dating, revealing so carefully what they want to have known about them. Couples who go out in complete ignorance of each other engage in what's called a "blind date." I met Nancy Berg—who would later become my wife—on such a date. Afterward, I wanted to see her again, but didn't know how to contact her. The only thing I knew about her was the name of the church she attended: Whittier Area Community Church. So I called the church, explaining I was a pastor at a church not far away, and I needed the phone number of a parishioner named Nancy Berg; it was more or less a ministry thing.

The receptionist put me on hold for about five minutes. What I did not know at the time was that the receptionist's name was Verna Berg—Nancy's mother. She put me on hold to call Nancy at home and ask her if she wanted me to have her number. Nancy, I add modestly, asked if her mother could somehow patch me through to the house right then and there. (I wasn't told this detail for some months.)

Part of what happens when we date someone or make a friend or see a therapist is the progressive disclosure of who we are. It is done cautiously, with the awareness that there are parts of us that are not too attractive.

So try to imagine, for a moment, the wonder of the first unfallen man and woman. Every deed they did, every word they spoke, every thought that passed through their minds brought unalloyed joy to the one they loved. The thought of hiding simply did not occur to them. They literally had nothing to hide. "Lookit me," Adam would say to Eve in perfect innocence, and looking brought Eve unfettered delight.

There was no hiddenness, no concealing, no guilty secrets to separate them. It is expressed physically ("naked and not ashamed") because the "language" of sexual love is the most intimate language available to human beings. In ancient Hebrew, the act of sexual love was referred to as "knowing" someone. It is the ultimate act of vulnerability and self-giving, and it expressed for the first man and woman complete transparency in every facet of their relationship.

They were fully known and fully accepted.

Then came the Fall. The man and the woman God had made disobeyed him.

What follows is an absolutely brilliant exposition of how temptation works. It begins with a clever question from a serpent: "Did God *really* say, 'You must not eat from any tree in the garden'?"

Now, God did not say they could not eat from *any* tree. God said they could eat from *every tree—except* this one. All sorts of trees that we're told were beautiful to see and delicious to eat. The whole variety pack. This is a misquote of litigious proportions.

The decision to sin always includes the thought that I cannot really trust God to watch out for my well-being.

What is the serpent up to? He wants to plant a seed in the woman's mind to raise doubts about God's goodness. *I don't think I can trust God really has my best interest at heart. I think that if I really obey God fully, I will miss out on something good. I think I will have to watch out for myself. I'd better be prepared to set aside what God says if necessary.* The decision to sin always includes the thought that I cannot really trust God to watch out for my well-being.

The woman corrects the serpent, but she, too, gives an inaccurate rendering of God's instructions. Eve says, "God did say, . . . 'you must not touch it, or you will die.'" God had forbidden eating this fruit, but said nothing about touching it. The woman is making God a little severe, a little unreasonable, so that disobeying him becomes a little justifiable.

Notice something else: The Evil One will strike at people's vulnerable points. When God originally gave the command, only the man was present. Presumably, the woman gained from the man her information about what God said. So let me pose a question just for the women reading this book: Have you ever known a man to have any kind of communication difficulties, to not always give detailed accounts of his conversations?

The serpent goes after the one who was not directly present to hear what God said. Notice also that she does not involve the man in this process.

When we are playing with temptation and do it in isolation—don't tell anyone what we're tempted by—we make ourselves all the more vulnerable.

The text tells how the woman is captivated by the fruit, believing that it is both good to eat and pleasing to the eye and desirable for gaining wisdom. We get the impression that she is obsessed with the fruit. She keeps thinking of what she would miss if she didn't eat it. Without God or another person to challenge her thinking, the next step becomes inevitable. She eats it.

The man's fall is much simpler: "She also gave some to her husband, who was with her, and he ate."

Does it strike you that the man is a little passive here? Sin is often like that. Ask a child, "Why did you do that foolish, destructive act?" What will the child say? "I don't know."

If you were to ask Adam, "Why did you do it? Why did you disobey God?" what do you think he would say? "I don't know. Seemed like a good idea at the time." Just a casual act—a bite of fruit. But it's the end of paradise.

The Butterfly and the Hurricane

There's a saying in a field known as chaos theory that a butterfly fluttering its wings in one part of the world can set in motion a chain of events that will lead to a hurricane somewhere else. In Genesis 3:6, the butterfly has fluttered its wings. In verse 7, the hurricane begins. The hurricane is with us still. Its name is sin. We read about it in the newspaper every day.

"The eyes of both were opened." That's what the man and woman had been hoping for! But they saw a nightmare beyond belief. This was the birth of shame, of guilt.

The man and the woman looked at each other, and the beauty of the image of God—*imago dei*—had become horribly twisted and marred.

They looked at each other and saw strangers. They covered themselves with fig leaves. They wanted to hide. The spiritual hurricane that struck the earth that day deeply affected human nature. This is an important part of Christian doctrine about the fallenness of humankind.

People in our day speak of believing in the basic goodness of mankind.

Christians believe it is very good that God made people. They matter to him; they often do good things. But Christians also believe that human beings are not simply morally neutral agents who can always choose to do good if we just try hard enough. In the Fall something happened to human nature. That something is called "depravity."

We see it early in life. What are the odds that if you make a two-year-old share a toy he's been hogging all day, he'll say, "I'm so glad it brings you joy—would you like to use my blankie as well?"

Depravity is a spiritual condition—our readiness to harm others or let harm come to them if it will help us reach our goals of security, ego gratification, or the satisfaction of desire.

God is giving the man and the woman a choice. True community is never forced on anyone.

We want to do what's right, but we are prepared to do what's wrong. Just as glass is predisposed to shatter or nitroglycerin is predisposed to explode; we are predisposed to do wrong when conditions are right. That predisposition is called depravity. This is what's behind all our little "as-is" tags. This is why "everybody's weird." Our weirdness is not just about psychological eccentricities or about wounds that someone else has inflicted on us.

The Reformers called this predisposition *total depravity* because it affects every part of us—our behavior, our thoughts, and our feelings. We can't fix this condition on our own. We have fallen, and we can't get up. And the consequences are horrific.

Adam and Eve knew shame and the pain of being alienated from themselves; from each other; from God; from creation.

Sometimes people wonder, "Why did God forbid the man and woman from eating from one tree? If there had been no such rule, they never would have disobeyed."

But in this detail of the story, God is doing something of fundamental importance for community: God is giving the man and the woman a choice. True community is never forced on anyone.

The man and the woman decide there is something they want more than community with God. They do not trust him. They disobey. And the hurricane struck community. Sin always does. Anger hurts people, pride belittles people, lust uses people, deceit mocks people—sin always kills relationship.

Adam hears God's footsteps in the garden at the accustomed time. Always before, that sound filled him with joy. Always before, when he heard those footsteps, he ran toward them like a little child playing "Daddy's home" when the front door opens at five o'clock.

But this time, Adam's body is flooded with feelings he has never known before. This time the sound that until this day brought only eagerness and delight now brings terror and shame. This time he runs, not toward the footsteps, but away from them. Now he knows shame and fear. This time he hides.

There is a difference between what might be called solitude and hiding. Solitude is a gift from God. It existed before the Fall. It is the experience of being a unique person with the ability to think, feel, value, and choose on our own. Solitude enriches our contributions to community. The poet Rainer Maria Rilke wrote, "Love consists in this, that two solitudes protect and touch and greet each other." The capacity for solitude is an indication of strength.

Hiding is a curse. It came into being after the Fall. Hiding is motivated by shame. It involves pretending and deceiving. Hiding is the place of fear and anxiety. It always diminishes our contributions to community.

Adam hides. And God says, "Adam, where are you?"

This is one of the most astounding questions in Scripture. Why does God ask it? The psalmist wrote that no matter where he went, he could never travel beyond the range of God's knowledge: "If I make my bed in Sheol, you are there." The thought of Adam trying to hide from God would be funny if it weren't so sad—like a four-year-old playing hide-and-seek in a telephone booth with Sherlock Holmes. Yet here is the omniscient Maker of heaven and earth asking for the location of one human being who hasn't even left the garden. Why doesn't God just use his X-ray vision to locate Adam?

The reason is that, of course, this question is not really about Adam's geographical location. It is not really a request for information at all, as if God needed a global tracking system for his creatures. It is an invitation.

God allows Adam to hide.

God offers him the opportunity to reveal himself.

God has the audacious grace to treat Adam as a person, even when Adam has defied him. God does this because no one—not even he himself—can get another person to be in a relationship by brute force.

One of the marks that distinguishes a healthy church from a cult (or an unhealthy church, for that matter) is that in authentic community, people are never coerced or manipulated into self-disclosure. A friend of mine was once in a small group where the leader would try to verbally embarrass people into prematurely disclosing intimate details about their financial lives or past sexual history: "What—you don't trust the other members of the group? You're too narcissistic to share openly?" If you ever find yourself in a relationship or group where that's going on, run—do not walk—in the other direction. You can pressure someone into conformity, but not into community. Dallas Willard writes, "God has placed the only key to the innermost parts of the human soul in its own hands and will never take it back himself or give it to another. You may even be able to destroy the soul of another, but you will never unlock it against his or her will."

"Adam, where are you?"

Adam responds, "I heard you . . . , and I was afraid. . .; so I hid." This is the first mention of fear in the Bible. There was no fear before the Fall!

God asks, "Who told you that you were naked? Have you eaten from the tree?"

Adam reflects on the importance of taking personal responsibility for his actions, summons his courage, and responds, "The woman." Worse than that, he says, "The woman *you* put here with me." In other words: "Let's think, O Lord, whose idea was it to create that woman in the first place? When it was just me and the animals everything was okay." Adam has moved a long way from his "bone of my bones" speech of the previous chapter.

So now blaming enters human history. Do you think they will be the last married couple to blame each other? Blame, denial, evasion—

these are all forms of hiding that have marked the human race ever since that day. Even though Adam has brought his body out into the open, he is still trying to hide at least a little of his guilt. He is pretending to be more innocent than he really is.

Adam and Eve are not just hiding from God. They are also hiding from each other, both physically (that's what the fig leaves are about) and spiritually.

To know and be known—which had always been the greatest joy of the human race—now becomes the greatest fear of the human race.

And hiding becomes universal. It, too, is part of the legacy of the hurricane.

A man who is desperate for work applies to a zoo that he's heard has some openings. "Well, it's a little unusual, but I do have something," said the zoo director. "Our gorilla died sometime ago, and we haven't had the money to replace him. If you're willing to wear a monkey suit and impersonate an ape, you've got the job."

It didn't feel terribly authentic, but the man figured a job's a job, so he signed on. After a few awkward days he began to get into the spirit of the thing, and soon he became one of the zoo's prime attractions. One morning he was swinging from one vine to the next with a little too much animation and inadvertently swung himself right over the wall into the cage next to his—which was occupied by an enormous African lion.

The man could feel the lion's hot breath on his face. He knew he was a goner. Reflexively, he began screaming for help, when suddenly the lion whispered urgently to him, "Shut up, you idiot, or we'll both be out of a job!"

The tendency to hide is so strong that psychologists sometimes speak of the "imposter's phenomenon": the universal sense that at some level I'm faking it, that if others knew the truth about me, the jig would be up. The more skillful we are at impression management, the more we are trapped in our true aloneness. But we were not made to live this way. The apostle Paul says that in true community love is to be genuine. The writer of Acts says that in the new community, people met with "glad and *sincere* hearts"; they learned to stop pretending to be other than they were.

Imagine what your life would be like if all pretense were to vanish from it. Imagine the freedom and relief of not trying to convince anyone you were smarter or better than you are. This really is God's plan for human life.

So let's look at three stages of openness or disclosure that lead us toward greater levels of authenticity.

Guarded Communication

Some people—especially some psychologists—have said you should always let it all hang out and never have an unexpressed thought or feeling. I don't think that is either wise or biblical.

There is a time to be deliberately selective about what we reveal and what we do not. One of those times, to paraphrase Neil Plantinga, comes when Aunt Edna says, "How did you like my lima-bean, spam, Velveeta cheese, rasberry jello salad?"

You don't have to say, "Aunt Edna, I could be polite and speak in superficial generalities, but I want to be deeply authentic with you. I'm aware that at the core of my being—that core right near where your salad is—I'm experiencing revulsion and disgust. Aunt Edna—what were you thinking? You should never be allowed in a kitchen again for the rest of your life."

In this moment, be polite and superficial. When you're in business, it can be very appropriate to be guarded. I would not want to hire a real estate agent who said to the people whose house I want to buy, "Well, here's the offer we're making; but I want to be deeply open and transparent with you—I don't want there to be any masks. My clients would be willing to pay twenty thousand more than this if they have to in order to get the house."

In particular, you will run across certain people with whom you should always remain quite guarded. The writer of Proverbs says, "A gossip can never keep a secret; be careful around people who talk too much."

Scripture writers caution people to use wisdom about what they reveal. In particular, don't do deep disclosure with an untrustworthy person. You can get badly hurt. There *is* a place for guarded communication. But that's not where true community lies.

Everyday Authenticity

There is nothing more winsome or attractive than a person who is secure enough in being loved by God that he or she lives with a spirit of openness and transparency and without guile. This is one of the qualities that most attracted me to my wife. I'll give you kind of a picture if you promise to keep it between you and me.

One of the defining moments in any dating relationship is the first time the man sees the woman without makeup. Makeup is the art of "facial management." You don't want to let a guy look at your actual, unadorned face. So makeup is designed to make eyes look bigger, to make lips look fuller, nose look nosier, enhance your face to hide the blemishes and flaws.

Nancy and I had been dating a few months. I went to her apartment unannounced, and she and her roommate were putting up wallpaper. Nancy was wearing blue jeans and a ratty maroon sweatshirt. It was the first time I had seen her when she wasn't wearing contacts; she wore a pair of oversized tortoise-frame glasses. Her hair was everywhere, and she wasn't wearing a speck of makeup—no lipstick, nothing.

Suddenly I knew her in a way I had never known her before.

Actually, one of the ways I knew I was attracted to her was that I found myself thinking: "I like this look. I like her face with no makeup at all."

But it is not just our physical blemishes that we try to hide. Most of us work pretty hard to conceal the flaws that mar our character. Besides her physical transparency—no makeup—one of the things that drew me to Nancy, one of the things I admire most, is a kind of transparency of spirit.

Just for the record, like me, she is not a perfect person. We have a very human marriage with ups and downs. Yet I found a kind of freedom in Nancy—a capacity for authenticity, a lack of pretension. There is a down-to-earth quality about her—a readiness to let people know who she is, what she thinks, what is in her heart—without worrying much who they are or what the consequences might be.

I think I was drawn to this in large part because there is a part of me that struggles to be free like this. There are many situations in which I find myself being much more measured or calculating than I wish I were; situations where I work as hard—and subtly—as I can to try to manage what the other person is thinking of me; situations in which I emphasize opinions I think they might agree with, or tell stories that make me sound smarter or stronger or more successful than I really am.

I wear too much makeup.

Authenticity is one of the areas I most want to grow in.

The apostle Paul has a wonderful line to a church in Corinth about how it is possible for people to live in community—with "unveiled faces." Paul uses this line in retelling the story of Moses' meeting with God on Mount Sinai. Moses' face glowed.

In our day we talk about happy people having faces that beam. People always have one adjective to describe a bride: "radiant."

Moses' face was radiant. I would guess that his contemporaries were very impressed by this. Word spread: "Moses has a shiny face." When they looked at him, people would say, "Wow!" He was special.

One morning Moses woke up, looked in the mirror while shaving or something, and noticed his face was not glowing quite so much. He was losing his radiance the way a Midwesterner loses a tan in September.

He knew that when people saw his face now, they would be less impressed with him. He wouldn't be so special anymore.

Paul writes that Moses "put a veil over his face to keep the Israelites from gazing at it while the radiance was fading away." New Testament scholars differ as to what exactly Paul's point is in all this. But I wonder if part of what was going on is that Moses wanted the people to think he was more spiritually radiant than he really was. So Moses wore a veil.

We don't know how long he wore it or when he finally decided to take it off. My guess is it was when his wife said to him: "Moses, take off that stupid veil. You're not fooling anybody!" She might have added, "Personally, I'm glad your face isn't glowing any more. I couldn't get any sleep at night; it was like going to bed with a giant firefly. Take off the veil!"

What a relief it must have been to take it off—to let people see that he was just plain old Moses.

Paul goes on to say that since we have the assurance of God's love no matter what, we can do a very bold thing. We don't have to pretend to be more radiant than we really are. We can live with "unveiled faces."

Since we have the assurance of God's love no matter what, we can do a very bold thing. We don't have to pretend to be more radiant than we really are. We can live with "unveiled faces."

No concealing. No masks. No hiding.

We are talking here about something more than the pursuit of emotional health. Our problem is not simply that we are bashful children who hide when we ought to be open. Self-disclosure alone doesn't cure our deeper fallenness—as if Hitler were to say, "Well, I may be a genocidal psychopath, but that's just who I am, like it or not." We don't just need disclosure. We need forgiveness, healing, and grace.

That is why Jesus went to the cross. At the cross are disclosed the full measure of our sin and the full measure of God's grace. The only place where disclosure is truly safe is at the foot of the cross.

Richard Foster writes,

> Without the cross, the discipline of confession would be only psychologically therapeutic. But it is so much more. It involves an objective change in our relationship with God and a subjective change in us. It is a means of healing and transforming the inner spirit.

So let me ask you a personal question: What's your veil? What do you hide behind to keep from being known?

Some people hide behind superficial conversation. They may make lots of small talk and may even be quite good at it. They may talk freely about the weather or their work or their favorite team. But all their words are a shield. They are hiding their hearts.

Some people hide behind humor. They may have a great gift for making you laugh. But you notice, over time, that when the conversation gets tense or sad or begins to get personal, they find some way to make a joke. They hide behind a smiling face.

"Each of us does his best to hide behind a shield," writes Paul Tournier. "For one it is a mysterious silence which constitutes an impenetrable retreat. For another it is facile chit-chat. . . . One hides behind his timidity so that we cannot find anything to say to him; another behind a brazen self-assurance which renders him invulnerable."

Some people use their intelligence as a veil. Others use ignorance. Some veil themselves in busyness, in their work, in their vast competence and success. Some people have high-tech veils with remote controls or mouse pads. Ironically, many people in the church veil themselves in spirituality. They quote Bible verses or speak of "having deep peace" or speak of "God being in control." They may say things that sound impossible to argue with, but their words are moats of protection, not bridges of relationship. It may be a stained-glass veil, but it's a veil just the same.

What's your veil? If you're not sure, the people closest to you can tell you.

If you wear a veil around your heart, if you get really good at figuring out what other people want and then delivering it, if you perfect the art of projecting the right kind of image—you may impress some people. But you will become a little less radiant, a little less alive every day.

You may impress people, but you won't make friends.

The irony is that we are drawn to people who live with unveiled faces.

A friend of mine said that one wonderful thing we like so much about children is that they haven't learned to manage their faces. Whether the ice cream truck comes, or they have to eat spinach, or there's a monster under their bed—their faces tell you what's in their hearts.

When we get older, we learn to manage our faces. We teach them to conceal and guard. We train our faces to look confident when our hearts are scared, to look pious when our hearts are wild with temptation or guilt. We often admire people who have learned to manage their faces.

But that's not whom we're drawn to.

We are drawn to people with unveiled faces.

Alan McGinnis writes that Pope John XXIII, one of most beloved religious leaders of the twentieth century, elicited warmth from people everywhere he went, in part because he completely lacked pretense. "He never pretended to be more than he was." He struggled with weight all his life. He was the son of a poor peasant family. One of his first acts after being elected pope was to visit a large jail in Rome. As he was giving the prisoners his blessing, he remarked that the last time he had been in jail was to visit his cousin.

The irony of the masks is that although we wear them to make other people think well of us, they are drawn to us only when we take them off.

One time the pope was at a party when a woman wearing a low-cut dress walked in. John commented afterward that "one of the hard things about being pope is—usually if a woman like that walks into a party, everybody looks at her. If *I'm* at a party and a woman like that walks in—everybody looks at me."

To live with an unveiled face means I make a covenant that I will try to never pretend to be more than I really am. This means I will

—Give up trying to please everyone in my life.

—Pursue the courage to express what I truly value, enjoy, and love even if I think the person I'm talking to will disagree or disapprove.

—Acknowledge it openly when I get something wrong, instead of giving in to the temptation to hide it or manage it or put a positive spin on it.

The irony of the masks is that although we wear them to make other people think well of us, they are drawn to us only when we take them off.

If you want to be in a relationship where people share deeply with you, there is one single step you need to take. In the words of Sidney Jourard, who spent years researching this field, "disclosure begets disclosure." Self-disclosure has enormous power. A therapist once said the single most compelling way to get a client to open up is to tell a secret that the client could hurt the therapist with if he were to break confidence.

Deep Disclosure with a Few Trusted Friends

This leads us to the deepest level of disclosure: telling another human being those aspects of our lives that make us most vulnerable. At this level we dare to unveil areas of failure or embarrassment that are quite intimate. This kind of disclosure should not be entered into lightly. One of the great writers on friendship, a twelfth-century English abbot named Aelred of Rievaulx, wrote that we owe love to all people, but only to a proven friend are we to entrust "the secrets of the heart."

Alan McGinnis notes that one of the most unique and attractive aspects of the life of Jesus was his utter transparency. Unlike so many leaders who go through life at a distance from their followers—remote, inaccessible, unknowable—Jesus lived a common life. He let his friends see him in unveiled moments of joy, sadness, anger, and fatigue.

Jesus' followers never had to guess whether he was delighted or disappointed. As his life was nearing its end, he did not try to convince them he was filled with optimism. He was so transparent, he took the risk of openness and said to them, "My soul is overwhelmed with sorrow to the point of death."

Jesus was the one adult human being who ever lived who never learned to manage his face.

To make sure that his disciples understood that this strategy of self-disclosure was deliberate, he said to them just before he died:

> "No longer do I call you servants, for a servant does not know what his master is doing; but I have called you friends, for all things that I heard from My Father I have made known to you."

Jesus modeled deep disclosure to a few trusted friends.

How are you doing with this? Is there anyone in your life who knows everything about you?

Everybody on this planet carries a few *deep* secrets:

—Maybe you've done things that you are desperately ashamed of, or made choices that are so painful that you try not even to think about them.

—Maybe things were done to you that have such a sense of darkness about them that you can't talk about them.

—Maybe they involve feelings of depression or anxiety so deep you didn't know if you could go on.

—Maybe they involve habits or behavioral patterns that you can't break—you feel so weak.

Every human being carries hurts or scars or wounds. Our tendency since the Fall is to hide as if our life depended on it.

This is exactly wrong.

Our life depends on getting found. *There is no healing in hiding.*

This is true even at the physical level. Contemporary research indicates a connection between self-disclosure and physical health. Timothy Jones notes that studies have shown that people who confess wrong things they've done and discuss traits that disturb them actually experience both short-term and long-term gains in physical well-being. Researcher James Pennebaker writes, "There appears to be [within us] something akin to an urge to confess. Not disclosing our thoughts and feelings can be unhealthy. Disclosing them can be healthy."

This sounds a lot like what is written in the book of James: "Confess your faults one to another, and pray one for another, that ye may be healed."

But coming out of hiding isn't just necessary for our bodies; it is needed for our souls. God still patiently asks us the question he asked in the garden so long ago: "Adam, where are you? Will you trust me? Will you stop hiding? Will you come back into community?"

You can only be loved to the extent that you are known. You can only be completely loved if you are completely known.

Maybe you have been carrying a secret for years. You try not to think about it—but it's always there. It keeps you from ever fully experiencing love.

Even when someone tells you they love you, inside you say to yourself: *Yes, but you don't know the whole truth about me. You might not say these things if you really knew.*

This is why knowing and being known go to the core of life: You cannot be fully loved if you are not fully known. You can only be loved to the extent that you are known. You can only be completely loved if you are completely known.

This is also why the practice of confession has always been at the heart of great renewal movements in the church. Sin causes us to seek hiddenness and separation, which in turn destroy community. In confession, we enter back into community. We come out of hiding. Dietrich Bonhoeffer wrote, "If a Christian is in the fellowship of confession with a brother, he will never be alone again, anywhere."

Two primary words describe this deep level of openness: self-disclosure and confession. They overlap, of course, but both are useful. *Disclosure* comes from the language of therapy. It includes telling about not only wrong things we have done but also things that have not traditionally fallen under the category of confession: shame about physical appearance, for instance, or anguish over having been sexually abused. These secrets need to come into the light.

Confession, by contrast, is a spiritual and moral term. It involves the naming of specific sins as part of the process of repentance and reconciliation. It is a reminder that we don't just need empathy and healing—we also need to be cleansed and forgiven. I believe that confessing our sins to another human being is crucial, not because God requires it before he'll forgive us, but because there is tremendous power in being fully known and in hearing another voice remind us that God *has* forgiven us. As Bonhoeffer—whose father was a psychiatrist—put it, "In the presence of a psychiatrist I can only be a sick man; in the presence of a Christian brother I can dare to be a sinner."

When people begin to open up at this deep level, then true community—the kind God intended for us—begins to become possible.

I think of a married couple I know. The husband wrestled with patterns of compulsive sexual behavior. On business trips, he would watch adult movies. He had secrets he knew were damaging to his marriage.

One of the hardest things he ever did was to tell his wife his secrets. He was so ashamed, he could not bring himself to look her in the eye as he revealed his struggles to her. He asked her for forgiveness. He promised her he would find support and accountability in a trustworthy relationship. He said he would do whatever was needed to overcome these habits.

He had tried to guess what her response would be. He pictured a hundred different scenarios. He knew she would be hurt; he thought she would be surprised. He hoped she would forgive him; he feared she might despise him. But when she responded, it was in a way he never dreamed.

She was silent. Her eyes filled with tears. Then, haltingly, she began to tell him her story. It turned out she had secrets of her own. While she was in high school, a youth pastor at her church had betrayed his position of trust to enter a sexual relationship with her. She had carried the burden of guilt and remorse over that relationship—alone—for fifteen years.

Because of her husband's decision, she gained the courage to be transparent with him.

To disclose at this level was messy, embarrassing, risky, and painful.

But this couple experienced a level of healing, closeness, and intimacy with each other they had never known.

If they had not opened up to each other, they could have been married for forty or fifty years, yet gone to their graves to some extent strangers to each other.

This couple would tell you that the decision to be transparent was the greatest gift they ever gave their relationship. After years of wretched hiding, they learned at least a little of what it means to be fully revealed "and not ashamed."

One of the greatest steps you can take toward living in community is this: *Move toward having someone in your life who knows all about you.*

Of course, we can't do this all at once. Sometimes out of emotional neediness or bad judgment or hurt somebody will share too deeply and too fast with another person they don't know. There are certain warning signs to watch for that will tell you when to slow down with a person or a small group:

—*Inappropriate use of humor.* Some people are embarrassed by deep honesty, and they attempt to relieve their embarrassment by using a little humor to create distance. Or they may mock the person who is disclosing. When this happens, you can see masks go back on.

—*Judgmental statements or premature advice.* A friend of mine talked with his small group once about his struggle with lust. It was a significant disclosure. He was taking a risk. The immediate response of another man in the group was, "I can't relate to that at all." I wanted to ask him, "What kind of hormone-challenged, libidinally repressed, passion-deficit robot are you, anyway? Maybe you're not that much more spiritually advanced—maybe you just have no mojo. You have a mojo problem."

—*Violating a confidence*. When you tell someone something in confidence, you are entrusting to them a little piece of your heart. It takes great verbal discipline to honor this, and some people simply don't have the character to do it. Test someone's ability to keep small confidences before you trust them with big ones. In Bonhoeffer's words, a trustworthy friend "keeps the secret of our confession as God keeps it."

Since we began this chapter with a children's game, it might be appropriate to end it with one as well. This game goes by a variety of names; my children used to call it "trust-ee."

It requires two people—the trust-er, and the trust-ee. The trust-er stands three feet or so in front of the trust-ee and falls backwards. To play the game right is to be utterly vulnerable—no looking, no sliding one foot back to protect yourself just in case. Your life is in the hands of the trust-ee.

Why play such a risky game? We play it, I suppose, because something inside us knows life is not worth living if we cannot trust. We play it because every time we fall back and get caught, our ability to trust gets a little stronger.

I believe it is inevitable that relationships will stagnate and die when people quit taking the risk of self-disclosure. I was a member of one small group that was becoming increasingly bland. It wasn't awful; people weren't getting damaged by it. It was just getting a little sterile. Even though we talked about our families and personal lives, we had a hard time getting beneath the surface.

Then one afternoon, a member of the group talked about an important project that was not going well. His eyes filled with tears as he spoke of his fear of failure.

He played trustee.

It is always a risk to do this. Risk is an indispensable aspect of authentic self-disclosure.

In this sense, being in a relationship is like riding a bicycle. Relationships never stand still. Relationships are always moving—either toward greater depth or toward more superficiality. Like the Dead Sea, a person who keeps everything trapped inside becomes stagnant and sterile.

It seems that relationships—marriages, friendships, small groups—require a kind of quota of risk-taking disclosure if they are to stay fresh and growing.

But especially, if we are going to play trustee, we look for faithfulness. We look for a loyal heart.

In the children's game, falling is optional, avoidable. In real life, however, we live in a fallen world. We all fall, we fall often, and sometimes hard. If we try to handle our fallenness on our own, if we try to keep it secret, eventually it will destroy us.

God has made a better way. He has formed a community in which people can live with unveiled faces. It really is possible to do life without hiding. All it takes is trust.

Learning to Dance

1. Think about a time when someone violated your trust. What happened? How easy or difficult is it for you to trust people now?

2. Rate yourself on the following scale:

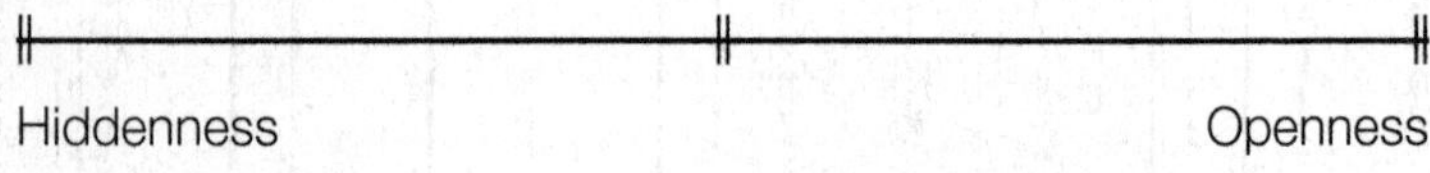

Where are you these days? Where would you like to be?

3. What are the qualities you look for in a trustworthy person?

4. Both solitude and hiding take place in aloneness. How do you define each, and how do you believe each affects community?

5. If a veil is something you hide behind, what is your veil?

   —Superficial conversation
   —Humor

—Intelligence
—Busyness/success
—Shyness
—Spirituality

6. What is one step you could take to reveal a little more of the truth about yourself in a close relationship?

7. Think about a community you are a part of: a small group or your family, for example. Are any dynamics present that might prevent intimacy?

   —Inappropriate use of humor
   —Violation of confidentiality
   —Judgmental statements
   —Premature advice-giving

   How might you best address this?

8. Notice attempts that you may make through the day to cover up. Practice "freedom of speech" today. See how well you can do to cultivate a sense of transparency.

PUT DOWN YOUR STONES: ACCEPTANCE

I really only love God as much as
I love the person I love the least.
DOROTHY DAY

You can safely assume you've created God
in your own image when it turns out that God hates
all the same people you do.
ANNE LAMOTT

Some years ago I visited a little museum on Nantucket Island devoted to a volunteer organization formed centuries ago. In those days, travel by sea was extremely dangerous. Because of the storms in the Atlantic along the rocky coast of Massachusetts, many lives would be lost within a mile or so of land. So a group of volunteers went into the life-saving business. They banded together to form what was called the Humane Society.

These people built little huts all along the shore. They had people watching the sea all the time. Whenever a ship went down, the word would go out, and these people would devote everything to save every life they could.

They did not put themselves at risk for money or recognition, but only because they prized human life. To remind them what was at stake, they adopted a motto:

You have to go out, but you don't have to come back.

This doesn't sound like a very catchy little recruiting slogan, does it? But it was.

It is fascinating to read accounts of people who would risk everything—even their lives—to save people they had never met.

Over time, things changed. After a while, the U.S. Coast Guard began to take over the task of rescue. For a while, the coast guard and the life-saving society worked side-by-side. Eventually, the idea that carried the day was, "'Let the professionals do it. They're better trained. They get paid for it."

Volunteers stopped manning the little huts. They stopped searching the coastlines for ships in danger. They stopped sending teams out to rescue drowning people.

Yet, a strange thing happened: They couldn't bring themselves to disband. The life-saving society still exists today. The members meet every once in a while to have dinners. They enjoy one another's company.

They're just not in the life-saving business anymore.

You and I were made to be in the life-saving business. We don't always see it, because we can be blinded by our self-preoccupation, but people around us have little mini-shipwrecks every day: A friend gets chewed out by her boss, a child fails in school, a wife fights with her husband and gets a little more disappointed in her marriage, a coworker makes foolish financial choices, a high school girl doesn't get asked to the prom, somebody at church gets caught in a lie.

Mostly, the lifelines we have to offer are words. Every word we speak has the power either to give a little life to people or to destroy a little bit of their spirit and vitality. We have the ability to offer acceptance, love, and hope; we also have the ability to judge, condemn, and wound.

"Accept one another," the apostle Paul says. What exactly do we do when we accept someone? It is a remarkable action, difficult to define, yet unmistakable when we experience it. To accept people is to be *for* them. It is to recognize that it is a very good thing that these people are alive, and to long for the best for them. It does not, of course, mean to approve of everything they do. It means to continue to want what is best for their souls no matter *what* they do.

Jesus, a Woman, and a Bunch of Stone Throwers

This is the story of a woman who was about to go under, a group of men who forgot they were supposed to be in the life-saving business, and the One who keeps searching the shipwrecks for what he treasures most.

We read about this woman in the eighth chapter of the gospel of John. She had been a young bride with dreams about married life. She had dreamt perhaps of having a husband who loved her, of praying and worshiping with him, of having children and raising a family.

But somehow, things did not turn out the way she had planned. She was disappointed in her marriage. Maybe it was her husband's fault, maybe it was hers; probably—as is usually the case—it was some of both.

Somewhere along the line the woman met another man. He noticed her. He seemed to want to listen to the things she had to say. This is a powerful thing for an aching heart, as the following story shows:

> My great-aunt, for many years a widow, fell in love when she was in her seventies. Obese, balding, her hands and legs misshapen by arthritis, she did not fit the stereotype of a woman romantically loved. But she was—by a man also in his seventies who lived in a nursing home....
>
> In trying to tell me what this relationship meant to her, my great-aunt told of a conversation. One evening she had had dinner out with friends. When she returned home, her male friend called, and she told him about the dinner. He listened with interest and asked her: "What did you wear?" When she told me this, she began to cry: "Do you know how many years it's been since anyone asked me what I wore?"

The woman in John's story met a man who seemed to care. At first it was all quite innocent. Then one day they crossed a line. Maybe it was a touch that lingered too long. Maybe it was a shared look that implied a kind of illicit promise. Maybe it was the sharing of secrets that violated her husband's confidence and trust.

That day she crossed a line. Maybe she didn't even notice it or think about it at the time. The Evil One always prefers to keep such moments dark and hazy so that we are hardly even aware of what we're choosing.

But she chose.

Then she started crossing other lines, until this became a full-blown affair. She entered into a state of spiritual despair, though she didn't know it yet.

As long as it was secret, it was as if she were living two lives in different worlds.

When she was in one world, she could pretend the other one did not exist. She kept from thinking about what this might do to her children. She kept herself from thinking about how this was damaging her soul—but it was!

Sin unchecked always leads to more sin:

She used to be a truthful person. The first time she lied to her husband about where she was going so she could be with this man, her heart was pounding, she was blushing, and she was sure her husband would sense she wasn't telling the truth.

Now she has become so expert at deceiving her husband and children that she can lie without showing it. *She* doesn't even notice, let alone her husband. She has become a liar.

The first time she went to the synagogue and heard the Scriptures read after sleeping with this other man, she was sure everyone could read the guilt on her face. She thought they would all find out. She thought God would strike her dead with a bolt of lightning. She vowed to God she would never see this man again.

But no one found out. There was no lightning. God did nothing.

Now she is able to go to the synagogue and hardly think about her affair at all. She doesn't think much about God, either. She tries to think about other things during the prayers.

She has become a hypocrite.

As long as her secret is intact, she hardly thinks about these things. Every once in a while she wakes up in the middle of the night in a cold sweat, but it usually passes. She doesn't notice what is happening to her—not really.

Then comes this night. She is with this man that she has been with we don't know how many times before. But this time it happens. The door opens. There have been men outside waiting and watching, and now they come in and seize her. She screams, she cries, she begs for mercy.

She would give anything if she could go back to where she first crossed the line. But she can't. You can never go back. This unreal haze that she has been living in for so long is ripped away. As happened at the Fall, her eyes are opened. She sees herself naked and is ashamed. She wants to hide, but has no place to go.

She suddenly realizes why she's here: She chose it. She chose this life.

That's not all there is to it. She was hurt and wounded and had needs that went unmet. But she is not just a victim. She made a thousand choices that led inevitably, inexorably to a moment like this.

She would kill herself right then if they would let her—they do not.

They wrap her up in sheets and lead her away.

Like the paralytic, she is taken to Jesus by a band of men while he is teaching a crowd. Only she is not carried on a mat but is wrapped up in sheets. The men who bring her are not her friends but her enemies. She is brought, not to be healed, but to be killed.

Jesus had just sat down to teach the people. In those days the way a rabbi signaled that formal teaching time has begun was by sitting down. If anyone needed to stand so people could see, the listeners would. That way the teacher could go on talking for hours. (Speaking as a teacher, I think that was a good arrangement.)

The point John wants us to catch is that this is not a private conversation to figure out constructive action. These men are more than willing to humiliate this woman publicly because frankly, it's Jesus they're after. The text says they were looking for something with which to accuse him. So they accuse this woman in an attempt to put him on the spot and gather material against him. They do not have much joy in life, but they do find delight in accusing people they don't like.

"Teacher," they say—as if they were honoring him, "this woman was caught in the very act. . . ."

The law was quite clear about what was required to be "caught in the act." Circumstantial evidence didn't cut it. "One witness is not enough to convict a man accused of any crime or offense he may have committed," Moses had said. "A matter must be established by the testimony of two or three witnesses."

This means that for some time two or more of these men had been hanging around this woman's house. They kept watching in her window. We are not told how long they watched and how much they saw. But the cold-blooded premeditation of their spying tells us about the depth of their contempt for the woman—and Jesus.

Scholars have pointed out that the other man is not brought here, even though the law said he should be stoned, too. One speculation is that the religious leaders were colluding with this man to set up the whole deal, so they let him slip away when they grabbed the woman.

At any rate, they bring her before Jesus: "She was caught redhanded. The law is very clear—stone her. What do you say?"

They think to themselves, *We've got him now. If he shows mercy, we get him for being soft on the law; if he says, "Stone her," the crowds will never forgive him.* In addition, the Roman authorities had forbidden the Jewish authorities from executing anyone, so if Jesus said, "Stone her," he would be in trouble with Rome.

Here is this woman—trembling with guilt and fear, wishing she could die, believing she is about to. But her accusers don't even see her. All they can think is, "We've got him now." They stand there, with stones in their hands, just waiting for the word.

Before we go on, before you judge them too quickly, let me ask you a question: Have you ever held a stone in your hand?

Sins of the Spirit

Historically, Christian thinkers have divided sin into two categories: "sins of the flesh" and "sins of the spirit." Sins of the flesh generally involve appetites that get out of control: lust, greed, gluttony, drunkenness, laziness. Our flesh is fallen enough that, given enough time, we can turn almost anything into the idol of our lives: *Playboy* magazines, Krispy Kreme donuts, BMW automobiles, even the television remote control. As was the case with the woman in this story, these idols will inevitably lead to other sins as well: deceit, betrayal, despair.

The second category is called "sins of the spirit." These have less to do with our biology than with our souls. They have names like pride, arrogance, self-righteousness, and judgmentalism. They are generally not as colorful as sins of the flesh. They don't provoke nearly as much gossip—perhaps because gossip is itself a sin of the spirit. Rarely does a church exercise discipline over one of these sins. If you hear of a pastor having to leave a church for "moral reasons," you can be pretty sure it's not pride. Churches in our day are not usually scandalized by sins like arrogance or self-righteousness.

_We_ are most scandalized by sins of the flesh. _Jesus_ was most scandalized by sins of the spirit.

But Jesus was. The New Testament tells a striking number of stories that involve the triad of a "sinner of the flesh," a "sinner of the spirit," and Jesus. There is the story of the Pharisee and the sinful woman who anointed Jesus' feet, of the Pharisee and the tax collector, of the prodigal son and his older brother, and—yes—of the religious leaders versus the woman caught in adultery.

In all these stories, the people guilty of the "sins of the flesh" knew they were in big trouble. They also saw Jesus as a person they could run to. They finally came home.

In all these stories, the people guilty of pride and arrogance were also blind. They thought it was possible to love God and despise people. They actually thought they were paragons of spiritual maturity because they avoided sins of the flesh. They had no idea that their sin crippled their ability to love—which makes sins of the spirit the most dangerous and destructive sins of all.

We are most scandalized by sins of the flesh. *Jesus* was most scandalized by sins of the spirit.

C. S. Lewis wrote,

> The sins of the flesh are bad, but they are the least bad of all sins. All the worst pleasures are purely spiritual: the pleasure of putting other people in the wrong, of bossing and patronizing;. . . the pleasures of power, of hatred. For there are two things inside me, competing with the human self which I must

> try to become. They are the Animal self, and the Diabolical self. The Diabolical self is the worse of the two. That is why a cold, self-righteous prig who goes regularly to church may be far nearer to hell than a prostitute.

I wonder whether, when these teachers of the law first signed up as young men to devote themselves to a life of service, they had warm hearts for God and others. Weren't they in fact motivated by love? But over time something happened. All their learning about Scripture filled them with pride. All their efforts at obedience filled them with disdain for the less devout. All their giftedness filled them with impatience toward those who were weaker.

All their spiritual power filled them with contempt for the weak. And they became as enslaved by a cold heart as an addict can become enslaved by crack cocaine.

What is so insidious about the sins of the spirit is that the carriers don't have a clue. At least with sins of the flesh, you find out you have messed up. With the sins of the spirit, you may not even know.

You just walk through life with a stone in your hand:

—Judgmental thoughts

—A superior attitude

—Impatient words

—Bitter resentments

—Little room for love

People stand around you—trembling in brokenness, guilt, fear, lostness—but you're so caught up in your own self-righteousness you don't even see them. Or worse yet, you see them and are not moved. You don't even notice—you're not in the life-saving business anymore.

A Church of Stone Throwers

I wonder about this a lot. I have been in the church my whole life. I love the church. But I wonder sometimes: *Why do churches produce so many stone throwers?*

I think of a church I was a part of many years ago where many people—not all, but too many—were just cold. They didn't dance, they didn't laugh, they had little capacity for joy.

But there is one thing they enjoyed: passing judgment on the spiritual inferiority of others.

—Somebody's kids were a little wild—people would pick up stones.

—Somebody's marriage wasn't working—another stone.

—The music minister chose the wrong kind of song, or played it too loudly—more stones.

Somebody crossed a line, violated a code, had a problem—word spread. People picked up stones. The truth is—though they would never admit this—it energized them, gathering stones. They looked forward to it.

It is never done openly. It happens like this: A woman is caught in adultery. Other women in the church talk about it: "Did you hear? What a shame. The poor children. How could she?" They shake their heads, cluck their tongues, and carefully adopt a pose of concerned disappointment.

Inside, they think the words they won't speak: *I never liked her. I've always been jealous. She is more attractive than me—I've always felt plain and undesirable with her around.* Just beneath the surface are barely disguised feelings of smug satisfaction and a kind of superiority at being "one of the faithful ones."

The stones may be highly polished, but they will kill all the same.

Sometime ago I worked at a Baptist church that had a sudden, large influx of unchurched people. They sometimes preferred music and language and living arrangements and beverages that came as an unpleasant shock to folks who had been around the church all their lives. So we brought in an expert—a New Testament professor known as "Dr. B"—to talk about communities and grace.

A stone thrower from way back complained to Dr. B about how she did not approve much of these newcomers and complained, "Shouldn't they clean up their act before they come to church?"

Dr. B can get quite passionate about this subject, and he did then. "If you want to go to a church where such people are not welcome and never darken the door, you will find many such churches in any city. You may attend there if you wish. But who will welcome those who are far from the church? What about"—and here Dr. B off the top of his head whipped off a long string of adjectives I can only partly remember—"what about the chain-smoking, adult-channel-watching, *Playboy*-reading, whiskey-guzzling, wife-swapping, tax-cheating, child-neglecting SOB?"

There was a long pause. People were not expecting that term from a New Testament professor. Then out of the silence, one of the deacons in the back, asked, "You mean Sons Of Baptists?"

Who will welcome the Sons of Baptists?

Philip Yancey begins his book *What's So Amazing About Grace?* with a story he heard from a friend:

> A prostitute came to me in wretched straits, homeless, sick, unable to buy food for her two-year-old daughter. Through sobs and tears, she told me she had been renting out her daughter—two years old!—to men interested in kinky sex. She made more renting out her daughter for an hour than she could earn on her own in a night. She had to do it, she said, to support her own drug habit. I could hardly bare hearing her sordid story. . . .
>
> At last I asked if she had ever thought of going to a church for help. I will never forget the look of pure, naive shock that crossed her face. "Church!" she cried. "Why would I ever go there? I was already feeling terrible about myself. They'd just make me feel worse."

Why is it that in ancient times women like this so often ran toward Jesus, where in our day they so often run from his followers? What might a little community look like if nobody in it were to pick up a stone?

So there they stand. This woman waiting to die; her judges, with stones in their hands; and this man, Jesus. The stone throwers ask him, "What do you say?"

Then Jesus does a curious thing. He bends down and starts writing in the sand. Ironically, this is the only time in the Gospels that we are shown Jesus writing—and he writes not on paper or papyrus, but on sand, where the words will quickly be lost.

This act of writing bothers the stone throwers. It is odd behavior on Jesus' part. There used to be a detective character on television named Columbo; you were never sure whether or not he was really noticing what was going on. Jesus is doing a Columbo kind of thing. He doesn't seem to be paying attention. So the teachers of the law keep pressing him: "You're the rabbi, so make the call. What do you say?"

Jesus stands up and speaks: "Go ahead and stone her. That's what the law says. Just one rule: Let the man without sin go first." Then Jesus goes back to writing on the ground.

What was Jesus writing? Unfortunately, John doesn't tell us. But it hasn't kept scholars from guessing:

—It was the custom in Roman law for a judge to first write the sentence and then read it, so some people think Jesus was doing that as a way to express his authority to judge.

—Some think Jesus was writing the Ten Commandments.

—There is another possibility. We have a word for the scribblings some people make when they are in a meeting or on the telephone: doodling. Maybe Jesus was a doodler.

—One intriguing idea dating back to the fifth century is that Jesus was writing down the names of the sins of the leaders in the group. For instance: "standing at the window watching adultery take place a lot longer than was necessary to gather evidence. . . ."

Maybe, one by one, he is naming the sins of the people standing in the circle of self-righteousness.

Condemnation and judgment have become so deeply rooted in the human spirit that most of us can't imagine having to function without them.

Whatever he is writing, whatever he is doing, he confronts these men with a decision: "Go ahead and throw your stone if you want. Pass judgment. Condemn her. Your call. Just make sure that you are sinless yourself. Just remember that sinful people—fallen people—are in no position to throw stones. When sinful people start passing judgment, they end up passing judgment on themselves."

It may be that Jesus is writing down their sins. But he writes them down on sand, where it can be quickly erased. Then an amazing thing happens.

Somebody lets go of his stone. Someone else, then a third person. The older and wiser ones first, according to Jewish custom, we are told.

Maybe their hearts melt a little bit and they become a little more human. Maybe they remember what it is like to stand in need of forgiveness. None of the stones get thrown in anger.

There is no room in Jesus' community for throwing stones. We are all too broken. Philip Yancey says that Jesus' audience would have divided people into two categories: sinners (like the woman) and the righteous (like the men). Yet Jesus in one brilliant stroke replaces them with two different categories: sinners who admit, and sinners who deny.

Letting Go of Our Stones

Do you have any stones you need to let go of?

Condemnation and judgment have become so deeply rooted in the human spirit that most of us can't imagine having to function without them. We *must* let people know how much we disapprove of them—particularly those we don't like. And of course, we are richly rewarded by the sense of superiority such condemnation breeds in us.

Dallas Willard writes about the remarkable way in which his future brother-in-law's family, in which he was raised,

> had a spirit in them that I, at least, had never before encountered, and perhaps never since. They did not condemn. They worked hard, were upright almost to a fault, and carefully disciplined their children. But I never saw or felt with them the slightest element of condemnation or condemnatory blaming.... [They] demonstrated to me how one could live a strong and good life without using condemnation to punish and control others.... When we enter the life of friendship with the Jesus who is now at work in the universe, we stand in a new reality where condemnation is simply irrelevant.

The apostle Paul says there is simply "no condemnation" anymore for those who are in Christ Jesus. "If God is for us, who can be against us?" Paul demands to know.

So, do you have any stones you need to let go of? Maybe against your mother or father, or against an ex-spouse, or against a boss or coworker, or against someone who has hurt you.

You have carried the stone for so long you don't remember life without it.

Put down the stone.

This may mean you need to take action:

—If you have spread gossip—go to the person you talked to, and apologize. Set things right.

—If your heart is hard toward someone—do an act of service for them. Don't tell anyone else. Ask God to change your heart.

—If you have behaved badly toward someone—go to them. Today. Ask forgiveness.

Sometimes stone-throwing happens in families. It may involve only little pebbles, but it becomes so habitual that the throwers hardly even notice it anymore. C. S Lewis asks,

> Who has not been the embarrassed guest at family meals where the father or mother treated their grown-up offspring with an incivility which, offered to any other young people, would simply have terminated the acquaintance? Dogmatic assertions on matters which the children understand and their elders don't, ruthless interruptions, flat contradictions, ridicule of things the young take seriously, . . . insulting references to their friends, all provide an easy answer to the question "Why are they always out? Why do they like every house better than their home?" Who does not prefer civility to barbarism?

Dorothy Bass writes about a family that found a novel way to honor the Sabbath. On Sundays they have an agreement that there will be no criticism in the house. The most striking result, she relates, is the way their children's friends end up spending Sundays at their home.

Paul Tournier was a brilliant thinker and writer, perhaps the most influential Christian therapist of the twentieth century. Doctors from around the world traveled to his home in Geneva, Switzerland, to learn from him. "It is a little embarrassing for students to come over and study my 'techniques,'" he once said, "because they always go away disappointed. All I do is accept people."

As I have said, accepting a person is not the same thing as approving all of one's behavior. We will see that Jesus himself does not approve of much about this woman's past. Nor is acceptance the same as toleration. Someone may tolerate me—may put up with my existence and even my faults—but there's no healing in that. People need more than toleration. Bertrand Russell wrote, "A sense of duty is useful in work but offensive in personal relationships. People wish to be liked, not to be endured with patient resignation."

This is part of the reason Jesus was such a magnet for people. As a general rule, when we come to those superior to us in some respect, to be endured with patient resignation is about the best we can hope for. The wise do not suffer fools gladly; all-stars don't usually ride the bus with third-stringers. But when messed-up sinners came to the only sinless person who ever lived, he did not merely endure them with patient resignation. He genuinely liked them.

Acceptance is an act of the heart. To accept someone is to affirm to them that you think it's a very good thing they are alive.

Acceptance is an act of the heart. To accept someone is to affirm to them that you think it's a very good thing they are alive. We communicate this in a hundred ways, but the most powerful way is to listen with patience and compassion as they reveal their dark secrets. A mother resents her young children and sometimes gets angry with the demands they place on her, then she is also filled with guilt and is sure this makes her a monster. A businessman finds himself wanting to have an affair with a woman in sales twenty years younger than he is. A pastor finds himself filled with secret doubts about the God he proclaims to others. A fifteen-year-old boy is flooded with feelings of attraction toward other men; he cries and prays, but the feelings won't go away, and he despises himself.

These people tell no one their secrets, because they are sure that the stone-throwing would begin in earnest. They know, because they often throw rocks at themselves. If they are fortunate, they find someone who listens and does not turn their face away in disgust. Someone who listens with something more than the endurance of patient resignation. Someone who sees the darkness, yet continues to love. Someone who has no rocks to throw.

This woman has found such a man. At the end of the story, the only ones left are Jesus and the woman—and a bunch of stones. Jesus could become the stone thrower. He has the right.

Instead, he does a wonderful thing. He asks the woman, "Where are all the stone throwers? Has no one condemned you?"

Jesus is not really asking for their whereabouts. He is making a point. He is saying, "You and these men are really not so different after all. They are broken sinners; you are a broken sinner. For all their spiritual superiority, you all are really in the same boat. Is there not a single sinless stone thrower left to let you have it?"

"No one, sir."

"Okay. Me neither, then. No more condemnation."

"Go, and Sin No More"

Jesus doesn't stop there. He has one more thing to say—another Columbo moment: "Just one more thing, ma'am. . . ."

Then Jesus says the words that cut her to the heart and bring her back to life. They fill her with pain because they reveal to her that he knows all about her past. They fill her with hope because they tell her that Someone believes in her. These words will remain with her until she is old and wrinkled and gray, surrounded by a husband and children and grandchildren who love her. Jesus says, "Go, and sin no more."

This is very important: *acceptance is not the same thing as tolerating any behavior she chooses to indulge in*.

People sometimes think acceptance means an abused wife has to tolerate whatever suffering her spouse chooses to damage her with; that a concerned friend must watch in silence as her friend makes choices that will wreck her life.

Accepting another human being does not mean we refuse to confront or challenge that in them which could harm others and damage their soul.

Jean Vanier writes, "To accept our weaknesses and those of others is the very opposite of sloppy complacency. It is not fatalistic and hopeless acceptance. It is essentially a concern for the truth."

Failure to confront, to speak truth in love, can ultimately be as fatal to the growth of community as judgmentalism. To paraphrase Bonhoeffer, "In daily, earnest living with the Cross of Christ the Christian loses the spirit of human judgmentalism on the one hand and apathetic indulgence on the other. He receives instead the spirit of divine severity and divine love."

There is a world of difference between *making judgments* and *being judgmental*. Dallas Willard writes,

> We do not have to—we *cannot*—surrender the valid practice of distinguishing and discerning how things are in order to avoid condemning others. We *can*, however, train ourselves to hold people responsible and discuss their failures with them—and even assign them penalities, if we are, for example, in some position over them—without attacking their worth as human beings or marking them as rejects.

Jesus accepted the woman in John 8. He forgave her sin—it is never possible to offer acceptance yet withhold forgiveness. But this acceptance and forgiveness came at enormous cost to himself. In defending her, he has made powerful enemies. He is under no illusions. As Kenneth Bailey says, "They will be back with a bigger stick. Jesus is in the process of getting hurt because of what he is doing—for her. Isaiah wrote, 'By his stripes we are healed.'"

"Go and sin no more." Jesus' acceptance is free, undeserved, unmerited—but it is also demanding. For the woman to fully examine her acceptance will require entering into a new way of life. The same grace that liberates her from past sin calls her to walk free of them in the future.

Amazingly enough, radical acceptance does what condemnation and judgmentalism and self-superiority could not do: produce a changed life. Imagine what might happen in your little world and my little world if we were to adopt the way of Jesus. What if we were to cease ever again attacking people's worth or holding them in contempt? Imagine becoming known as one who will never pick up a stone.

Then we, too, will become part of Jesus' community of radical acceptance. Then we will join him in the life-saving business. Then we, in our own smaller ways, will reflect the One who on the cross lived out the aspiration of the Humane Society: "You have to go out. You don't have to come back."

Learning to Dance

1. When was a time you failed or erred and someone offered you acceptance instead of the condemnation you expected? How did this affect you?

2. Here is an exercise to help you reflect on your experience of community. You may want to apply this to a friendship, a small group, or your marriage. Think about the way you relate to each other along this spectrum. Place an "x" where you think it would best describe your current level of community.

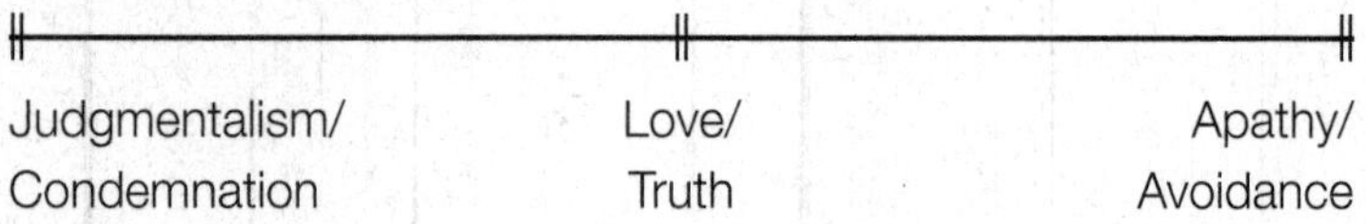

3. What is the next step you need to take to move closer to speaking truth and love?

4. Why do you think a church might produce stone throwers?

5. Are you holding onto any stones right now?

6. What people or problems tend to bring out the stone thrower in you? Why?

7. Think about the words you have spoken today. Did they give life to those around you? Make a list of the words or actions that most powerfully communicate acceptance to you. Spend some time practicing them with the people you encounter today.

CHAPTER 6

THE ART OF READING PEOPLE: EMPATHY

You say you know the inwardness of men,
As well as of a hundred other things.
Dare to speak out and tell me about myself.

ROBERT FROST

There is a book that at one time in your life was about the most important piece of literature in the world to you. It is not a well-written book; there isn't a single quotable line in it. It is not a particularly memorable book, and I doubt that you can identify the author. Yet, apart from the Bible, it may be the most widely read book in American society.

It's called *Rules of the Road*. There was a time in your life when you devoted yourself to studying and knowing the contents of this book.

It's fresh in my mind because I received a phone call this week from my daughter, who recently turned sixteen. She was calling me from the car. She has just received her driver's license. She can drive all by herself.

So if you're in the Chicago area anytime soon and you see a red-haired girl driving around—in the words of Elmer Fudd—be vewy vewy careful.

Before you are allowed to get a license, you have to demonstrate a certain level of competence. You have to have a working knowledge of certain basic signs and show that you are able to read and respond to them appropriately. These signs are so important that people who design them work to make them clear enough that you don't even need words.

—If you see a "U" inside a red circle with a line running through it, it means no U-turns.

—If you see two lines joining together to form a single line that terminates in an arrow, it means two lanes are merging to form one.

—If you see the number "55" on an expressway, it doesn't mean much, as a general rule.

Road signs aren't always helpful. Ken Davis writes that Trail Ridge Road, one of the highest paved roads in the continental United States, reaching 12,183 feet at its crest, has a sign at the summit, erected by some overachiever employed by the state of Colorado. The full text of the sign is "Hill."

Davis adds,

> They've also included a picture of a hill, just in case you might mistake the next fifteen-mile luge ride as a large dip.
>
> Speaking of which, who decides the location of those signs? Usually it's only after peeling myself off the ceiling of the car that I see the "dip" sign. I feel strongly that a "dip" sign should be more of a warning than an acknowledgment. All these signs do is accurately describe the person who placed them there.

But the general idea behind road signs is that it is possible—at least in theory—to always know what you should be doing behind the wheel. The sign makers seek to remove the guesswork.

Relational Education

The thought occurred to me: Wouldn't it be nice if they didn't just have signs for roads but also had signs for people:

You come to work, and there's a big sign around your boss's neck: "Had huge fight with spouse this morning—proceed with caution."

You go to tuck your child in late at night, and you're tired and tempted to rush the moment, when you see the sign: "Growing up too fast—reduce speed."

You go out on a date with someone you don't know very well: "Severely and breathtakingly dysfunctional—run for your life. Backing up will cause severe tire damage." Or possibly the sign would simply read: "Dip."

What if we all had to take "relationship education" in school, the way we take driver's ed, and had to get licensed before we could start navigating relationships on our own?

People could get pulled over by relationship police for talking too fast or too long or too loud, for failure to come to a complete and thoughtful "stop" before executing a proper confrontation, or for trying to merge when all the signs said "road closed."

It would be a great help if people had signs telling us how to respond to them as we try to navigate our relational lives.

The truth is, they do. But we have to learn how to read them.

The writer of Proverbs says, "The lamp of the LORD searches the spirit of a person; it searches out the inmost being."

To the writers of Scripture, one of the glorious characteristics of God is that he doesn't just look at the outward, obvious dimensions of a human being. He discerns the heart. He pays attention to the spirit. "You have searched me and you know me," the psalmist says. "You perceive my thoughts;... you are familiar with all my ways."

Because we have been made in God's image, because we were created for community, we have a little of this ability ourselves. God wants us to know one another, to pay attention to what's going on underneath the surface, to listen to what's happening in someone else's heart.

Here is the key: People's hearts (feelings) are not usually put into words. Most of the time they are expressed in subtle ways: body language, tone of voice, facial expressions, gestures. A person may give a nervous laugh or sit with slumped shoulders or speak with animation and energy. Primarily through their bodies, people are sending you thousands of signals all the time: "Keep talking. Stop talking. I'm feeling stressed. I disagree with you. I'm enjoying this interaction. I'm bored. I wish I was in Milwaukee. I wish *you* were in Milwaukee."

People are sending messages all the time without saying a word, usually with their bodies.

I believe God gave us bodies in part because they offer a brilliant way for us to speak the language of the heart. There are many examples in Scripture.

The writer of Genesis says that when Cain was jealous of Abel, "his face was downcast."

God asked him, "Why are you angry? Why is your face downcast?"

God was *reading* Cain's face.

Dallas Willard puts it like this:

> The tendencies and feelings that run our life, whether we are aware of it or not, reside in fairly specific parts of our body, and they reveal themselves to others through our body language—in how we "carry" our bodily parts. They not only govern our immediate responses in action, but also are read with great accuracy by observant people around us and then determine how they react to us. We wear our souls "on our sleeve," even when we ourselves are oblivious to them, and that governs the quality of our relations to others.

Researcher Daniel Stern calls the ability to read and respond well to someone's heart *attunement*. Relationally intelligent people are geniuses at it. You can see it at work between mothers and infants. The infant picks up a rattle and shakes it and smiles, and the mother gives a little shake of her shoulder. The infant squeals with delight, and the mother gives him a smile and a little squeeze, or matches the pitch of her voice to the baby's squeal.

The mother is attuned to—in tune with—what is happening in that little infant's heart. She is giving a sense of emotional connection to that child, helping him know his feelings are understood. Stern finds that mothers do this about once a minute with their children.

When this happens well, the child grows up to be able to read his own heart—that is, have self-awareness—and can tune in to others also.

One dangerous aspect of this skill is that generally people who don't read others well aren't aware that they don't. It is like being emotionally tone-deaf. Ever sing next to someone who had a tin ear and a loud voice? If you have one tone-deaf person singing off-key in a room full of people with perfect pitch, who is the one person that doesn't know someone's singing off-key?

It is much the same with being relationally tone-deaf. These folks are not aware that they're doing anything wrong. Thus, why relational intelligence is important. At work, certain people consistently transmit anger, judgmentalism, or discouragement. They may know the technical aspects of their job well. They may be right a lot. They may even get many tasks done. But other people don't want to be around them. They are stuck at a low level in their vocational lives and don't know why. They just find themselves feeling left out or isolated. They find that relationships will hit a wall. Growth and opportunities at work will get cut off at a certain level. People will have a way of distancing themselves after a time. This may be quite painful.

The truth is that they may be doing things that keep people from entering into intimate relationships with them—but they *never know!* Their isolation is a mystery to them.

The good news is that relational intelligence can be learned. Develop this skill, get it right, and you will have opportunities to influence, comfort, challenge, and love people on a regular basis. You will have friendships characterized by a deep sense of openness and intimacy. You will be sought out by others at work. You will be much more effective as a parent or a friend.

Relational Rules of the Road

Let's walk through some relational rules of the road. These are some of the key signals people send to guide us in the way that we relate to them. For these, I draw on the substantial research compiled by David Givens in *The Nonverbal Dictionary of Gestures, Signs, and Body Language Cues*. But I want to present these signals in the form you might actually see while you're out driving. What major signs have to be read to become a master in the art of people-reading?

1. Stop

We start with a very simple sign. People will send out signals all the time: "Stop talking, stop advising, stop rambling, stop criticizing, stop gossiping, stop hogging the verbal spotlight—just stop."

Have you ever gone through a clearly marked conversational intersection without coming to a full and complete stop? It is amazing to me how many people run through nonverbal stop signs.

The most common way people send this signal is with their eyes. Eye contact produces strong emotions; in normal conversation it rarely lasts more than three seconds before one or both people experience a powerful urge to glance away. People who like each other tend to engage in longer direct gazes; lovers say, "Drink to me only with thine eyes." But when someone wants you to stop talking, they will lower eye contact to a minimum.

Confession time: Have you ever gone through a clearly marked conversational intersection without coming to a full and complete stop? It is amazing to me how many people run through nonverbal stop signs.

Years ago my family and I were stuck in a room with a mother and her eight-year-old son as we each waited for a family member during Parents' Day at college. We had never met before. For one hour this mother did not stop talking. She told us about herself, her husband, her kids, her neighbors, and her neighbor's kids. After an hour we knew more about her than we did some of our own relatives. She made Don King look like an introvert.

It's not that we weren't sending signals. We were. No one would make eye contact with her, because we were afraid it might encourage her. No one was nodding their head in response to what she was saying. Our bodies were facing the other direction. We tapped our feet, we drummed our fingers, we did everything but go out and rent a large neon sign: *Please pause for a breath*. She couldn't stop. It was as if she had taken some powerful verbal laxative and the words were out of her control.

Finally her daughter arrived. She and her son stood up to go, but she kept the word faucet turned on: "Well, we've got to go, kids. I've got to get some things for dinner, I've got to pick up Dad, and—oh yes—I've got to stop and get some buttons."

Then her son spoke; the only words he said the entire afternoon: "Mother, you need some buttons for your mouth."

We all felt this was probably a prompting from the Holy Spirit.

It is possible, at least in some of your encounters with people, that the single most important tool you could add to your relational intelligence tool kit is a button for your mouth. In your interactions, look for nonverbal stop signs: People start looking away; they stop giving you little verbal cues that say they're listening; they lean backwards; they stop interacting and asking questions. Don't say to yourself, *I've talked them into submission—now they're mine!*

Stop talking! Give someone else a chance.

If you keep running nonverbal stop signs, you may have an audience for a moment, but you will lose the chance to make a friend.

Maybe you're doing okay in this regard, but there is someone in your relational world who needs to have their conversational license revoked. Maybe it's a trusted friend, a family member, or a close coworker. Do the person a favor. Take that person aside, and gently give him or her a little remedial class on nonverbal stop signs.

There is another reason for observing this sign as it relates to spiritual growth. The writer of Proverbs put it like this: "When words are many, sin is not absent, but he who holds his tongue is wise."

This remarkable statement says there is a direct correlation between the number of words you say and the number of sins you commit. It also means that one of the simplest ways to cut down on sin is to stop talking so much.

Bill Hybels wrote in *Making Life Work* that it is as if the writer of this proverb is saying we can calculate the relationship between words and sin.

So let's try it. Let's generate a Sin Prediction Index. Assume for the sake of argument that we speak an average of 10,000 words per day. How many sins would that involve? It is a little hard to calculate, but here is a start: William Backus cites research that indicates the average person in our society lies 200 times a day.

And lying is just one form of verbal sin. Add gossip, slander, anger, bragging, insults, flattery, unkept promises, impression management—it starts to pile up. So let's estimate the sin quotient at 1,000 per day. That would yield a ratio of 10 words for every sin. If you could cut the amount of talking you do in half, you bring the sin factor down to 500.

If you can get the word total down to 10 a day, you would be down to one sin. And if you could get it to 9 or less—you'd be a saint!

Obviously, the goal of life is not to produce people who avoid sinning by staying mute all day. But before you write off this proverb altogether, you should know that some wise people in the early church, known as the Desert Fathers, strongly recommended the practice of silence as a spiritual discipline. The number one reason they gave is that it is hard to talk without sinning. Henri Nouwen tells how when Abba Arsenius, a wealthy Roman senator who abandoned his social prominence to become a monk, prayed, "Lord, lead me into the way of salvation," he heard a voice saying, "Be silent."

When we practice the proverb, we begin to learn amazing things. We can live without getting the last word. We can live without trying to make sure we control how other people are thinking about us. We can live without winning every argument, without powering up over every decision, without always drawing attention to ourselves.

One last observation here: Use wisdom in using silence.

If you're a husband arriving home from work, and your wife wants to connect soul-to-soul and asks how your day went, you might not want to say, "When words are many, sin is not absent."

If the wife is wise, she may reply with Proverbs 25:11: "A word aptly spoken is like apples of gold in settings of silver." Which means, "Start talking or I'm going to go buy jewelry."

It is no accident that we speak of *paying* attention to people; attention is the most valuable currency we have.

When we stop talking, we also have the opportunity to engage in the most important intimacy-building skill in the world: listening. The New Testament writer James says, in one of the most often violated commands in all Scripture, that everyone should be "quick to listen, slow to speak." Listening, writes Daniel Goleman, is the single most important relational skill a person can develop. "Asking astute questions, being open-minded and understanding, not interrupting, seeking suggestions" are all ways of communicating to other human beings that they matter. An engaging aspect of Jesus' life is that although he was the greatest teacher who ever lived, he spent an enormous amount of time simply listening to people. He especially listened to people whom no one else bothered with, such as Zacchaeus the tax collector and the paralytic at the pool of Bethesda.

It is ironic that we try to impress people by saying clever or funny things, yet nothing binds one human being to another more than the sense that they have been deeply, carefully listened to. It is no accident that we speak of *paying* attention to people; attention is the most valuable currency we have.

2. Sobriety Checkpoint Ahead

On the road, sobriety is a necessity. But in life, an attitude of joyless, glum, somber, self-preoccupation is lethal. So this sign might simply read, "Lighten up."

The writer of Proverbs says, "A cheerful look brings joy to the heart." Recent studies have found that the contagion of joy is so powerful that when we see even a *picture* of someone smiling—a "cheerful look"—we tend to smile back. Smiling and laughter produce relief from stress by releasing pain-killing, euphoria-producing endorphins, enkephalins, dopamine, noradrenaline, and adrenaline. Proverbs 15:30 turns out to be true at the most physiological level.

There are people (I'm told) who genuinely don't like chocolate. There are tea drinkers who find the aroma of fresh-brewed Starbucks in the morning eminently resistible. But one hunger is universal. You have never met a person who doesn't long for more joy. W. H. Auden wrote, "Among those whom I like or admire, I can find no common denominator, but among those whom I love, I can: all of them make me laugh." More often than you can imagine, when people are stressed, worried, preoccupied, lonely, or afraid, they carry this sign just beneath the surface: "Joy needed—please lighten up."

More often than you can imagine, when people are stressed, worried, preoccupied, lonely, or afraid, they carry this sign just beneath the surface: "Joy needed—please lighten up."

The expression of authentic happiness is what researchers call a *zygomatic* smile. It takes its name from the zygomaticus muscles that produce it. The signs of a zygomatic smile are the lip corners turning upward and also crow's-feet showing around the eyes. Here is where the connection between the human body and the human spirit is truly amazing. We can show a polite grin or a camera smile at will. In such cases, people make their lips go up, but no crow's-feet are visible.

The polite smile can be manipulated; that is why the smiles that people put on their faces for photographs often look forced. But the zygomatic smile is hard to fake. It is a smile that goes all the way up to the eyes. This distinction begins early; five-month-old infants show the eye-muscle smile when the mother approaches, but a smile without the eye muscle when a stranger approaches.

People who don't take themselves too seriously give a great gift to those around them. In contrast, joy-challenged people face a serious handicap in trying to live in community.

I had lunch sometime ago with a man I'll call Allen. He is one of the smartest guys I know. He made a boatload of money in his profession, but has always been fascinated by theology and ventured out to pursue an advanced degree in graduate school. He genuinely loves to study, but people get the sense when they are with him that mostly what he loves is to be right. When he was in high school, he was on the debate squad, and he's never really graduated.

Allen approaches conversations like a prosecuting attorney marshaling evidence to prove his case. He is very good at pointing out logical flaws to people who disagree with him—especially his wife, whose self-esteem has gradually withered during their marriage. He wins many arguments. He has a gift for sarcasm. He has a way of communicating—by tone of voice, dismissive gestures, the way he cocks his head—that conveys impatience, cool disdain, or condescension. He takes himself, his opinions, and his prestige with deadly seriousness.

He is very alone. He doesn't think about his aloneness much, and he wouldn't like to think of himself as lonely. He does make relationships with like-minded people occasionally, but they don't run too deep or last too long. He keeps winning disagreements and losing friends. He doesn't seem to realize that every time people are with him, they come away a little emotionally bruised.

Allen asked to meet with me because he has a son whom he's nuts about, who is now ten years old. He wants to express love to his son; but all too often what comes out is his impatience that his son is not as smart as he is. He is seeing now, in his son's eyes, the hurt and pain that his arrogance gives birth to. He finally sees that he has a very difficult addiction: his need to be right. And he's not sure he'll ever be free.

A friend of mine says that one of the hardest things in the world is to be right and not hurt anybody with it. If you have any doubts about that, remember some time in school when you sat next to the smartest kid in class. Did you enjoy it? Being right (or more precisely, having the need to be right) is a terrible burden. An amazing thing about Jesus is that he was always right and never hurt anyone by it.

Maybe you are in a position of power or authority and can impose your will if you choose. You may be a supervisor or a parent or just someone with the more dominant personality. You can steamroll others if you want to and win lots of arguments and feel right a lot, but you won't have many friends.

In contrast, if you're willing to lighten up, even your mistakes can become bridges. The church where I work videotapes most of the services, so I have hundreds of messages on tape. Only one of them gets shown repeatedly.

This video is a clip from the beginning of one of our services. A high school worship dance team had just brought the house down to get things started, and I was supposed to transition us into some high-energy worship by reading Psalm 150. This was a last-second decision, so I had to read it cold, but with great passion: "Praise the LORD! Praise God in his sanctuary; praise him in his mighty firmament!" The psalm consists of one command after another to praise, working its way through each instrument of the orchestra. My voice is building in a steady crescendo; by the end of the psalm I practically shout the final line, only mispronouncing one word slightly: "Let everything that has breasts, praise the LORD."

A moment of silence. The same thought passes through four thousand brains: *Did he just say what I think he did? In church? Is this some exciting new translation I can get at the bookstore?*

Then everybody in the place just lost it. They laughed so hard for so long, I couldn't say a thing. It was zygomatic. I finally just walked off the stage, and we went on with the next part of the service.

I have been teaching at that church for eight years. Of all the passages I have exegeted and all the messages I have preached, that is the one moment that gets replayed before conferences and workshops. Over and over.

It's an amazing truth: Being fully right rarely brings as much life to people as simply being human. Sometime ago a psychology journal published an article entitled "The Effect of a Pratfall on Increasing Interpersonal Attractiveness." The surprising conclusion: "Seeing someone you admire do something stupid or clumsy will make you like him more." People are hungry for joy-bringers. We are about thirty times more likely to laugh when we are with other people than when we are alone. Research indicates that people in good spirits may laugh one hundred to four hundred times a day. (Go ahead and do a quick review of your day.) Other folks may go through a day without a single smile.

3. Warning: Construction Zone

When our children were small, there were three words I hated more than any others in the English language. Sometimes the phrase read, "Easy to assemble," but nothing ever was. Tab A never fit into slot B.

One Christmas Eve we foolishly purchased three "easy-to-assemble" gifts. At about one in the morning, after two and a half hours of frustration and anger, I finally said to my wife, "Do you want some help with that?"

Every relationship you have ever been or ever will be a part of comes with this phrase on the outside of the box: "Some assembly required."

We would all like for relationships to simply flourish on their own, without any attention from us, but they don't.

Every relationship is a construction zone.

Early in our marriage, Nancy and I would occasionally have quite idealized pictures in our minds of what our yard could look like. We would ask friends who had beautiful gardens if they could help us plan a landscaping scheme that would have beauty but be "low maintenance." They would claim to design just such a plan, but it always turned out that our idea of "low maintenance" differed from theirs. The truth is that to us, low maintenance pretty much meant no maintenance. And there's just no such thing as a no-maintenance garden. Where living things are involved, some assembly is required.

This is no less true of human gardens. Without proper attention, relationships tend to drift. Conflict tends to go unresolved. Work teams tend to break down. Small groups tend to lose touch. Families tend to get busy. Sports teams tend to go south.

If you are part of a family, friendship, club, organization, department, small group, or church, you are part of what Daniel Goleman calls an "emotional economy." Every single interaction we have with another person involves not simply exchanging information or performing tasks but also influencing each other's moods and attitudes. The emotional economy is "the sum total of exchanges of feeling among us." Emotions are more contagious than the flu. This dynamic is so powerful that in one study, three volunteers sat silently in a circle for two minutes, and at the end of that time the most emotionally expressive person transmitted his or her mood to the other two without saying a word. "In every such session, the mood the most expressive person had going in was also the mood the other two felt coming out—whether happy, bored, anxious, or angry," Goleman says.

Every time two people make contact, they come away feeling either better and more energized or worse and more depleted. It is as if we carry our own little emotional ATMs around with us all the time, and at each encounter we are either making deposits or withdrawals on the vitality of those around us.

This is true even for interactions between people and animals. It is why people have pets and why some pets are more life-giving than others. According to received wisdom, there is the difference between dogs and cats. A dog says, "You love me, feed me, shelter me, care for me—*you* must be God." A cat says, "You love me, feed me, shelter me, care for me—*I* must be God."

You have dog people in your life, and you have cat people in your life. A good question members of families and churches and organizations and small groups can ask is, "What are the dominant moods in our emotional economy: fear, joy, anger, complaint, hope, discouragement, or compassion?"

Relationally intelligent people ask, "Who are the biggest contributors to our emotional economy?"

Goleman calls these contributors "glue people"—the folks who help a community stick together. In the Baptist circles where I grew up, we called these people "pillars of the church." But there were also those who were drains on the emotional economy. In Baptist circles where I grew up, we called these people ... *deacons*.

This is why some people at work call a meeting and you look forward to going, no matter what the topic. Someone else calls a meeting, and you look for an excuse to leave early. The issue is not whether the people have technical excellence, but whether they are assets or debtors in the emotional economy. As Anne Lamott writes, there are certain people

> whose company you love, whose mind you love to pick, whose running commentary totally holds your attention, who makes you laugh out loud....
>
> When you have a friend like this, she can say: "Hey, I've got to drive up to the dump in Petaluma—wanna come along?" and you honestly can't think of anything in the world you'd rather do. By the same token, a boring or annoying person can offer to buy you an expensive dinner, followed by tickets to a great show, and in all honesty you'd rather stay home and watch the Jello harden.

4. Road Closed

People often use what researchers call "spatial orientation" to assess the state of a relationship. Our upper body unwittingly squares up, addresses, and "aims" at those we like and feel close to. We will tend to lean toward them. However, someone who is uncomfortable in a conversation will begin to angle their body away from the other person. The tendency to express relational dynamics by "angular distance" is so strong that it is often possible to identify the most powerful or high-status person seated at a conference table by the relative number of torsos aimed in her or his direction.

People with high relational intelligence recognize and respond to this reality intuitively. They build rapport with others by matching their posture and movements. They show that they are "in sync" with the other person by mirroring that person's tone and rate of speech.

On the other hand, some people are blind to these signs. Sometimes you can see a parent haranguing a child on some issue or other, maybe after a Little League game; or after report cards come out. It is very clear that emotionally, for whatever reason, the child is overwhelmed or completely tuned out; he's looking the other way, his head is hanging down, he's responding with monosyllables or not at all.

This conversation is not serving any productive purpose; it's just an exercise in catharsis for the parent. The child is sending signals: "Road closed."

I remember taking our dog to obedience school. It was a fascinating learning experience. The trainer said sometimes a dog just won't learn. People who are skilled with animals can read the indicators: their eyes, their posture, their level of restlessness, and so on. (A dog's verbal skills are uniformly bad, so you have to pay attention to nonverbal cues.) The trainer told us that wise dog owners don't try to force things. I thought about some of my recent parenting interventions. Ouch!

Parents with high relational intelligence will say in those moments, "I've got to find another road." Maybe that means we should have this conversation another time. Maybe that means we will have to find another way to discuss the matter. Maybe we will need to use fewer words and more questions.

One of the more remarkable statements in Scripture was made when Jesus said, "I stand at the door and knock. If anyone hears my voice and opens the door, I will come in and eat with them, and they with me."

Relationally intelligent people know that God has given to every human being the key to the door of one's heart. There can be no forced entry. Jesus himself does not try to force his way inside; he stands at the door and honors our choice. We may be able to push and manipulate somebody's behavior, but not their heart.

People with high relational intelligence become experts at reading the signs of loss of community breakdown:

—A loss of morale
—The presence of unresolved conflict
—The misuse of humor—team members engaging in sarcasm or ridicule to send barbed messages to one another
—Factions and divisions
—An inappropriate sense of competitiveness
—People complaining about other members of the community to third parties rather than going directly to the person they are at odds with
—A lack of civility

Being able to discern the state of an emotional economy is a great gift. No one ever mastered this the way Jesus did. Simply by walking with his friends, he was immediately aware of the presence of tension and would skillfully use questions to surface and learn from problems: "What were you arguing about?"

You may wonder when the other people in your life will be mature enough not to have to work on relational skills anymore. It will never happen. People you know will never be that normal. Neither will you.

You may wonder when the other people in your life will be mature enough, healthy enough, or normal enough to become a finely tuned machine and not have to work on relational skills anymore. It will never happen. People you know will never be that normal. Neither will you. "Everybody's weird."

Relationally intelligent people regularly ask the question, "What kind of community do we want to be? How are we doing at it?" They become experts at knowing when the road is shut down.

5. Shoulder Work

Every human being you know is making a request of their friends, though it usually goes unspoken. Here's what they ask: "Motivate me. Call out the best in me. Believe in me. Encourage me when I'm tempted to quit. Speak truth to me and remind me of my deepest values. Help me achieve my greatest potential. Tell me again what God called me to be, what I might yet become.

"Inspire me."

You have no idea what it means to the people when you respond to this need. The truth is, often people just get beaten down in life:

—Beaten down by their failures
—Beaten down by their jobs
—Beaten down in their families
—Beaten down by their disappointments
—Beaten down by voices inside themselves

People's bodies have ways of signaling this sign as well. Often it is done with the shoulders. The shoulder shrug is a subtle but universal sign of resignation, uncertainty, and surrender. Squared shoulders suggest confidence and certainty. Hunched-up shoulders are a sign of a cringing spirit. Sometimes our shoulders speak a truth that our mouths are afraid to say. We may say, "Yes, I'm sure," at the same time our hunched shoulders say, "I'm not really so sure."

We speak of someone with a capacity to handle anything life throws at them as having broad shoulders. We show our strength when we shoulder difficult burdens. We were not made to go through life with shoulders slumped in defeat.

We start out with bright dreams, high hopes, noble aspirations, and sometimes they just get worn down by sheer challenge of survival. We have the right intentions, but get ground down by life. We forget the kind of person—friend, parent, servant, giver—that we set out to be. Deep in the heart of everyone you work with, play with, live with, is a sign, if only you will take the time to read it:

"Inspire me." Challenge me to grow, and then celebrate with me when I stretch. Help me shoulder whatever burden life throws my way.

You can do this. Remember the proverb we heard earlier: "A word aptly spoken is like apples of gold in settings of silver."

You are surrounded by people whose lives can be touched a little by a word aptly spoken from you. Sometimes it's only a small word. One year on the Fourth of July, the *Chicago Tribune* printed the Declaration of Independence. When I noticed it in the paper, I said rather breezily to my kids, "I'll give a hundred dollars to any of you who memorize this today."

Mallory immediately made eye contact, aligned her body, squared her shoulders, and gave me a zygomatic smile. She picked up the newspaper and didn't put it down until five o'clock that evening. She memorized the whole thing in a single day. (I would never have offered the money if I'd thought someone would actually take me seriously!)

When she had finished and recited it all for me, she felt a great sense of accomplishment. Her face was beaming because she had tackled a hard challenge. This was a face begging to be celebrated with.

This was a face just wanting to hear somebody say, "Way to go!"

Mostly, that face wanted a hundred dollars, but also she wanted to hear "way to go!" A word aptly spoken.

We were not made to go through life with hunched shoulders. We were made to face life squarely. But none of us will do this on our own. This is a gift we can help each other attain.

At the end of the movie *Apollo 13*, three astronauts in a spaceship far from earth hang in the balance. They depend on a little community of engineers in Houston who find themselves in the life-saving business. One of the engineers says to his superiors that he fears this will be the worst catastrophe in the history of the National Aeronautics and Space Administration (NASA). The character played by Ed Harris straightens up, squares his shoulders and says, "To the contrary—with all due respect—I believe this will be our finest hour."

All through the film Harris's character has laid out before his team the seemingly impossible problems they must solve, the resources at their disposal, the size of the stakes at risk: "Failure is not an option." Time after time you can see the team members' shoulders straighten as he speaks to them; they sweat, they pray, they work, always he goads them on, always he believes they can do it.

It is not at all certain that the space capsule will withstand the heat of reentry into the earth's atmosphere. The suspense is heightened when, during the reentry, the crew of the Apollo 13 is out of radio contact for four minutes. Life and death are on the line. The silence lasts an eternity. The whole world holds its breath: Will they make it home?

Finally, out of the silence, amid a rumbling of static, a voice is heard: "This is Apollo." The men are safe. They are home.

People on-screen start jumping up and down. Engineers who wouldn't know a feeling if it smacked them upside the head are dancing and embracing and pounding each other on the back. People in the theater watching the film are laughing and crying.

And I thought, as I watched the scene unfold, about Jesus' statement that there will be joy in heaven over one sinner who repents. I thought of the joy that will occur one day when God's dream of community is finally fully realized. The day when even the most nonexpressive people on earth—engineers and accountants and Swedes and Baptists—will laugh and hug and dance and sing and weep and shout in heaven.

Then, in the midst of all the pandemonium, the camera pans back to Ed Harris in the control room at NASA. He is simply standing there, with emotion too deep for words. And you realize, watching, that his whole life—his work as a scientist, his dreams and labor, his every thought—have led up to this one shining moment. And you realize that though he may live many more years, grow to be an old man, and do many things, this is his finest hour.

You are a guardian of the human spirit. You have the power to manipulate and coerce if you want to. You can avoid and ignore if you choose. But you can also ennoble and inspire.

All around us are people searching, seeking, attempting reentry, for whom life and death hang in the balance. Everyone we know needs someone who believes, someone who will remind them: This could be your finest hour.

You are a guardian of the human spirit. You have the power to manipulate and coerce if you want to. You can avoid and ignore if you choose. But you can also ennoble and inspire. You can lift up and appeal to all that is good and honorable and holy. You can remind fallible and finite people around you that they hold their lives and calling as a sacred trust, that their best efforts matter, that their worst failures will one day be redeemed.

This is all because the Crucified One, who shouldered the burdens of the whole human race, who rose again, will come back one day to honor all that is good and set right all that has gone wrong.

Jesus said those who follow him will know he is coming. They will remember to read the signs.

Learning to Dance

1. "People are sending messages all the time without saying a word, usually with their bodies." How well do you do at reading people? Take a few days to practice noticing what people are saying to you with their faces, their body language, and the tone of their voices.

2. From whom did you most learn how to be "in tune" with other people?

3. How do you recognize nonverbal "stop" signs? When do you tend to run through them?

4. Who are the biggest contributors to your "emotional economy"? How can you make sure to get large chunks of time with these people? Who are the biggest drains?

5. What relationship for you is currently "under construction"? What can you do to help get it on firmer ground?

6. When someone in your life, such as a coworker or a child, is sending you "road closed" signs, how do you tend to respond?

7. Ask a trusted friend to tell you which of the relational signs you most need to work on.

8. Just for today, be on the lookout for someone who needs inspiration. Ask God to help give you the right words or gesture.

CHAPTER 7

COMMUNITY IS WORTH FIGHTING FOR: CONFLICT

Communities need tensions if they are to grow and deepen. Tensions come from conflicts. . . . A tension or difficulty can signal the approach of a new grace of God. But it has to be looked at wisely and humanly.

JEAN VANIER

I'm warning you ahead of time: What you are about to read contains an undignified level of self-disclosure. If you have good taste or a squeamish stomach, you will now skip ahead to the first subheading in this chapter.

(That's what I thought.)

One day many years ago when we had three children under the age of five, we were taking a long drive. All three of the children were asleep, which meant my wife, who was normally home with them all day, had a few golden moments of silence.

What's most embarrassing for me is that when we go for a long drive, the person who has to make the most pit stops all the time is me.

Everyone else in the family has a retention capacity that is frankly inhuman. It's like traveling with four camels.

At one point I said to my wife, "I have to make a stop."

"No, you don't!" she said. "The kids are all asleep. If you stop this car, they'll wake up. I'll lose this quiet. If you love me, if you're any kind of a man, you won't stop this car."

I held out as long as I could (thirty seconds), then stopped at the next service station.

I quietly got back into the car and gently eased the door shut. Click. But there was the tiniest little stirring in the backseat.

"The baby's awake," Nancy said. That's all. Three words, then silence. But do you think she was just passing me neutral information about the baby's state of consciousness?

When you know someone well enough, you learn to read between the lines: "The baby's awake. He wouldn't be, if it weren't for you. There would be peace in the valley, if it weren't for you. I, their mother, who am at home all day with three children pulling me, tugging me, chanting, 'Mommy, Mommy, Mommy,' as if it were some kind of Eastern mantra—I would be experiencing a rare moment of quiet and serenity if you had the retention capacity of a six-year-old and weren't more concerned with your own comfort and convenience than the emotional survival needs of your wife and children."

All that in just three words: "The baby's awake."

A few months later, we were on another marathon journey, this time through the deserts of Arizona. It was a blisteringly hot day. The kids were asleep. I had made the mistake of purchasing and consuming a "44-oz. Big Gulp" ice tea. Nature took its cruel course.

"I need to stop," I said.

"I need not to stop," Nancy said.

"I have a passionate, burning need to stop. Believe me, if there was a way not to stop, I wouldn't stop."

We had been down this road before.

But this time Nancy broke the cycle. She empathized with my situation and got a horribly creative gleam in her eye. She came up with a solution that could accommodate both our needs and have a clear win-win outcome. She handed me the now-empty 44-oz. Big Gulp cup. "You promised."

"Greater love hath no man."

The Art of Handling Conflict

There is no greater challenge in building community than to master the art of handling anger and conflict. According to recent FBI statistics, there is one violent crime every 24 seconds, an aggravated assault every 48 seconds, a murder every 23 minutes. Murder is one of the leading causes of death for both young men and women in America today. Domestic violence is the top cause of visits to emergency rooms by women. During the war in Vietnam, more women were murdered at home than men were slain on the battlefield.

Furthermore, the damage anger causes is not limited to physical violence. Mismanaged anger plays a major role in virtually every divorce (50 percent of all marriages in America) and wreaks havoc in many other marriages where people are separated emotionally if not legally. Parents who do not learn to manage anger wound children, who grow up to repeat the pattern. Many jobs are lost to anger problems: One boss was nicknamed "Old Faithful" by her employees—not because she was reliable, but because she "went off at least once a month."

Most importantly, we must consider how important this topic is in God's eyes. It is both remarkable and appalling that by and large in churches today we are not scandalized by broken relationships and chronic enmity between people. When I was growing up, I knew of many churches where the sins that *really* got people into trouble revolved around lifestyle issues: sneaking a cigarette, having a beer, going to the wrong kind of movie, or listening to the wrong kind of music. Even today, if you hear of a pastor being fired from a church for "moral reasons," you can make a pretty safe bet (except that you're not supposed to gamble) that "moral" involves either sex or money. We are not scandalized by lack of love.

But Jesus is. Love was his supreme value. His summation of the total teaching of divine revelation is captured in that single word: love for God, and love for people. Therefore, the greatest crimes against the kingdom of God are crimes against love. To slander another human being, to carry a grudge against someone who I think has hurt me, to gossip about someone I have not even confronted—these are direct violations of Jesus' fundamental command. Yet these behaviors go on all the time—even in churches. We are not shocked by them. We would be shocked if they suddenly ceased.

But Jesus is shocked by them. We have already seen why this should be a matter of supreme importance. We have been invited into the Fellowship of the Trinity. "As you, Father, are in me and I am in you, may they also be in us, so that the world may believe that you have sent me," Jesus prayed. When we violate oneness, when we contribute to relational brokenness, it doesn't just affect us. It doesn't just affect the other person. We are contributing to the destruction of that which is most prized by God and was purchased by him at greatest cost—the oneness of the Trinitarian community. We are, in a real sense, committing treason against the Trinity. To the New Testament writers, such action was unthinkable. "You are still worldly," Paul writes to the church at Corinth. He then spells out what worldliness—opposition to God's way of life—looks like, and he doesn't talk about things like wearing too much lipstick. "For since there is jealousy and quarreling among you, are you not worldly?"

So anyone who takes God's dream of community seriously will have to come to grips with conflict. Let's start with a little pop quiz to test your IQ (irritation quotient):

When driving, how often do you use your horn?

1. Rarely if ever.
2. As needed; at least once a day.
3. It is the most used part of my car.

At a restaurant, how often do you complain about food?

1. Never.
2. Only if it's cold, or there are too many bugs in it.
3. Regularly, and I go out to my car and honk the horn until they get it right.

While waiting in an express checkout line at the supermarket, I—
1. Meditate quietly or visualize world peace.
2. Count to see if anyone has more than twelve items.
3. Threaten anyone who looks as if they're going to use coupons.

The earliest research on anger, done a hundred years ago, found two main categories of causes of anger.

The first involves what is sometimes called the "stupid inanimate object." This is the shoelace that breaks when you try to tie it in a hurry, the ATM that swallows your card or keeps your money, the computer that eats your file, the toy that comes in a box marked "easy to assemble." You have experienced this if you've ever pushed the button repeatedly on the theory that the foolish elevator will then sense your urgency and bypass all those people waiting on other floors. (The author of *A Geography of Time* discusses an ingenious theory that the angry, hurried type A personality is contagious, passed on by touching the "door close" button inside the elevator.)

Here is the ultimate example: Police Chief Jack Kellem of Bellevue, Washington, reported that a motorist became so irate when his vehicle got stuck in six inches of snow that he pulled a tire iron from the trunk and smashed all the windows. Then he hauled out a pistol and shot all four tires, reloaded the gun, and emptied half of a second clip of bullets into the car. "He killed it," Kellem said. "It's a case of autocide." Kellem said the man was sober and rational, but very perturbed.

But the main target of our anger is other people. Often the people we're closest to. One research study asked a large population of children this question: "How do you wish your mom was different?"

The number one answer was, "I wish my mom didn't yell at me so much." This was the response of 98 percent of those who answered; it was fifty times more popular than all the other answers put together!

Seven Steps for Resolving Conflict

I want to structure this chapter around a single statement of Jesus, recorded in the gospel of Matthew: "If your brother or sister sins against you, go and show them their fault, just between the two of you. If they listen to you, you have won them over."

This topic is so crucial, and this one statement of Jesus is so important, that it has become a part of the language at the church where I serve. If somebody says, "We need to have a little 'Matthew 18:15' conversation," you know exactly what's coming. Also, although Jesus is speaking specifically of dealing with sin within the church, I want to apply it to conflict in general.

Jesus' command can be broken down like this:

1. If there is conflict
2. You
3. Go
4. To the person
5. In private
6. And discuss the problem
7. For the purpose of reconciliation

Dealing with conflict always involves a series of choices. With each choice, our natural inclination is to handle the conflict in a *destructive* manner. So if we want to live in the Fellowship of the Trinity, we will have to be guided by Jesus into a better way.

Jesus gave a set of instructions about what to do in case of relational breakdown. They're in the manual—the Bible. The good news is that they're so simple, a child can follow them. Jesus' wisdom can be summarized in a single phrase: "Go and tell." Go to the other person and directly discuss the problem.

The odd thing is, we don't do it. This may be the single most violated of all the instructions Jesus ever gave the human race. Why?

Because, at each point in his teaching, we face a crossroads. We face powerful reasons to ignore his instructions. We are tempted to go the other way. So let's walk through what he said one small step at a time.

1. Acknowledge Conflict

"If your brother [or sister] sins against you, . . ." the text says but we might replace the word *if* with *when*. To be alive means to be in conflict. People fight. Sometimes they fight a lot, sometimes a little; sometimes constructively, sometimes destructively; sometimes fairly, sometimes unfairly. Sometimes fights end in hugs and kisses and new depths of intimacy; sometimes they end in screaming and loss of control; sometimes they end in coldness and withdrawal.

To be alive means to be in conflict. It's part of the Dance of the Porcupines. People may not be normal, but conflict surely is—at least in our world. It is an inescapable part of being an "as-is" human being.

Many people prefer to pretend that conflict doesn't exist. Sometimes people think that a lack of conflict is automatically a sign of spiritual maturity. Unfortunately, that's not necessarily the case.

To be alive means to be in conflict.

If you are married to someone who is passive around the house, you may not experience much open conflict. However, the lack of open conflict does not mean the passive person is spiritually mature; they are merely apathetic. (What's worse, when you try to confront them on it, they don't care.)

The place to start is honestly admitting there is unresolved conflict in your life. There has been a breakdown.

Some relationships that were once a significant part of your life have deteriorated to the point of breakdown. Perhaps they involve a friend or a parent. Some of you just try to "junk" the relationship, but it may not be simple. Truth about conflict is often complex and hard to resolve even with goodwill. But let us begin with a deep commitment to face relational breakdown squarely in the eye.

If we are going to enter life in little communities, unaddressed and unresolved breakdowns are not acceptable.

2. I must own responsibility

The next word Jesus uses is "you." He calls on everyone who will listen to own the task of seeking reconciliation.

We don't want to do that. These kinds of thoughts come to us all the time: "Let the other person come to me," and "It's not fair that I should have to be the one to take the first step."

Anger often contains an element of self-righteousness that causes me to want to blame the other person and avoid owning responsibility. I remember seeing a television documentary that featured the story of two drivers in conflict. One man felt the other driver had cut him off. He tailgated, then pulled alongside the other driver, and they made angry gestures toward each other. As his anger escalated, the first pulled out a semiautomatic pistol and emptied into the other car, hitting and killing the driver, a seventeen-year-old girl.

What struck me was this comment, made during an interview with him in prison: "She started it. I am just as much a victim as she is."

Do not play the game of justifying your mismanaged anger because of what someone else has done.

Interestingly, while Jesus tells his hearers they should take the responsibility to set things right if the other person has sinned, in another setting he tells his hearers to take the first step if *they* are the ones in the wrong. Jesus puts the burden on you in both cases. If *you've* done something wrong, take the first step, he says; if the other person has done something wrong, you still take the first step.

Why? Because porcupines are stubborn, prickly little creatures. Because we have a surplus of weapons and a deficit of peacemakers in this world. Because people who value community are people who own responsibility to deal with relational breakdowns.

3. Approach, don't avoid, the person you are in conflict with

"Go," Jesus says. Take action. Don't let resentment fester.

But often I don't want to go. I want to stay and stew. I would rather just be mad. It's more fun to pout. Besides, if I go it may get ugly.

This is the huge step. It is important to remember that when you approach the other person, you may not even do it well. You may stutter and stammer and stumble over your words. Don't let that stop you.

It is important to try to use as much skill and wisdom as you can. If you wait until you can do it perfectly, you will never go at all. Doing it flawlessly is not the main concern. The main thing is to go.

Avoidance kills community. Avoidance causes resentment to fester inside you.

Avoidance kills community. Avoidance causes resentment to fester inside you.

Anger is physiological arousal. More adrenaline is secreted, more sugar is released, your heart beats faster, your blood pressure rises, your pupils open wide. Anger is a form of power. It is a signal that something needs your attention. It prepares you to act.

Some people grow up in homes where family members never acknowledge anger. Often they learn to "stuff" it. Sometimes they grow up with the thought, "I should never experience anger. It means I'm a terrible person."

It is a good thing that you have the capacity to be angry. It's part of the ability to live a passionate life. But you were not meant to live in an extended state of anger. Anger is like a smoke detector: It's very good to have one. When it buzzes, it signals that something needs to be fixed. Maybe the problem is external—you need to put out a fire. Maybe the problem is internal—the batteries may be out, in which case you need to fix the detector. It's good that you have the detector, but it's not good to live with the smoke detector constantly making noise.

Anger exists to tell you something is wrong and to move you to action. Anger exists so you will be motivated to make it go away.

However, taking wise action while you are angry is exceedingly difficult. As the arousal level goes up, you suffer from what therapists sometimes call "cognitive incapacitation." You can't think straight. Anger produces what might be called the Jim Carrey effect: As you get mad and madder, you get dumb and dumber. Neil Warren puts it like this: "When your inner gauge reads 'red-hot anger,' delay response."

You need to buy time. You need to allow your body and your emotions to cool down, so you can behave intentionally instead of going on autopilot.

The writer of Proverbs says, "People with a hot temper do foolish things; wiser people remain calm."

We may want to physically leave the situation and go somewhere until our emotions are out of the red zone. One researcher found that for men, their favorite strategy when they get extremely angry is to go off alone for a drive.

This makes you think twice. A long walk may be a better idea.

However, here is a key: A cooling-down period will not work if you use the time to pursue an anger-inducing train of thought. If you rehearse reasons for anger, you just get madder. You must find a way to reroute your thoughts.

There are a couple of ways to do this. One is, when we find ourselves thinking hostile thoughts that continue to feed anger, simply yell the word "stop" out loud if appropriate. Another way is to have an alternate thought at hand. For instance, anger makes us feel that we are absolutely in the right and are justified to do anything to hurt the other person. So a very good thing for people with anger issues to say is, "I could be wrong." You may want to practice saying this out loud right now. (Go ahead. I'll wait.) The problem is, we get angry just saying that. It helps to smile. It may help us to find some reason to say, "I could be wrong," twice a day this week.

Also, before we follow Jesus' command and "go," it may be helpful to ask two key questions. Champions at anger management ask them intuitively; anger mismanagers never think about them.

The first key question is, "Why am I angry?"

Remember how you learned in grade school that red, blue, and yellow are primary colors and that other colors can be made from a mixture of them? In a similar way, anger is not a primary emotion. It is virtually always the result of a mixture of other emotions, such as hurt, frustration, or fear. If we want to manage anger constructively, we need to step back and ask what is underneath the anger. Otherwise, we are not dealing with the root cause.

A few examples may help:

—Let's say you let someone of the opposite sex know you're attracted to them. They respond by saying, "I'm not going out because I just don't find you attractive—though I could be wrong." You're flat-out rejected. You feel anger, but what's underneath it? Hurt.

—Or, let's say she warms up to you. You're on the way to pick her up for your first date, running a little late because your boss gave you a last-minute project, and you get pulled over for going thirty-six miles an hour in a thirty-five zone. You are highly aware of your anger, but what's fueling it? Frustration.

—Another scenario, compliments of Ken Davis. Things work out very well, and the two of you get married. It's two o'clock in the morning. She hears a loud thumping noise downstairs, like someone walking around and bumping into things. She says, "What's that noise?" You say, "I don't hear anything." (This has actually happened to me. I had to say it loudly, so Nancy could hear me over the thumping noise.) She says, "I know. I heard the story on the radio. It's some ax-wielding, bloodthirsty, mouth-foaming, homicidal maniac who's escaped from the maximum security penitentiary for the criminally insane. Go check it out."

"All right, then. I'll go down in my B.V.D.s—that'll scare him." Now you're angry about having to go down and look for a homicidal maniac. What's beneath the anger? Fear.

The second question to ask is, "What do I want?"

It is an amazing dynamic: Once people get to a certain level of anger, their only focus is to win an argument or to inflict pain or to get away. They forget to ask a crucial question: What would I like the outcome of this situation to be? What lies in accord with my desires and deepest values?

When we get angry, we start thinking about what we can say that will win the argument or inflict pain. Instead of listening, we just use the time the other person is talking to reload our thoughts. Or we listen for any misstatement they might make that we can jump on to our own advantage.

But once we have cooled down and thought things through— "Go!" The apostle Paul wrote to one community that was having conflict problems, "Be angry but do not sin; do not let the sun go down on your anger."

Make sure you follow through. Many people have only two gears. First, they get really mad and say or do anything. Then when they cool down, they avoid confrontation because it is unpleasant. They don't do anything to correct what the anger was about.

Certain thoughts lead to anger. People who have trouble managing anger are people who habitually tend to think hostile, cynical thoughts about others.

To become a champion of anger management, you must become *aware* of your thoughts and begin to think different thoughts.

Your thoughts lead to anger. Consider this example:

It is nine o'clock in the evening. My four-year old gets out of bed and cautiously, tentatively, comes downstairs, violating curfew. However, I have nothing to do, nowhere to go; I am relaxed and at peace with the world. *Look at the little tyke. Only a few more years to enjoy Kodak moments like this, then he'll be grown. How brave and adventurous he is, risking punishment to explore the unknown world of the night! He's just like his father.*

Another night: Same time, same child, same father. But now it's the end of a long, stressful day, and I still have to put together a message on anger before I go to bed. The tyke comes downstairs, and my mind takes a different turn: *Only a few precious moments to get my work done, and Eddie Munster here can't stay in bed. Sure, sneak down the stairs, kid! Go ahead, make my day. The question you gotta ask yourself is, do I feel lucky? How rebellious and disobedient he is, defying parental authority ordained by God because of his relativistic narcissism! He didn't get those genes from my side of the family.*

Notice that the external situation is identical in both cases. It is the thought process that makes the difference. Of course, that doesn't mean the thoughts that lead to anger are *always* irrational. If you're with a person who is abusive and who deliberately insults you, your thoughts will lead to angry feelings. Those thoughts are on target; they are accurate thoughts.

Sometimes you should become angry. However, even then you still must decide how to express your anger.

But often we feel anger because we are thinking distorted, hostile, cynical thoughts.

Paul wrote to the church at Philippi, "Finally, brothers and sisters, whatever is true, whatever is noble, whatever is right, whatever is pure, whatever is lovely, whatever is admirable—if anything is excellent or praiseworthy—think about such things."

Sometimes you should become angry. However, even then you still must decide how to express your anger.

One research team working on road rage taught drivers a cognitive strategy: Anytime they found themselves getting angry with another driver, they were to stop and think, "There goes my mom." (If you have mother issues, this may just make you madder. You may have to think about somebody else's mother.) Or the drivers were to think of possible reasons other people might have for making a driving mistake. Maybe they are in an emergency. Maybe they are having a horrible day.

For the most part, you won't want to invite other drivers into deep conversations about your anger with them. But off-road, Jesus says we must learn to approach and not avoid the people with whom we have conflict.

4. "No third parties"

Go directly to the other person involved, Jesus says. As a general rule, I don't want to go to the person I'm having conflict with. That's the last person I want to go to.

I want to go to someone else, and say, "Let me tell you what's going on here. I just want to lay it out objectively and get some feedback from a neutral third party. Don't you share my concerns about this person, who is my brother in Christ and a deeply disturbed psychopath?"

It's more fun to go to someone else. I can commiserate with the third party.

We tend to idealize the first-century church and think that it had a conflict-free environment. But the same New Testament that tells us how they were of one mind and devoted themselves to one another also paints a picture of communities in which conflict was alive and well. The Greek-speaking members had a big ruckus with the Hebrew-speaking members over whose widows were getting taken care of. Ananias and Sapphira were so jealous of other people's reputation for generosity that it seriously damaged their health. Paul and Barnabas had such a strong disagreement over a colleague that they dissolved their partnership.

The early church was not a place where conflict didn't exist. It was a place where people were committed and accountable to manage conflict well.

Paul wrote to the community at Philippi, where two prominent women, Euodia and Syntyche, were locked in a difficult conflict. We don't know what the issue was—maybe it was over who had the goofier first name.

What is interesting is what Paul *doesn't* advise. He doesn't say, "Euodia, talk to some other people about how unfair Syntyche is being to you. Thoroughly discuss her character flaws and neuroses so that others can pray for her more intelligently." He doesn't say, "Syntyche, let three or four of your close friends know how Euodia has mistreated you so they can reinforce your self-righteous sense of martyrdom."

Instead, Paul strongly asks them ("I plead …") to resolve this conflict directly—to "agree with each other;" to be of one mind. It is striking that in this same little paragraph he commends both women. He says they have "contended at my side in the cause of the gospel"—one of the strongest commendations he can give. He says their names are written "in the book of life." Their difficulties with conflict do not diminish their standings in Paul's eyes at all. The litmus test of spirituality is not the absence of conflict; conflict will not disappear until we die. The litmus test is how we handle it. Conflict is inevitable. Resentment is optional.

Problems emerge when we talk about the conflict with somebody else instead of dealing directly with the person involved. So instead of going to Synteche directly, Euodia goes to someone else: "Do you know what Syntyche did?" Then, inevitably the word gets back to Synteche: "Do you know what Euodia said about you? Of course, don't tell her I told you because this is confidential." Instead of two people trying to hammer out an honest disagreement, we now have three people involved—all of whom are avoiding confronting the conflict directly, but all of whom now have reason to dislike one another.

One of the great myths of our day is that "talking anger out" with a third party will help us become less angry. Often, if people decide they won't ventilate directly, they handle anger by going to a third party, someone they know will be sympathetic, and telling that third party why they are so upset.

Talking things over often does make us *feel* better. That's what friends and therapists and bartenders are for. But again, the research on this is very clear. Carol Tavris reports, "'Talking out' an emotion doesn't reduce it, *it rehearses it*. . . . As you recite your grievances, your emotional arousal builds up again, making you feel as angry as you did when the infuriating event first happened, and, in addition, establishing an attitude [of hostility] about the source of your rage."

This doesn't mean you should never talk about your anger. You may need a sounding board to help you plan how to resolve the conflict. But generally, if you're going to involve a third party, you should do it with the goal of finding reconciliation.

It is the height of irony that few organizations have fought more often or split more bitterly than the church. In the twentieth century there were more than a hundred varieties of Baptist churches alone, including the Northern Baptists, Southern Baptists, General Baptists, Particular Baptists, Seventh-day Baptists, Hard Shell Baptists, Free Will Baptists, Duck River and Kindred Association Baptists, and my favorite: the Two-Seed-in-the-Spirit Predestinarian Baptists. A group called the Church of God had a branch break off, calling itself the True Church of God, and a group split off from that calling itself the Only True Church of God. A researcher points out that there are more than 33,000 denominations of Christianity in the world. And every one of them was a split. Almost all of them were born out of anger and hostility and withdrawal between people who claimed to follow the teachings of Jesus. This is the same Jesus who prayed to his Father that all his followers might "be brought to complete unity to let the world know that you sent me."

A man is rescued from a desert island where he survived alone for fifteen years. Before leaving, he gave his rescuers a little tour of the buildings he had constructed as a sort of one-man town over the years: "That was my house, that was my store, this building was a kind cabana, and over here is where I go to church."

"What's the building next to it?"

"Oh, that's where I *used* to go to church."

The need for sensitivity is one of the most important—and often misunderstood—aspects of healthy anger management.

5. "Use sensitivity"

Jesus says that we are to approach the object of our anger in private and deal with it "just between the two of you." One consequence of this strategy is that we don't needlessly embarrass another person by forcing them to respond in front of an audience. We approach him or her in the way *we* would want to be approached.

This need for sensitivity is one of the most important—and often misunderstood—aspects of healthy anger management.

Another myth is that the best way to handle anger is to ventilate it. This view was popular among psychologists during the 1960s and 1970s. The idea is that unexpressed anger gets stored up in a kind of inner psychological reservoir, so when we become angry, the main thing we must do is discharge our feelings. "Get it off your chest." "Blow off steam." "Let it all hang out." Throw something, hit something, scream something—ventilate.

According to this theory, if we don't let the anger fly, it doesn't go away. It builds up like steam inside a tea kettle, and if there's not some release, we will just blow up some day when we least expect it. We become like a volcano, waiting for the "river of rage" inside to overflow.

Why do we think that way about anger? We don't think that way about other emotions. No one says, "I've been holding in joy all these years; people tell funny jokes, and I just repress all my laughter; I haven't released it and it's been building up inside me. Now the joy dam is about to burst; I'm gonna spew joy all over everybody." Therapists don't say, "You've got to get in touch with your gratitude; for years your parents helped you and sacrificed for you, yet you never learned to verbalize your thankfulness. Now you've got all this gratitude bottled up inside you, and it's not healthy. You're like a walking time bomb of gratitude. Someday you're going to walk up to people you don't even know—and gush gratitude all over them."

It turns out that there is a problem with ventilating anger. The old theory was that you get angry, you ventilate, anger drains off, you get it "out of your system." The problem is, ventilation is tolerable. It is self-reinforcing. People hit, they feel powerful, they want to hit more. One review of a dozen studies in this area found that "both the observation of and participation in aggressive behavior leads to more, not less, anger and aggression."

I will sometimes demonstrate this with crowds of people by having them stand up and say "yes," and then I invite them to scream "NO!" while clenching their fists and shaking their heads. Inevitably, the amount of energy in the room is scary. When I tell them to sit down, they just keep standing there, yelling "NO!" and shaking their fists at me.

Carol Tavris wrote, "The contemporary ventilationist view [is] . . . that it is always important to express anger so that it won't clog your arteries or your relationships. . . . If your expressed rage causes another person to shoot you, it won't matter that you die with very healthy arteries."

There is another problem with ventilation. Researchers have discovered that people don't enjoy getting ventilated on. The ventilator has a good time, but the ventilatee tends to get angry.

How often do you see this scene? One man feels he's been cut off by another motorist. He pulls alongside the perpetrator, yelling, "What kind of an idiot are you? What were you thinking? Were you trying to kill me?"

The other person responds, "That's a point well taken. You've touched me deeply. I'm going to change. I want to thank you for taking the time to offer me that hand gesture as well."

Research on anger has reached a level of consensus rare in the social sciences. Three major reviews, covering dozens of studies over several decades, did not find a single study that demonstrates that catharsis—letting anger fly—is an effective way to manage anger. It just creates more anger.

The simplest guideline is to approach the other people the way you would want to be approached in their place.

People who let anger fly may get what they ask for in the short run, but they miss out on the intimacy that is their deepest need. Once a man approached me after I had covered some of this material in a talk that was launching a series on anger. He was a large hulk of a man, perhaps six-foot-five, and looked as if he might have had a job with the World Wrestling Federation. His right hand was in a cast. He wanted to talk to me about the message. "What you said about that ventilation business is true. Last week I got so mad I smashed a concrete wall with my fist and broke the bones in two of my fingers. I'm coming back for every talk in this series, and"—he fixed me with a fierce glare—"it better be good."

The simplest guideline is to approach the other people the way you would want to be approached in their place.

6. "Direct communication"

"Show him his fault," Jesus says. This, too, is often easier said than done. Very often, when an actual face-to-face confrontation takes place, people end up addressing the problem indirectly in an effort to soften the blow. For instance, a wife may be frustrated with her husband's failure to help around the house. But her frustration may come out in the form of a question instead of a direct statement: "Wouldn't you like to get the garage all cleaned up today?"

He reflects on the state of his heart and discovers that at the deepest level, at the intimate core of his true self, he really wouldn't like to get the garage all cleaned up today. And he tells her that, proud of his self-awareness and transparency. She goes away twice as conflicted, because she didn't really intend it to be a question; she wanted him to clean the garage.

On the management team where I work, we often talk about the "Last 10 Percent Rule." The idea is this: Often, after going through all the hard work of setting up a difficult conversation, we shrink back from saying the hardest but most important truth. We fail to say the last 10 percent. We get vague and fuzzy precisely when clarity is most needed by the other person. Instead of saying, "You talked too much at the meeting," I might say, "It was hard to have a good conversation." Instead of honestly naming rude behavior, I speak vaguely of not feeling connected to the other person and hope they will fill in the blanks. I do this not out of love for the other person, but because I don't want to go through the pain or fear involved in deeper conflict.

When I speak of the last 10 percent, I don't mean that I'm to take on the obligation of straightening everything out in every person. It certainly doesn't mean I am obliged to give every observation I have to everyone I know, whether they want it or not. It does mean that in loving confrontation I must watch my tendency to get fuzzy precisely when the truth is most needed and the most difficult to speak.

Here is a general framework for the last 10 percent:

a. Describe clearly what you observed: "You weren't really listening to me."
b. Explain how it hurt you: "I found myself feeling that I don't matter to you."

c. Tell what the consequences have been: "This could cause distance in our relationship, and I don't want that."
d. Ask for the change you would like: "I want to connect when we're together."

7. Aim at reconciliation

Jesus says, "If he listens to you, you have won your brother over." The goal in conflict situations is not to win or score points—it's reconciliation.

Your aim should be to restore the relationship. Reconciliation is rarely simple and almost never quick.

But it is Jesus' will for the human race. It is his express command for his church. If this is not the goal, all the rest of our work will be for nothing.

I was trying to parallel park on a congested one-way street in Pasadena, California, not long ago. The driver behind me was getting increasingly frustrated because he couldn't get around me; he just had to sit there and wait (and this was southern California, where people shoot first and honk later). Finally, I wedged my car in, and he pulled up next to me to share his deepest feelings. (Generally, in a situation like this you don't think of something really good to say until two o'clock the next morning when it's too late to use it.) "What's your problem . . . ?" he yelled at me, calling me a name. I won't repeat it, but it was a reference to part of my anatomy, not too far north, not too far south, just below the Equator, in the Western Hemisphere. Then he drove away.

It was a pretty profound question. I've thought about it often. It pretty much sums up the human condition.

But the man didn't stick around to discuss it with me. He didn't really care what my problem was. He just left me with this provocative question.

The man did many things right, according to Matthew 18:15. Did he acknowledge our conflict? Yes, with clarity and passion. He took initiative without waiting; he was not passive. He did not complain about me to other motorists or start a circle of gossip on the streets so that other drivers were talking about me; he spoke to no one but me. His communication was impressively direct; I knew exactly what he was thinking and feeling. He went the last 10 percent.

He got six out of seven steps right. Not bad! But he missed the one that matters most of all. If you're not ready to do this, you're probably not ready for the first six.

Direct confrontation doesn't always do good. Sometimes it escalates the conflict. Sometimes it leads to violence. Confrontation can do tremendous damage.

Sometimes that happens. Sometimes we get deep scars and wounds from people. Then we need something more than anger management. We need a miracle.

And God created one. It's called forgiveness. That's what we turn to next.

Learning to Dance

1. How did your family handle conflict when you were growing up?

2. What characterizes your approach to conflict?
   a. Avoid at all costs
   b. I can face it, but I don't like it
   c. A good argument every once in a while clears the air
   d. I do conflict recreationally

3. Pay attention to your anger today. What tends to trigger it? How do you tend to handle it? Is it most often fed by hurt, by frustration, or by fear?

4. Are there any people in your life who tend to drag you in as a third party to a conflict where you should not be involved? How can you handle this?

5. Think of a person whose conflict management skills you admire. What makes him or her effective? Ask them how they became skilled at dealing with anger.

6. How are you doing at speaking the last 10 percent? To whom do you need to tell the last 10 percent, and whom can you ask to hold you accountable to do it?

7. Is there *any* unresolved conflict in your life? If so, ruthlessly decide to seek to resolve it.

PART 3

THE SECRETS OF STRONG RELATIONSHIPS

CHAPTER 8

SPIRITUAL SURGERY: FORGIVENESS

When you forgive someone, you are dancing to the rhythm of the divine heartbeat . . . God invented forgiveness as the only way to keep his romance with the human race alive.

LEWIS SMEDES

"There are some people for whom friend making is effortless. They smile, they crack a joke, they shrug insouciantly, they offer something up, accept what has been offered, balance themselves delicately on the threshold. And when the door unlatches, they're in."

But for most of us, the door is harder to find. Beth Kephart, who wrote these words, tells of being the new kid in high school when her family moved from her old home, and of searching desperately for a friend.

> I had to think: who might have room for me? Who isn't taken? I had to shield myself from the hazards of rejection, send out just enough signals but not too many. . . . Walking up and down the halls I studied students at their lockers, tried on attitudes, sat front, back, middle on the bus. I strategized, adapted, hoped (without disclosing hope) that someone out there was looking

> too, that something about me would inspire. One can go one's whole life without a friend; I realized that. There's the possibility of perpetual loneliness.

In a vast field of isolation Beth found the pearl of great price—a friend; a best friend. Joanne was funny and bright and warm, and in the mysterious alchemy of human beings, two gawky fourteen-year-olds were alloyed in friendship. That year, Beth writes, the world became a different place for her. She belonged. The cafeteria was no longer a no-man's-land; someone was saving a place for her. Four years went by: birthdays, pizzas, projects, makeovers, and sleepovers. Because of her friend, Beth writes, she learned the music of that era; she learned about boys and secrets and other people's families and the fine art of passing notes in school.

She told Joanne everything, as best friends do. Her senior year, Beth told Joanne her biggest secret: She had fallen in love. It was an impossible crush. He was a blond-haired, back-of-the-bus Big Man on Campus who hardly knew Beth was alive. At best, he would occasionally grunt hello. Still, every night after school, after homework, Beth would call Joanne to tell her the details: where she had seen him, what he had worn or said, whether or not he had acknowledged her with a terse greeting. Joanne was always encouraging: "Maybe he likes you."

"Really?"

Beth wanted so badly to believe her friend, to think this BMOC might feel for her some echo of what she felt for him. "Love is stronger than death," the ancient writer says, and I suppose it's no less true when you're in high school. Beth could not stop hoping, even though he gave her so little reason, even though he didn't seem to notice her and never said much more than a grunt. She could not stop hoping, she writes, until the night Joanne showed up with him at the prom.

And a friendship that blossomed for four years, with the only best friend she ever had, was silenced for twenty years.

The ache of loneliness.

The hope of searching.

The joy of intimacy.

The anguish of betrayal.

The Law of Lamech

Community always involves a kind of promise, whether or not it ever gets stated out loud. It is a promise of commitment and loyalty. *In a world of uncertainty, you can count on me*. When that promise gets broken, so does someone's heart. No one can love us like someone we've given our heart to, but no one can wound us like that person either. This truth is the driving force behind country music. Someone sent me a list of classic country titles, and most of them revolve around the pain of betrayal:

"If You Leave Me, Can I Come Too?"
"I Bought the Shoes That Just Walked Out on Me"
"How Can I Miss You If You Won't Go Away?"

God created human beings in his image so they can be friends—intimate, love-filled companions—with him and one another. But soon they learn to live as enemies. To all the wonders that God has created, human beings add an invention of their own: revenge. You hurt me, and I'll hurt you back. A kind of Newtonian law becomes as inevitable as the law of gravity: For every infliction of pain there must be an equal and opposite act of vengeance.

To all the wonders that God has created, human beings add an invention of their own: revenge.

A character in the book of Genesis named Lamech takes this concept to its ultimate extreme. He kills a man for wounding him; he says he will seek revenge seventy-seven times over against anyone who hurts him. This is the Law of Lamech: If anyone inflicts pain on me, I must make them pay. One of the most poignant statements in Scripture comes shortly after the episode of Lamech as God views the violence and corruption that has spread like an epidemic through the creatures he loves: "The LORD was grieved that he had made man on the earth, and his heart was filled with pain."

God keeps giving his heart to the human race, and they keep showing up at the prom on somebody else's arm.

So God, who created the heavens and the earth in six days, has to create once more after the Fall. He invents a kind of spiritual surgery that can remove what is toxic to the heart and make dead relationships live again. This new creation is called forgiveness. It is in some ways his last, best gift to the human race. It is the only force strong enough to heal relationships damaged by hatred and betrayal. Porcupines can't live in community apart from the miracle of forgiveness.

Peter comes to Jesus one day: "Someone's hurt me. He's done me wrong. Not just once. I know I'm supposed to forgive him; but it feels so unfair. Why should *I* always have to be the one to forgive? How often do I have to forgive him—seven times?"

Most likely Peter is expecting Jesus to say that such magnanimity would be beyond the call of duty. The rabbis used to say there was an obligation to forgive someone three times; Peter here is doubling it and throwing in a bonus round for good measure.

And it's not just anyone who has hurt Peter. It's his brother. Somebody he trusts. How can he keep setting himself up for heartbreak?

The concern behind Peter's question has been felt by everyone who has ever been hurt. Why should I forgive? What if the other person doesn't deserve it? I might get hurt again. Forgiveness looks like a pretty risky business. Forgiveness looks to Peter like one of those activities that Jesus is always talking about, and it is probably a pretty spiritual thing to do, but it doesn't always work out so well for those of us who live in the real world.

Imagine Peter's response when, instead of commending him, Jesus tells him he still has seventy acts of forgiveness to go: "I tell you, not seven times, but seventy-seven times." Of course, Jesus doesn't mean that on the seventy-eighth violation Peter can let the man have it. Jesus is reversing the Law of Lamech. He is making a point that there are two ways to live with hurt: the way of vengeance and the way of forgiveness. The first way leads to death, and the second to life.

There is another reason, I think, that Jesus uses such large numbers. In a world of porcupines, you're going to receive a lot of quills. Forgiving is a little like breathing: If you try to keep track of every time you do it, you'll go crazy. Even seventy-seven times is just a warm-up. Forgiving will have to be a way of life.

Jesus makes this point, as he typically did, by telling a story. A number of years ago, my colleague Bill Hybels retold that story in a modern setting. Let me retell it in my own words as we explore what it means to forgive.

The CEO and the Embezzler

One day the founder-president-CEO of a large and thriving software company calls in his whole management team: all the vice presidents and department heads. It's tax time for the Roman government. Caesar's revenue agents have been auditing the books, and everybody around the firm is a little nervous. The Roman government has a flat-tax program: Pay what they tell you or get flattened.

It turns out that during the auditing process the Romans discover that one of the VPs has had his hand in the cookie jar. The VP has been working for the firm a long time, but he has an Achilles' heel: He wants to maintain a lifestyle he can't afford.

So the VP has been systematically embezzling from the company for years. Now he owes an astronomical sum of money. When Jesus tells the story, he grabs onto the largest number in the language and pluralizes it. It would be something like saying "zillions" in English. He wants us to appreciate the size of the debt. It's like the national debt or the trade deficit—more money than you will ever see. It's like your mortgage.

There is no possibility that the VP can ever pay the money back. To make matters worse, he has no positive financial prospects and no Swiss bank account. He didn't make shrewd investments; he just blew the money, shot the wad. He is left with no job, no job offers, and the prospect of a prison sentence hanging over his head. This is a case of plain, unadulterated, forget-about-tomorrow greed.

Now comes the day of reckoning. It is the firm's annual meeting. All the stockholders are there. This embezzler comes to the founder and principle owner—the man who had given him his chance, believed in him, and trusted him. The VP has to admit his greed, his theft, and his violation of trust. Imagine the tremors that will work their way through the firm. This is going to be bloody.

Imagine the employee's fear and utter humiliation. His head throbs, his heart pounds, his palms are sweaty. It's all over. No more bluffing. No more con games. There is no such thing as a Chapter 11 bankruptcy, no chance to reorganize, no hidden assets, no rich uncle, no horse that might come in, no lottery tickets. The VP is finished. He will be thrown into jail or sold into slavery—and not just him, but his whole family. And not just this generation, but for generations to come. The slave in Jesus' story was worth maybe two thousand dollars; his whole family wouldn't bring in one-tenth of one percent of the debt. This would mean slavery for his descendants for generations to come.

The VP stands before his peers, the stockholders, and his boss. The sentence is read: "Sell everything he owns, sell him into slavery, and his wife and children, and his children's children, until the unpayable debt is paid. Case closed. Take him away. Next item of business."

No surprise. Standard operating procedure. Right out of the policy manual.

But something happens in this embezzler. As the reality of what's happening to him registers in his mind, an idea comes to him: *What if I were to fall on my face, humble myself, and beg for mercy?* It's a long shot; a last-ditch effort, a bolt-out-of-the-blue million-to-one shot. But he reasons to himself, *What do I have to lose? This is my last option.*

So the VP falls to his knees. He blurts out, "I know I'm guilty. I know what I owe. Please show me some mercy! I'll pay back what I owe you. I just need some time. Give me a grace period. Give me grace."

Jesus' listeners would know that such a thing would never happen. When it comes to debt, every economy that has ever existed has been built on one simple rule: *You owe, you pay*. Certain people who lend money are always quite touchy about this. They keep careful accounts. You pay—or you get a visit from a large man named Vito.

We have a phrase for people on the street who lend money that reflects how seriously the "you owe, you pay" rule is taken. It's an aquatic metaphor: the "loan shark." Not "the loan bunny." Not "the loan poodle." It's a shark. Making debtors pay is serious business.

Imagine the scene in the boardroom. All the players avert their eyes and look down at their shoes. They're all thinking the same thoughts: *This is embarrassing. He's hit a new low. He lined his pockets, he knew the rules, he got caught, he can't pay—this is a just penalty. Standard operating procedure*. Mercy? *He must be joking. Even if he had a thousand years, he couldn't pay this debt. Give me a break. Get a clue*. *At least go down with some dignity.*

If they're surprised at the plea, imagine what happens when they look at the old man, the founder-president-CEO. He's no pushover. He's been through the wars. He didn't get where he is by being an easy mark for every con man that comes along.

But when they look over at him, the old man can't speak. He's all choked up.

The employees say to themselves, *He's not going to fall for this line, is he? He's not going to go soft on us now.*

But as the CEO thinks of the man before him and his family, something happens in his heart. His eyes are full of tears; his lips tremble a little as he speaks. In his account, Jesus calls this "pity" or "compassion."

For reasons no one understands, the CEO walks over to where the embezzler lies cringing on the ground and raises him to his feet. "All right," the CEO says, "I will rescind the sentence."

The man will not go to jail. He will not be a slave. He will not lose his family. He may keep what he owns.

But the CEO goes far beyond that. He releases the man from his debt. The unpayable debt doesn't have to be paid back. Grace will be extended indefinitely. This is more grace than the embezzler dreamed of asking for. It's more grace than anyone else imagined to exist.

It is crucial here to grasp what Jesus is saying about the heart of God. When the CEO forgives the debt, it doesn't simply disappear. There is still the loss of a vast fortune to be accounted for. Who absorbs it? The answer, of course, is the owner. When he forgives the embezzler, it is not a casual thing. Forgiveness comes with a price tag that no one in the room but the old man can ever fully understand. He comes up with a whole new system for handling the unpayable debt: *You owe, I'll pay.*

Imagine the embezzler's response. "I can't believe it! I didn't have a prayer, it was a total long shot—and it paid off! I threw myself on the mercy of the court, and he took the loss. I got grace. I'm free!" He goes home and tells his wife and hugs his children—who will *not* be slaves after all. They pass from death to life.

You Owe, I'll Pay

Now we need to step back from the story for a while. The master in Jesus' story, of course, is a stand-in for God. The other character, the embezzler, represents you and me. Jesus says we have accumulated a moral debt before a just and holy God, and it's been growing for years. Every time we are less than honest or fudge an expense account or tax return or treat a five-year-old too harshly or make a cutting remark we shouldn't or should speak truth in love but don't or gossip or tell a racist joke or have sexually impure thoughts—each act adds to a mountain of moral debt. All human beings owe that enormous debt.

As a pastor, I have devoted my life to spiritual growth, yet it took me only thirty seconds to come up with that list of sins. Know why? Because my wife has done every one of those things. (Not really. My own heart teaches me all I need to know about the reality of sin.)

So God himself uses the instrument he never would have had to invent if the human race had not sinned. God has developed a new possibility for dealing with betrayal and hurt: *You owe, I'll pay.* He forgives. But forgiveness does not come cheap.

This is where the story gets very personal for Jesus. Jesus knew all about friendship, pain, and betrayal. As a boy, he had to learn about friends the same way you and I do. God Incarnate learned what it is to be the new kid or to ask, *Who might have room for me? Who isn't taken?* He would have learned to run the hazards of rejection, to send out just enough signals, to strategize and adapt and hope that someone else was searching, too.

As an adult, Jesus would give himself to all people, and to twelve friends in particular. One of them would betray him, another would deny him, all would abandon him. On the cross, the entire weight of the unpayable debt owed by sinful humanity would fall on him. He would pay it all.

God has developed a new possibility for dealing with betrayal and hurt: *You owe, I'll pay.* He forgives. But forgiveness does not come cheap.

This is why the cross is at the heart of Christianity. It shows us the heart of God. He feels compassion, his eyes fill with tears, his lips tremble a little out of love for his children. He chooses to pay the debt we never could. He longs to forgive.

And what Jesus does at infinite cost, he invites us to do as well, though at much lesser expense. Jesus is telling this story, after all, in response to Peter's question about why he should forgive. So let's think about what we're being invited to do.

Some Things Forgiveness Is Not

What is it that we do, exactly, when we forgive? Lewis Smedes, who is the closest thing I know to an expert on forgiving, says we must start by understanding what forgiveness is *not* and then look at the three stages that are part of what forgiving *is*.

First, forgiving is not the same thing as *excusing*. Excusing is what we do when we consider extenuating circumstances for our behavior. We excuse expectant fathers for driving fast because they are taxiing a woman in labor. We excuse clumsy skiers for bumping into us when we find out they're beginners. We excuse eight-year-old boys for making bodily noises because they're eight-year-old boys.

People sometimes say that "to understand all is to forgive all," but in a sense that's exactly wrong. Forgiveness is what is required precisely when there is no good rationale to explain away why someone did what they did. Forgiving does not mean tolerating bad behavior or pretending that what someone did was not so bad. As Smedes says, excusing is an end run around the crisis of forgiving. When an action is excusable, it doesn't require forgiveness.

Forgiving is not *forgetting*. All that forgetting requires is a really bad memory. I forget where I parked my car or put my keys. This doesn't mean I have an advanced soul, just some badly misfiring neurons. Sometimes, if a hurt is severe enough, it can be buried away out of fear or trauma. It is in some sense forgotten, but it hasn't been forgiven. Scripture writers sometimes use the language of "'forgetting" to describe how God deals with our sin, but this doesn't mean that God has a memory retrieval problem. It means that our past sins become irrelevant to his dealings with us. Forgiving is what's required precisely when we *can't* forget.

Forgiving is not the same thing as *reconciling*. People sometimes think that forgiving someone means we must reunite with them no matter what—that a wife must move back in with a brute that beats her or a businessman must take back a dishonest partner as many times as requested. Although there is some disagreement about this among those who write about ethics, I think forgiveness and reconciliation are two separate things. Forgiveness takes place within the heart of one human being. It can be granted even if the other person does not ask for it or deserve it. C. S. Lewis once observed that he had finally forgiven a man who had been dead for more than thirty years. Reconciliation requires that the offender still be alive and be sincerely repentant for the wrong he or she committed. Reconciliation requires the rebuilding of trust, and that means good faith on the part of *both* parties.

What Forgiveness Is

Forgiving is required when excusing or condoning or tolerating or accepting are not big enough to do the job. The first stage of forgiveness is the decision not to try to inflict a reciprocal amount of pain on everyone who has caused hurt. When I forgive you, *I give up the right to hurt you back*. Even though you may hurt me deliberately, personally, and deeply, I suspend the law of vengeance. I refrain from the instinctive response of retaliation. I don't act on or indulge my desire to see you squirm. When I forgive you, I set you free from the little prison I have placed in my mind for holding you captive. I seek to stop entertaining fantasies of vengeance in which you are tortured or fired from your job or suddenly gain fifty pounds.

Forgiveness begins when we give up the quest to get even. This is difficult, because getting even is the natural obsession of the wounded soul. Stories about getting even always capture our attention. It wouldn't surprise me if revenge is the theme of as many as half the movies shown in theaters today.

Sometime ago Dave Hagler, who works as an umpire in a recreational baseball league, was pulled over for driving too fast in the snow in Boulder, Colorado. He tried to talk the officer out of giving him a ticket by telling him how worried he was about insurance and how he's normally a very safe driver, and so on. The officer said that if he didn't like receiving the ticket, he could take the matter to court.

At the first game in the next baseball season, Dave Hagler is umpiring behind the plate, and the first batter up is—can you believe it?—the policeman. As the officer is about to step into the batters box, they recognize each other. Long pause. The officer asks, "So how did the thing with the ticket go?"

Hagler says, "You'd better swing at everything."

Sweet revenge.

But for deep hurts, the way of vengeance has not proved so successful. The problem with getting even is that no two people weigh pain on the same scale. Will the Palestinians ever get even with the Israelis, or the Serbs with the Bosnians? Or, as Smedes puts it, "Will the Bloods ever get even with the Crips on the streets of Los Angeles? Never. They may go on killing each other until they are all dead, but they will never get even." Forgiving starts when we decide to stop trying to get even.

Of course, letting go of vengeance doesn't mean letting go of justice. Justice must still be honored. A kidnapper may be forgiven by his victim, but he still needs to pay his debt to society. Justice involves the pursuit of fairness. Vengeance is the desire for retribution. Vengeance by its nature is insatiable.

The next stage of forgiveness involves a new way of seeing and feeling. One thing that happens when we get deeply hurt is that as we look at the one who hurt us, we don't see a person—only the hurt. In Jesus' story, the unforgiving employee doesn't see another person; he only sees an uncollected debt.

When we hold fast to unforgiveness toward another person, we tend to believe only bad things about them. We want to think of them only in terms of the hurt they have caused us. We want to forget their humanity.

Sometime ago, a person whom I considered a trusted friend told someone else that I was the "difficult person" in his life. He had never said this to me. When I found out, I felt deeply wounded and betrayed. From that point on, the only thoughts I had toward him related to my feelings of being hurt by him. Of course, there was much more to him than this. He is a human being, just as I am, with the same share of wonder and waywardness that I participate in.

When we forgive each other, we begin to see more clearly. We do not ignore the hurts, but we see beyond them. We rediscover the humanity of the one who hurt us. He is no longer just an uncollected debt of pain. He is the product of a fallible mother and father; he is lonely or hurting or weak or nearsighted—just as I am. He is also a bearer of the image of God—just as I am. It was only when I saw this that my friend and I could begin the fitful journey of two porcupines traveling toward reconciliation.

The third stage of forgiving, the one that shows you have begun to make some real progress, is when you find yourself wishing the other person well. You no longer hope that the only calls they get will be from telemarketers and the IRS. You find that your prayers no longer drift into anger fantasies in which your enemy finally realizes he's treated you horribly but it's too late to make amends and he will spend eternity wallowing in unrelieved guilt.

You hope for good things for them. You can hear someone say a kind word about them without inwardly screaming for rebuttal time. You genuinely hope that things are well between them and God, that their relationships are healthy, and that their life is happy. Of course, this does not happen all at once. And it usually doesn't happen once-for-all; you will have some backsliding, some moments when you would like to hear they've gotten bald or fat or have been turned down by a dating service. But the trajectory of the heart is headed in the right direction. When you want good things for someone who hurt you badly, you can pretty much know that the Great Forgiver has been at work in your heart.

The Miracle of Forgiveness

We are always to pursue forgiving people who have hurt us, even when the offenders don't ask for or deserve it. God commands us to forgive because it is the best way to live. He commands us to forgive others because he has forgiven us; he is the Great Forgiver. He commands it because the only other way is to remain a prisoner of the hurt for as long as I live. God commands forgiving because to refuse to forgive means I allow the one who hurt me to keep me chained in a prison of bitterness and resentment year after year. No human beings are more miserable than the unforgiving.

But when the miracle of forgiveness takes place in a best-case scenario, it leads to the healing of a broken relationship. It leads to the reestablishment of community. In New Testament language, this is called "the ministry of reconciliation." This is a dance that demands the full cooperation of two partners: the forgiver and the forgivee. This is where our story diverges a bit from the one Jesus told. As a general rule, where there is hurt, I am both the victim of *and* the agent of wrongdoing. In most relationships where deep pain is involved, I must both forgive and seek forgiveness.

When reconciliation happens, it is a miracle and a mystery. It is hard to define, but it is unmistakable when we experience it.

Garrison Keillor has a wonderful story of reconciliation in his book *Leaving Home*. He was, he writes, part of a church that split into factions over very small points of doctrine. The congregation was cursed with a surplus of scholars and a deficit of peacemakers. One dispute had to do with whether or not it was right to show hospitality to those in doctrinal error—what they called the "Cup of Cold Water" debate.

Uncle Al decided to try to make peace between the warring factions, which were led by Brother William Miller and Brother James Johnson. Al worked through an intermediary, Brother Fields, who had never shown hospitality to anyone, whether they were in error or not, and was therefore judged to be neutral on the issue.

They all arrived one Sunday for Aunt Flo's famous fried chicken. They came in their Fords, being united on the General Motors question: gaunt, flinty-eyed, thin-lipped men in dark floppy suits and their plump, obedient wives.

The grace before the meal posed a problem. Church members were sometimes known to seize prayer and beat other people over the head with it, so Uncle Al had everyone pray silently—an excellent idea except that it soon turned into a contest to see who could pray the longest. Brother Miller snuck a glance at Brother Johnson. No signs of surfacing; Brother Johnson was deeply engaged with God, who agreed with Brother Johnson on so very many issues. So Brother Miller dove back down for some more prayer, too. No one would come up for air, because it might look as if they wanted to eat more than they wanted to pray.

> It was becoming the longest table grace in history, it ground on and on and on, and then Aunt Flo slid her chair

back, rose, went to the kitchen, and brought out the food that they were both competing to see who could be the most thankful for. She set the hay down where the goats could get it. Tears streamed down Brother Johnson's face, and so was Brother Miller weeping.

It's true what they say, that smell is the key that unlocks our deepest memories, and with their eyes closed, the smell of fried chicken and gravy made these men into boys again. It was years ago, they were fighting, and a mother's voice from on high said, "You two stop it and get in here and have your dinners. Now. I mean it." The blessed cornmeal crust and rapturous gravy brought the memory to mind, and the stony hearts of the two giants melted; they raised their heads and filled their plates and slowly peace was made over that glorious chicken.

It's Never Too Late

Because reconciliation is the healing of our deepest longing, it is never too late to seek it. You may have a relationship that broke decades ago; maybe it never worked right. Maybe you have been at war with someone close to you as long as you can remember.

It's never too late.

My wife and I have a friend we will call Sue, whose relationship with her mom was marked by friction her whole life. It alternated between uneasy cease-fires and all-out war. Sue never received a compliment. Her mom never told her she looked pretty. In time, the only way they could relate was to inflict pain on one another verbally, and in a family you know each other's most vulnerable areas.

Because reconciliation is the healing of our deepest longing, it is never too late to seek it.

Sue ended up in the state where people from troubled families usually find themselves (California) and entered the profession they usually enter (psychologist). She tried to avoid going home, and on occasions when she had to go back, she would stay with her brothers. But there was a hole in her heart.

One day Sue received a phone call. Her mom had been diagnosed with a degenerative neuromuscular disease and did not have long to live.

Sue began to pray, asking for a miracle. Maybe for her mother's body, maybe for her mother's heart; maybe for her own heart. Nothing happened.

Her mom went downhill rapidly. Sue got another call—the end was not far off. Sue flew home. The family gathered for a vigil that lasted days, but her mom survived the crisis, and everyone went home exhausted.

Sue stayed. She could not sleep that night. She went to her mother's bedside, and something began to melt her heart. "I'm sorry," she told her mom. "I know I wasn't easy to raise."

"Me, too," her mom said. "I'm sorry, too."

For the first time since she was a little girl, Sue's heart was flooded with love for her mother. She had been afraid that she would be cold toward her till the very end. She had not touched her mother for years; now she couldn't stop. She held her mother's hand and stroked her head and wouldn't let go.

Sue lay down on the bed next to her. "I love you, Mom. I really do. I was afraid you'd die without knowing it."

"I'll bet you were afraid you might not know, too," her mom said.

At that moment, Sue said, her mother looked radiant, the way some people look when heaven is not far off.

Mom was having trouble speaking now. She wrote a single word for Sue to read and pointed toward her daughter. *Pretty*.

"The nurse said I look like you, Mom."

Sue found herself with thoughts and feelings she wanted to express to her mother that she didn't even know she had. She was forty years old and had not been married. "I hoped to give you a grandchild."

You gave me a daughter, her mom wrote.

It was the last time Sue would see her mother. It was her mom's last night on earth. Her last, best night. And a prison door was unlocked. Two stony hearts melted. Two human beings who had lived as enemies became mother and daughter again.

God commands us to forgive whenever we're hurt, and reconcile whenever we can, because life is too short not to do so. We do not have another shot at it. If you don't forgive—if you let pride, resentment, stubbornness, and defensiveness stand in your way—you become a hard and bitter person. You carry a burden that will crush the humanity out of your spirit. You will grow a little colder every day. You will die.

The Rest of the Story

This is why Jesus adds a second act to his story. This crooked embezzler has received grace. The embezzler owes his life, freedom, family, possessions—everything—to the grace of the master. He doesn't have to repay a cent. But this is not the end of the story. It's a two-parter.

The embezzler is leaving the meeting when he spots an employee who owes him something. This debt is in the neighborhood of twenty dollars. Pocket change to the VP. But he demands it.

God commands us to forgive whenever we're hurt, and reconcile whenever we can, because life is too short not to do so.

In his opening words Jesus begins to hint at the difference between this man and the CEO. We're not told what the initial words of the CEO to his employee were; Jesus merely says he "wanted to settle accounts." But when this employee sees someone who owes him money, his immediate statement is, "Pay me what you owe me!" He does not simply state this, Jesus says the man demanded it.

The fellow worker hasn't got the cash. He is a desperately poor man. "Wait till the end of the month," he begs. "I won't stiff you. Give me a little time." He asks for grace. In fact (and this is part of Jesus' mastery in storytelling) this poor man uses exactly the same words that the VP himself used to the CEO. "He fell to his knees and begged him, 'Be patient with me, and I will pay you what I owe.'" The greatest difference is that this time around the amount is manageable. The debt is finite. The gap between these two is nothing compared with the gap between the first man and the CEO.

We wait to see the VP's response. Incredibly, this former embezzler, this cheat who was forgiven everything, thinks to himself, *I'm not going to make the same mistake the old man made with me. I'm not going to get stuck. I'm gonna make him pay.*

The VP says to his anxious colleague, "I'm not interested in excuses. Do you really think I'd fall for that bit? Don't make me laugh! What kind of sucker do you take me for?" He grabs the man by the throat, chokes him, and has him thrown into prison.

The VP doesn't see a human being. He just sees a debt. He will not pay the price. He will not forgive the debt. He lives by the old code: *You owe, you pay.*

Human beings have a tendency to think they can receive forgiveness from God without having to forgive others. In telling the story, Jesus doesn't say that this is a bad idea; he calls it impossible. In such cases what people want from God is not really forgiveness and reconciliation but merely punishment-avoidance. And forgiveness is not the same thing as allowing someone to avoid pain. It is longing for their spiritual well-being, which includes desiring that they become loving persons.

This is why Jesus says elsewhere that we are to pray, "Forgive us our debts *as* we forgive our debtors." Charles Williams wrote, "No word in English carries a greater possibility of terror than the little word 'as' in that clause." Interestingly, a recent study in the *Journal of Adult Development* found that 75 percent of those surveyed believe they have been forgiven by God for past mistakes and wrongdoing, but only 52 percent say they have forgiven others. Even fewer—43 percent—say they have actively sought forgiveness for harms they have done.

True forgiveness is never cheap. Hurt is deep; hurt is unfair. You want the offenders to know the pain they have inflicted on you. You want them to get paid back.

In fact, only one thing I know costs more than forgiving someone. Know what it is?

Not forgiving them. Non-forgiveness costs your heart.

Frederick Buechner wrote that of all the deadly sins, resentment appears to be the most fun. To lick your wounds and savor the pain you will give back is in many ways a feast fit for a king. But then it turns out that what you are eating at the banquet of bitterness is your own heart. The skeleton at the feast is you. You start out holding a grudge, but in the end the grudge holds you.

Jesus said that the unforgiving employee ended up in prison. I think that, spiritually speaking, the prison term for non-forgivers begins on earth. Bitterness and coldness of heart are far stronger than any iron bars.

Anne Lamott wrote,

> I went around saying for a long time that I am not one of the Christians who is heavily into forgiveness—that I am one of the other kind. But even though it was funny, and actually true, it started to be too painful to stay this way.... In fact, not forgiving is like drinking rat poison and waiting for the rat to die.

I cherish resentment and bitterness because I want to hurt the rat that caused my pain. But after resentment and bitterness have festered long enough, I find out that the rat is me, after all.

Don't forgive, and your anger will become your burden.

Don't forgive, and bit by bit all the joy will be choked out of you.

Don't forgive, and you will be unable to trust anybody, ever again.

Don't forgive, and the bitterness will crowd the compassion out of your heart slowly, utterly, forever.

Don't forgive, and that little grudge you nurse will grow larger, and stronger. Although you may think you can hide it from everyone you know, in time it will become a monster of hostility, and one day it will kill you. All that will be left of what was once a person is bitterness and hate. And that bitterness will spread.

Philip Yancey writes of a friend whose marriage was choked by hostility. One night the friend reached the breaking point: "I hate you!" he screamed at his wife. "I won't take it any more. I've had enough! I won't go on! I won't let it happen! No! No! No!"

Several months later, he woke up in the middle of the night to strange sounds coming from the room of his two-year-old son. He walked down the hall and stopped by his son's door. What he heard sent shivers down his spine and took away his breath. Inside, his son was repeating in a soft voice—with precisely the same inflection and intonation he had heard—the argument that had passed between his mother and father: "I hate you! . . . I won't take it! . . . No!"

This is life without forgiveness.

Epilogue

There is one more part to the story. To tell the truth, I wish there weren't, because it has fearful implications. But there is. Since this is Jesus' story, I can't leave it out.

The tale of the embezzler spreads through the whole corporation. Word gets to the CEO. By this time it is clear—he doesn't miss much. He's a pretty sharp guy, the old man.

The forgiven embezzler comes into the boardroom once more, for a second exchange. It is a different story this time around. In this interview, there are no tears, no pleading, no bargains.

The CEO says, "You didn't get it at all, did you! It didn't penetrate. You have gravely misunderstood me, my friend. You thought 'grace' meant I was a fuzzy-minded incompetent who would let you get away with whatever you want and abuse whomever you want. You thought that because you were 'in' with me, you could be the same old hurtful, self-centered, unforgiving person you were before.

"You were badly mistaken. I was willing to take the loss. Would be still, but you don't want what I offer. You were shown forgiveness but won't give it, offered grace but won't extend it, showered with love but you won't live in it. I offered you the miracle of forgiveness, a chance to live beyond a 'you hurt me I'll hurt you back' world. But you can't receive it for yourself and deny it to others. It's a package deal. You have rejected what I have, and there is nothing left to give you."

The CEO turns to the guards: "Take him away, throw him into prison, leave him there until he pays back the unpayable debt." End of interview. Beginning of sentence.

"This is how my heavenly Father will treat each of you unless you forgive your brother from your heart," Jesus says.

Now you must choose. Vengeance or mercy. Prison or freedom. Hatred or grace. Life or death.

Choose wisely.

Learning to Dance

1. What sorts of hurts are hardest for you to forgive? Why?
2. To what degree have you lived according to the Law of Lamech ("if anyone inflicts pain on me, I must make them pay")? Can you think of someone whom you have held captive in the little prison of your mind with a desire to get even? What is keeping you from giving up your right to hurt them back?
3. How do you distinguish between forgiving, forgetting, and excusing?
4. How easy or difficult is it for you to experience a sense of God's forgiveness in your life? Why?
5. How can you forgive someone when reconciliation does not seem possible?
6. What are the effects on you when you hang onto resentment and withhold forgiveness?
7. Is there anyone you need to offer forgiveness to? Anyone you need to seek forgiveness from?
8. Spend some time today reflecting on how God has forgiven you. See if this impacts your ability to forgive others.

CHAPTER 9

THE GIFT NOBODY WANTS: CONFRONTATION

Nothing can be more cruel than the leniency which abandons others to their sin. Nothing can be more compassionate than the severe reprimand which calls another Christian in one's community back from the path of sin.

DIETRICH BONHOEFFER

This is a foundational paradox about the porcupines in our world: We want to know the truth about ourselves, and we want very much not to know the truth about ourselves. We both seek and resist awareness about the reality of who we are.

Start with the truth about our bodies. We buy scales and mirrors and pants with measured waists to tell us the truth about the condition of our bodies, and then we avoid, argue with, or get rid of them when we don't like the truth they tell.

The problem with a scale is that it's hard to finesse. We try. Many people (particularly people of a certain gender that shall remain nameless) approach a scale with extreme caution. They take off their shoes before they get on it; in many cases they want as much privacy as a confessional booth. They will only get on during a certain time of the day—usually in the morning, before having eaten and after having gone to the bathroom. They remove whatever clothing they may be wearing as well as jewelry, hair accessories, loose tooth fillings, and heavy lipstick before they get on it. They exhale before looking at the numbers.

It turns out, experts tell us, that scales are not the most accurate tools to reveal the truth about our physical condition. (Good news—perhaps I'm in better shape than I thought.) Not far from our house is a facility that for a modest fee will measure the fat content in your body by having you expel all the breath out of your body and sit in a chair underwater until you can see an image of Jesus coming at the end of a long tunnel of white light.

Ken Davis says he has invented a less expensive (free!) method for measuring fat content:

> Next time you get out of a shower, grab a stopwatch and stand in front of a full-length mirror totally naked. Start the watch and stamp your foot on the floor as hard as you can. When stuff stops moving, punch the watch and check the time.
>
> I'm down to two days, three hours, and six minutes.

We try to finesse mirrors, too. Savvy department stores have people try on clothes in front of mirrors where the lighting is so dim that customers can't see any blemishes or wrinkles at all and in fact can barely make out their own features. The goal is to convince them that the clothes have smoothed their complexion and taken years off their appearance.

Our clothes, too, try to tell us the truth about our bodies, but we find ways around that as well. Clever marketers now sell clothes with wonderful euphemisms like "relaxed fit" jeans. (Were our old Levis really tense all those years?) The idea is that the fabric is so relaxed that it can be worn by someone two or three sizes larger than the one printed on the label. One entrepreneur said he was going to start a store called "Size Two" and have every garment in the place up to the size of a pup tent say "Size 2" on the label on the theory that women don't care what size their clothes really are as long as the number on the label is small.

Scales and mirrors are tools of accountability. They tell us about reality. We can try to outsmart them if we want, but if we allow them to, they will reveal the truth.

The Need for Truth-Tellers

Community is a place to get on the scale. I don't know if you need an instrument to tell you how many pounds you've gained or a tape measure to tell you how many inches you've added, but I know this: Every one of us needs a few people to tell us the truth about our hearts and souls. We all have weak spots and blind spots that we cannot navigate on our own. We need someone to remind us of our deepest aspirations and values and to warn us when we may be getting off track. We need someone to help us question our motives and examine our consciences. We need someone to perform spiritual surgery on us when our hearts get hard and our vision gets dim. We need a few Truth-Tellers.

We need Truth-Tellers because our capacity to live in denial is astounding. Self-deception, writes Neil Plantinga, is a mysterious process where we pull the wool over our own eyes.

> We deny, suppress, or minimize what we know to be true. We assert, adorn, and elevate what we know to be false. We prettify ugly realities and sell ourselves the prettified versions. Thus a liar might transform "I tell a lot of lies to shore up my pride" to "Occasionally, I finesse the truth in order to spare other people's feelings."

A whole field in social psychology—the study of what is called "cognitive dissonance"—is based on our nearly endless ability to justify what we do or say so that it is consistent with our self-concept. We are all like the man on a diet who drove past the bakery and said he would only stop for doughnuts if there was an available parking space in front of it, clearly indicating that it was God's will that he should eat a doughnut. Sure enough, his sixth time around the block, a parking space opened up.

Many of us have never invited someone else to be a Truth-Teller in our lives for the same reason we don't get on a scale: We are afraid of what we might find out. What if the truth about me is too painful for

Many of us have never invited someone else to be a Truth-Teller in our lives for the same reason we don't get on a scale: We are afraid of what we might find out.

me to bear? When I think about our longing for and fear of truth, I am reminded of two statements. One of them comes from actor Jack Nicholson in a film called *A Few Good Men*. Tom Cruise plays a lawyer cross-examining Nicholson's character. Cruise pleads, "All I want is the truth." To which Nicholson replies in his inimitable snarl, "You can't handle the truth."

Jesus had a fundamentally different take on the subject. Jesus said, "You will know the truth, and the truth will set you free."

You have to decide whom to believe: Jesus or Jack Nicholson.

Dietrich Bonhoeffer's words in this regard are simply too good not to be quoted in full.

> One who because of sensitivity and vanity rejects the serious words of another Christian cannot speak the truth in humility to others. Such a person is afraid of being rejected and feeling hurt by another's words. Sensitive, irritable people will always become flatterers, and very soon they will come to despise and slander other Christians in their community. . . . When another Christian falls into obvious sin, an admonition is imperative, because God's Word demands it. The practice of discipline in the community of faith begins with friends who are close to one another. Words of admonition and reproach *must be risked*.

We need Truth-Tellers who will help us grow in our acceptance of reality. But we also need them because they serve as anchors; they help hold us accountable to the commitments we make.

People need to make decisions about their spiritual life. William Paulson writes, "It is unlikely that we will deepen our relationship with God in a casual or haphazard way."

There is a big difference between deciding and preferring. For instance, have you ever tried journaling? Have you ever felt guilty that you didn't fill it out often enough? (My own advice is to keep two journals; if you write one day and then there's a gap of months or years before the next entry, just write, See other journal. Evasion, unfortunately, is one of my strong suits.)

People need to make decisions:

—What are my commitments about prayer?

—What are my commitments about Scripture?

—What are my commitments about stewardship?

We all need to make decisions about what values we want to honor, what spiritual practices we need to engage in, what kind of friends and neighbors and sons and daughters and husbands and wives we will be. But decisions alone are not enough. We need to go public with them. We need accountability. We also need someone who will ask us, "How's it going? Is your way of life working? Do some things need to change? What are you struggling with in regard to sin or temptation?"

We need others to help us live up to our best intentions and deepest values. Just as mountaineers rope together for a climb and athletes work out with trainers and coaches, so it is in every area of life. Organizations like Alcoholics Anonymous and Weight Watchers are carefully structured around this one constant truth. They know that for people to think that they can live up to their best intentions on their own is a recipe for disaster. These groups are made up of people who have faced up to the fact that they're not *normal* and are committed to help one another live one day at a time. David Watson says, "Anything that is subject to human limitation or error requires the collegial presence of another person to ensure responsibility. It is a fact of life."

Watson writes that in the movement associated with John Wesley, people met together in little communities to help hold each other accountable for their deepest values and most important decisions. Wesley had a beautiful phrase for this; he called it "watching over one another in love."

Before someone entered into this community, they would be asked a series of questions to see if they were serious about living in mutual accountability. Sometimes when I speak on the topic of community, I will read these questions to church leaders and ask them to imagine them being posed to the congregations.

- Does any sin, inward or outward, have dominion over you?
- Do you desire to be told of your faults?
- Do you desire to be told of all your faults—and that plain and clear? (By this point, church leaders are inevitably laughing at even the idea of people putting up with such pointed questions.)
- Consider! Do you desire that we should tell you whatsoever we think, whatsoever we fear, whatsoever we hear concerning you?
- Do you desire that in doing this we should come as close as possible, that we should cut to the quick, and search your heart to the bottom?
- Is it your desire and design to be on this and all other occasions entirely open, so as to speak everything that is in your heart, without exception, without disguise, and without reserve?

Can you imagine people in your family or your circle of friends answering yes to such questions? In Wesley's day they did—by the thousands. They did so simply because they knew they could never grow into the people they wanted to be without help.

Over time, however, the commitment to truth-telling got lost. Watson writes that when these small groups shifted their focus from mutual accountability to vague sharing, most of the power of these little communities was lost. Eventually they began to die out. People tend to drift away from truth-telling. As Scott Peck puts it,

> A life of total dedication to truth also means a life of willingness to be personally challenged . . . but the tendency to avoid challenge is so omnipresent in human beings that it can properly be considered a characteristic of human nature.

So I want to look at the story of one of the most famous men in the Old Testament. He made some horrible choices and knew deep failure. But he had a Truth-Teller in his life, and that meant that failure did not get the last word.

David: A Story of Life

We are told that one year when the armies went off to fight, King David stayed home. Kings went to war that time of year, the way the swallows go to Capistrano and the Cubs go to Arizona for spring training.

This year, David thinks to himself, *I don't want to go. I don't have to go. Let them go without me.*

There is something unusual going on with David. He isn't an old man yet, but he isn't the golden boy anymore, either. Women don't look at him the same way they used to.

He starts using Rogaine. He tells himself he is going to work out more and maybe have a jogging track installed around the palace. He doesn't tell anyone, but he has had a little Metamucil added to the royal diet.

He wants—what does he want? He isn't sure. He wants to feel young and alive. He is restless and lonely and a little bored.

As far as we can tell, David, being a king and all, does not talk about these feelings with anyone. Then one day he sees a woman bathing on the roof, and she is remarkably attractive. (People sometimes wonder, "Maybe it's not altogether David's fault—what's she doing taking a bath outside?" But nothing in the biblical text indicts her. In the afternoon, when water in the rain barrels was warmest and the men were away, this was probably the custom.)

David treats this woman as an object. (There is no mention anywhere in the text of her feelings, what she says, or what is said to her.) David thinks perhaps she will solve his boredom problem and make him feel younger. Perhaps she will take away his feelings of loneliness.

David sends someone to find out about her and in doing so actually receives a mild confrontation. He is told, "Isn't this Bathsheba, the daughter of Eliam and the wife of Uriah the Hittite?"

In ancient times, genealogies were not usually recorded for women. When they were, they took note of ancestors, not spouses. David's servant is saying to him, "This is somebody's wife. Somebody's daughter. Be careful."

If David were at a spiritually sensitive place with God, this statement would have stopped him in his tracks. But David is not interested in hearing truth right now. As many drivers do, when he sees the yellow light, he hits the accelerator. He thinks he's in control. (In the biblical account, he is initially the subject of all the verbs, especially the verb *send:* he sees her, he sends a messenger to find out about her, he sends for her, he sleeps with her, he sends her back home.)

But then comes the message: "The woman conceived and sent word to David, saying, 'I am pregnant.'"

David goes back into action. He sends word to Joab to release Uriah from duty for a few days, and he sends for Uriah to be brought to the palace. But he can't get Uriah to forget his fellow soldiers and go home to carouse. Ironically, this foreigner, this Hittite, is more faithful to God than David. So David goes into sending mode again; he sends Uriah back to the army and sends Joab word to make sure Uriah gets killed by the enemy. Then, after Uriah is dead, David sends for Bathsheba once more, and he marries her, and she bears their son.

Anytime we try to handle temptation in isolation, we are extremely vulnerable to deception.

And David thinks he has navigated this whole affair successfully. He thought the great danger was someone might find out. But that isn't the great danger. The great danger is that no one will find out.

How long does David live in hypocrisy and hiddenness? We don't know exactly, but we know that it lasted at least as long as it took for Bathsheba to give birth. In other words, David goes at least nine months being king, pretending to worship, and leading the people, while inside he carries the secret guilt of unconfessed, unrepentant murder and adultery. Every day he gets a little more used to his deception. Every day his heart gets a little harder; God gets a little farther away.

Up to this point, no one can see what is going on in David's life underneath the surface. Anytime we try to handle temptation in isolation, we are extremely vulnerable to deception.

Gary Richmond paints an unforgettable picture of this. Richmond used to work at a zoo that had a thirteen-foot-long king cobra. Its venom glands contained enough poison to kill a thousand adults. The cobra had a scar that made him look like the embodiment of evil, but worse, it meant that when the snake shed his skin, the eye cap did not come off. It had to be removed by hand. And, unfortunately, snakes don't have hands.

This required a team of five people: two keepers, the zoo's curator, a veterinarian, and Gary—whose job was to furnish the scalpel and sponge to the vet. The cobra slithered from its den, spread its cape, raised itself up to full stature, and looked at the five intruders, deciding on his first victim. He chose the curator. With lightning speed the keepers threw their nets around the writhing snake, the curator grasped it behind the venom glands, and the vet said, "Let's get this over." His hands were trembling; beads of sweat were dripping off everyone's forehead but the snake's.

The vet asked if Gary had any cuts on his hands.

"No."

He told Gary to wad up paper towels and stuff them in the cobra's mouth.

"Okay."

The cobra bit and chewed until the towels were yellow and dripping with venom.

As the team worked, the curator explained that every year several full-grown elephants die from king cobra bites. A man could never survive a bite with a full load of venom. This is why he was having Gary drain the snake's venom sacs. The curator's hands were sweating, and his muscles were weakening; his fingers were starting to cramp—which could not have been good news to anyone except maybe the snake. The curator wasn't sure they could move quickly enough when it was time for the release. Then he explained what we might call the secret of the snake: *More people are bitten trying to let go of snakes than when they grab them*.

Easy to grab, hard to let go. This is true of everything that can destroy human character: deceit, bitterness, pornography, greed, debt, workaholism. This is the power of addiction, and sin is, among other things, addictive. These sins are serpents that will quickly weaken the human spirit.

It is a fatal tendency of human beings to think we can handle the snake on our own. This has been going on since the Garden of Eden. When the serpent tempted Eve, what she did *not* do is signficant. She did not talk about this temptation with Adam. She did not discuss it with God. One of the first signs that we're in trouble with a temptation is that we don't reveal it to anybody else. We keep the snake a secret because at some level we want to retain the option of grabbing it. We keep temptation a secret because we want the option of giving in to it undiscovered.

David grabs the snake. And he thinks he can handle it on his own.

Until one day God goes into sending mode: "The LORD sent Nathan. . . ."

David has been playing god with people's lives: Bathsheba, Uriah, Joab, the army, all Israel. This time God does the sending. He sends David a prophet named Nathan. Nathan is going to tell the truth. Nathan is going to hold David accountable to live up to all those psalms he wrote.

For a moment, think about what must have been going on in Nathan's heart. Imagine how it must have felt to schedule this interview, to utter the first sentence, from which there is no going back. This is not a casual conversation. There is no guarantee that David will be responsive to what Nathan says. There are all kinds of reasons Nathan could tell himself to avoid having this talk: *Who do I think I am to confront David? I've lusted in my heart—I'm no better than he is. Maybe he's confessed all this to God. Besides, it would be embarrassing to bring the whole subject up. Probably there's somebody else in David's life that's closer to him who should talk to him about it.*

Nathan knows what could happen. If David doesn't respond positively, Nathan is in serious trouble. David has already killed one man to cover up his crimes; he could do the same thing to Nathan.

It's worth noting that before he says a word, Nathan has clearly given much thought and prayer to how he will approach the king. Nathan knows that after a year of hiding, David will be quite resistant to truth. Nathan has to find a way to get past all David's defenses and hardness of heart. He wants to capture David's heart; to maximize the odds of David's opening his heart to the truth.

I mention this because there are people—sometimes even people in churches—who love to go around correcting other folks. Jean Vanier writes, "I am struck by the people who come into our communities . . . and very quickly put their finger on failings—of which, God knows, there are enough!—without being able to see anything good. . . . They believe that their gift is to be a savior." There is a kind of person who speaks "truth" recreationally, but does it without love. Such a person blasts away and passes judgment in a spirit of arrogant superiority, which they cover up by saying. "I am a prophet."

There is a very important theological distinction between being a prophet and being a jerk. What burns deeply in the heart of a true prophet is not just anger but love.

There is a very important theological distinction between being a prophet and being a jerk. What burns deeply in the heart of a true prophet is not just anger but love.

To hold others accountable does *not* mean that we get to view ourselves as being in charge of their lives. Periodically in religious communities the idea of accountability gets twisted into a system wherein certain people try to take control over the lives of others. In authentic community each person is responsible for one's own life. We cannot abdicate this responsibility even if we want to.

Accountability is a tool and a gift we give to one another to try to realize the growth we could never know all by ourselves.

Nathan is angry with David, but he also loves him. So with enormous skill and art he tells David a story about a rich man who rips off a little sheep that is the only possession and prized treasure of a desperately poor man. It is a story designed to capture David's sympathy and passion for justice, and the arrow finds its mark. David is indignant: "The man . . . deserves to die!"

(We can be like that. We can get all fired up about somebody else's sin and forget about our own. We are capable of guilt and righteous indignation at the same time.)

Now is the moment when Nathan must decide how much he's willing to risk. He knows what he's doing. The king is a ruthless character these days. Nathan would be risking his own life to speak out. But he doesn't hesitate.

Nathan looks straight in the eye of the most powerful man in his world—a man who could have him put to death for speaking these

Accountability is a tool and a gift we give to one another to try to realize the growth we could never know all by ourselves.

words, who has already killed before to keep a secret. Nathan says, "You are the man!" He tells the king, "This is your story. This is your sin. This is the depth to which you have fallen."

Let us consider the cost of truth-telling and why it happens so rarely in our world. If truth-telling is so important, if we all agree we need it to grow, if it is an act of love—why does so little of it go on?

The answer, simply, is fear. It takes enormous courage to be a Truth-Teller. If we speak painful truth to someone, things get messy. We might be rejected. We might get into a long, difficult discussion. There is a good chance that we will be accused of meddling in what's not our business. It will cost us time and energy. It gets frightening. We usually tell the truth until it's costly, and then we trade truth for peace.

Scott Peck says that most of the time we live in what he calls *pseudocommunity*. Its hallmark is the avoidance of conflict. In pseudocommunity we keep things safe; we speak in generalities, we say things that those around us will agree with. We tell little white lies to make sure no one's feelings get hurt, no one gets tense. We keep relationships pleasant and well-oiled. Conversations are carefully filtered to make sure no one gets offended; if we feel hurt or irritated, we are careful to hide it. Pseudocommunity is agreeable and polite and gentle and stagnant—and ultimately fatal.

Marriages can last for decades—sometimes for a lifetime—and look quite pleasant from the outside. Not much conflict, not many storms. But the reality is that the husband and wife are living in pseudocommunity. They talk about the kids or the job or the mortgage, but it doesn't go beneath the surface. They haven't told the truth in years about their loneliness or hurt or anger. Their sexual desires and frustrations go unnamed. They are disappointed in their marriage and each other, but neither has the guts to speak frankly and honestly. So every day they die a little more.

To go beyond pseudocommunity, Peck says, we have to be willing to enter into chaos. Chaos happens when someone is willing to speak risky truth. Chaos is always unpleasant. When we are in chaos, we feel out of control. There is no guarantee that you are going to agree with what I say. Negative emotions will have to be acknowledged and discussed.

The New Testament records a surprising amount of chaos. Jesus himself was never frightened by it and often invited people into it. "What were you arguing about along the way?" he asked his disciples, when he knew this would get into a messy discussion about who was the greatest. He asked people why they called him "Lord" without doing what he said; he asked a promiscuous woman to fetch her husband; he called religious leaders "corpses with expensive makeup jobs" ("whitewashed tombs"), knowing full well things would get messy.

There was chaos in his church as well after Jesus was gone. Hebrew-speaking Christians got tangled up with Greek-speaking ones about whose poor were getting cared for. Paul went after Peter for caving in to legalists. People who love authentic community always prefer the pain of temporary chaos to the peace of permanent superficiality.

People who love authentic community always prefer the pain of temporary chaos to the peace of permanent superficiality.

Telling people what they want to hear is not love. When people are engaged in destructive, soul-threatening behavior, they need a mirror. They need someone who will tell them the truth. Nathan loved David so much he was willing to risk his life to be a Truth-Teller. Ironically, we often chicken out of speaking the truth for infinitely lower stakes.

Nathan tells David the truth.

For who knows how long, all is silence. The thought surely occurs to David: *I can manage this problem as well. No one knows but Nathan. If I get rid of him, I'm home free.*

But David hears a voice. This voice whispers to David of days when he was an innocent shepherd boy and God cared for him. It reminds him of the exhilaration he had once known fighting for God. It recalls the days when he danced before the ark. It remembers when his best friend, Jonathan, had given up his own ambitions for the sake of David and affirmed that David was God's choice to be king.

For who knows how long, Nathan's fate hangs in the balance. And although perhaps he didn't know it, David's does as well.

And then the miracle happens. A heart that has been hard and stony and cold and dead for a long time melts: "I have sinned against the LORD." David confesses, "I am the man."

What if David did not have a Nathan in his relational world? How would his life turn out? We don't know the whole answer, of course, but David has gone for at least the better part of a year without getting straightened out. All indications are that without Nathan to interrupt him, this slide would go on indefinitely.

This is not just true for David. Without a Nathan in our lives, we have a way of drifting off course. David—"a man after God's own heart"—didn't set out to become a murderer and an adulterer. We generally don't intend to make a mess of our lives.

Nobody takes a vow of marriage and plans on ending up in divorce court.

No dad welcomes children into this world and plans on being so busy with meetings and briefcases that he ends up a distant, polite stranger.

No disappointed homemaker picks up a glass of wine to take the edge off her boredom and plans on entering the life of a secret alcoholic.

No out-of-shape person embarks on an exercise program planning to binge their way into physical collapse.

No businessperson makes a first deal and plans on becoming so consumed with expanding his lifestyle that all generosity and compassion dry up in his soul.

No one graduates from school and decides to become so pressured and preoccupied and self-absorbed that they end up without a single friend worthy of the title.

No one plans these things. But they happen every day. Why?

Here is at least one major reason: *We have no one in our lives whom we have invited to tell us the truth*. We think we can handle the serpent by ourselves. When we have nobody to answer to—no one holding us accountable for living up to the values we most deeply hold—we become very vulnerable.

Without someone to hold him accountable for what he had done, David's life might have ended quite tragically. That's why accountability is indispensable for community.

So, let me get personal for a moment. Who is the Nathan in your life? Is there anyone you have asked to be a Truth-Teller to you? Patrick Morley writes that accountability means to be "regularly accountable for each of the key areas in our life to qualified people." Do you have a person or two with whom you meet regularly to do that?

If you don't, I urge you to start looking and praying for one. Choose very carefully. It needs to be someone whose confidentiality and discernment you can trust. As with self-disclosure, you must travel this road one step at a time.

But you do need a Nathan. So do I. We can't handle the serpent on our own.

Learning to Dance

1. Recall Bonhoeffer's words from the beginning of the chapter: "Nothing can be more cruel than the leniency which abandons others to their sin. Nothing can be more compassionate than the severe reprimand which calls another Christian in one's community back from the path of sin."

   Do you think this is true? If so, why do people often practice the "cruel leniency" of abandoning others to unconfronted problems?

2. What is the difference between seeking another person to hold you accountable and trying to abdicate responsibility for your life?

3. On a scale of 1 to 10, 1 being pseudocommunity and 10 being authentic community, where would you rate your closest relationships? Why do you give them this rating?

4. Are you in chaos in any relationships? How can you move toward resolution?

5. How defensive do you tend to get when someone tries to give you feedback that is painful to you?

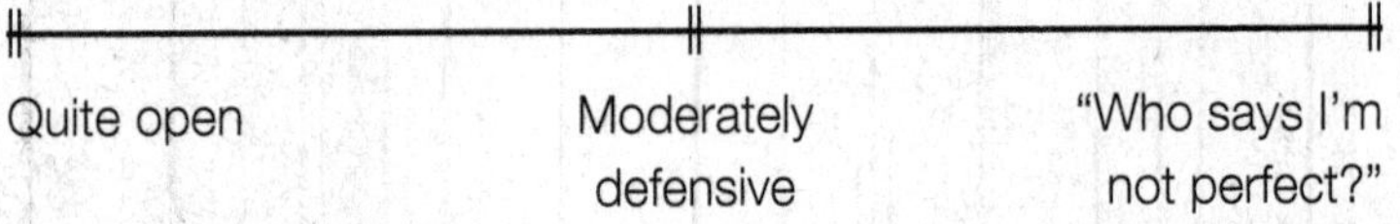

6. What do you see as the most important element in confrontation? Why?

7. Who is your Nathan? Whom have you invited to speak truth to you? If you don't have anyone now, who has the potential to be this person in your life? What is the next step you can take to deepen the relationship toward this goal?

CHAPTER 10

BREAKING DOWN BARRIERS: INCLUSION

Of all passions the passion for the Inner Ring is most skillful in making a man who is not yet very bad do very bad things.

C. S. LEWIS

When our children were ages five, seven, and nine, we decided to move from southern California to the northwest suburbs of Chicago. We left mountains and palm trees and beaches and sunshine for a part of the country that looks—as my wife memorably put it—as though God took an iron and flattened the whole place out.

The move was the biggest change we had ever gone through as a family. The responses of two of our children were pretty easy to read. On the day Nancy and I announced our decision to move, our oldest daughter ran sobbing out of my office and locked herself in the car. This wasn't the response I had been hoping for, but at least it was a clear indicator of her emotions. Our youngest was excited that we were moving to a land of basements and snow. But our middle daughter was—as is often the case with those of us who are middle children—somewhere in the middle. She seemed to be okay with the move. Or perhaps I just wasn't looking very closely.

One night several months after we were settled in Illinois, I was sitting on the side of her bed tucking our middle daughter in. She had been getting into more trouble than usual lately, but I hadn't connected this pattern to anything in particular. Then, in the quiet moments that come before sleep, the dam broke, and the tears began to flow: "Daddy, it's so hard living here! Nobody knows me. I go to a new school, a new church; everybody already seems to have friends. I don't belong. I don't have anybody that I can really talk to; I don't have people who want to have lunch with me or choose me for their team. I just try to get through the day."

Then my daughter said the words that stabbed me. She painted a one-phrase picture of vulnerability I will never forget: "I feel like a little mouse that doesn't have a hole."

This was the pain of feeling like an outsider. Kids are resilient, as the saying goes, and my daughter soon adjusted to her new home. But the picture has always stayed with me: a vulnerable little creature scampering about in the midst of dangers it cannot control, desperately trying to find a safe place to be welcomed into.

There are few joys in life like being wanted, chosen, embraced. There are few pains like being excluded, rejected, left out. At the core of Christian community is the choice, in the words of Miroslav Volf's great book on the subject, between exclusion and embrace.

The Inner Ring

It is a part of our fallenness that makes us want to be in not just any group but an *exclusive* group. By definition, every society includes people who connect, who belong to one another. Yet every society includes people who feel left out, who don't get chosen at recess, whose invitations to dance get turned down, who get blackballed and cold-shouldered and voted off the island. We exclude others because of pride or fear or ignorance or the desire to feel superior.

I thought of this tendency we have to divide people the last time I was on a plane. The first-class people were served gourmet food on china and crystal by their own flight attendants; those of us in coach ate "snacks" served in paper bags with plastic wrappers. The first-class passengers had room to stretch and sleep; those of us in coach were sitting with a proximity usually reserved for engaged couples in the back row of a movie. The first-class passengers had flight attendants bring them moist Towelettes for comfort and personal hygiene; those of us in coach had to sit and stew in our facial sweat.

On almost every flight, once the plane is under way, a curtain gets drawn to separate the two compartments. It is not to be violated; it is like the Berlin Wall or the veil that separated the Court of the Gentiles from the Holy of Holies in the temple at Jerusalem. The curtain is a reminder throughout the flight that some people are first class and some aren't. Those who aren't first class are not to violate the boundary. They can't even see what's going on behind the other side of the curtain.

On my recent flight, a voice came on the intercom system a few minutes into the flight, telling us that because of new security measures, the attendants were not allowed to fasten the curtain. But the airline wanted all of us in the Court of the Gentiles to know that we were not allowed to use the facilities in the Holy of Holies, even though there was one restroom for eight people up there and two restrooms for several hundred of us (mostly children under six who had been drinking Jolt Cola the whole flight) on the other side.

Let the curtain stand for a tendency deep inside the fallen human spirit—the tendency to *exclude*. In the act of exclusion, we divide the world up into "us" and "them." These terms do not simply point out that we're different—differences between human beings are as old as Adam and Eve and can enrich community enormously. They also mean that we take a posture of rejection and withdrawal toward the others. We refuse to offer them any heart or goodwill. We deliberately indulge in feelings of superiority at their expense.

We see the ultimate damage of exclusion in phrases like "ethnic cleansing," which suggests that someone who is "other" than me is dirty and needs to be removed.

C. S. Lewis wrote a brilliant essay on this subject called "The Inner Ring." In every society, in every school and church and workplace, there are little groups of people who are on the "inside." These groups are almost never formal; no one votes on who gets in. Yet whether or not you're a member will be reflected in subtle things—use of nicknames, inside jokes, invitations to certain events. Once you get inside, of course, you discover that there are further rings that are even *more* inside. The further in the ring is, the more status and prestige it bestows on the members.

Today we become quite aware of these groups in high school. Jocks and cheerleaders are usually at the innermost rings, with preppies and brains and boarders in various orbits, and wanna-bes and geeks on the far outer fringes. (*Geek* is currently preferred to *nerd;* nowadays, if you use the term *nerd*, you're a geek.)

As we get older, the names of the groups change, but the dynamics stay the same.

Lewis writes, "I believe that in all men's lives . . . one of the most dominant elements is the desire to be inside the local Ring and the terror of being left outside." The existence of such rings, he says, is not necessarily bad. We are all finite, and we can have deeply intimate friendships with only a limited number of people.

But the desire to gain status by being part of a high-status Inner Ring is a deeply dangerous one. This desire leads us to constantly compare ourselves with others, to feel anguish when we get left out and deeper anguish when someone close to us gets ushered in. We begin to compromise. We say something we don't really believe because we think it might make us look good to someone deeper in and higher up. We laugh at that person's jokes a little too eagerly, pretend to agree when we secretly differ, or give a compliment that is partly sincere but also partly self-serving. We get a little surge of pleasure when we think that we are in a more inner ring than somebody else. Seeing others excluded makes us feel more special.

The Inner Ring turns out to be like an onion. Once we make it to a certain circle, we find out there is yet another one. But no circle is so far inside that it can confer on us that sense of permanent worth we want so badly, because inside we know we're still the same person. Groucho Marx once said he would never join a club whose standards were so low they would let someone like him become a member.

Jesus' disciples wrestled with this desire. Two of them, James and John, actually approached Jesus and asked if they could be in the Inner Ring when they got to heaven. "Could we have the two seats next to yours, one on your left and one on your right?" Surely if they got those two seats, their desire to be on the inside would finally be satisfied. They even had their mom working on this request for them. And of course, the other disciples got mad when they heard about this request, because it would mean that even though they were apostles, they would not quite be in the *innermost* circle. Jesus must have just shaken his head. He was constantly teaching about and getting in trouble for his views about who was in and who was out, and about God's desire to let anyone who wanted come into the Inner Ring.

Women, Dogs, and Other Outcasts

One of the most striking stories about status is told by Matthew.

> Jesus withdrew to the region of Tyre and Sidon. A Canaanite woman from that vicinity came to him, crying out, "Lord, Son of David, have mercy on me! My daughter is suffering terribly from demon-possession."
>
> Jesus did not answer a word. So his disciples came to him and urged him, "Send her away, for she keeps crying out after us."
>
> He answered, "I was sent only to the lost sheep of Israel."
>
> The woman came and knelt before him. "Lord, help me!" she said.
>
> He replied, "It is not right to take the children's bread and toss it to their dogs."
>
> "Yes, Lord," she said, "but even the dogs eat the crumbs that fall from their masters' table.
>
> Then Jesus answered, "Woman, you have great faith! Your request is granted." And her daughter was healed from that very hour.

This story used to be confusing to me. At first glance, it can make Jesus look almost mean. But it has become one of my favorite stories about him. I think this is actually a passage about a master teacher trying to help his students understand God's desire to exclude no one, to bring all who will allow him into his embrace.

Ken Bailey writes that to grasp the point of this passage we have to see that in this encounter Jesus is giving a test—for two sets of people. He is testing the disciples, and he is testing the woman. Who aces the test, and who gets an "incomplete"? What does the test teach us about the pain of being left out and the power of being welcomed in?

The story takes place in a foreign region far north of Jewish territory. Tyre and Sidon were two Phoenician cities located on the Mediterranean coast. The Jews despised the people who lived there. The first-century Jewish historian Josephus wrote that "the people of Tyre are our bitterest enemy." Jesus said once that on the Day of Judgment, even Tyre and Sidon will be better off than the cities that saw his miracles but didn't respond. He was saying, "Even the most wicked people you think you know—even those you regard as the bottom of the barrel—would have repented if they had seen the miracles you have seen."

So this woman would be regarded by the disciples as an outcast. She was a member of the most spiritually degraded people they knew. Her people were their enemies.

But the woman comes to Jesus with the traditional cry of a beggar: "Have mercy on me." She humbles herself. She adds a title to it: "Lord." (The Greek word *kurios* could mean "sir" or "master." She will repeat this title two more times in the story.) She calls Jesus, "Son of David," so she knows something of Judaism. She is deeply respectful. Her desperation causes her to cross boundaries of ethnicity and gender that were plainly not crossed in her day.

Jesus does not say a word. This woman's daughter is suffering terribly, she appeals to Jesus with humility and reverence, and he acts as if he didn't hear. He responds with apparent silence, indifference, and rejection.

(Notice that Matthew doesn't try to hide this. He deliberately draws our attention to this fact. Matthew knows something we don't know yet. He knows this is a test. He knows how this story will end. For now, he wants us to have to grapple with whatever it is that Jesus is up to.)

The woman could walk away at this point. She has to decide, *How deeply do I want healing for my daughter? How much am I willing to trust this man?*

This is part one of the Canaanite woman's exam. But now let's turn our attention to the disciples.

Jesus is giving the disciples a test as well. They are not surprised Jesus doesn't talk with her. What rabbi would? There is a rabbinic saying from ancient times that goes,

> He that talks with womankind brings evil on himself,
> Neglects the study of the law,
> And at the last will inherit gehenna.

So Jesus deliberately ignores the woman and watches the disciples to see what they will do. Do they get it yet? Do they understand what he's about?

They respond strongly, and they are quite confident their words will meet with his approval: "Send her away, for she keeps crying out after us."

The "us" is a little grandiose. She hasn't said anything to them at all. But they generously include themselves in Jesus' power and ministry: "She's bothering *us!* We came north for a little R and R, and everybody wants a piece of us. *You* send her away."

This is reminiscent of a time when children tried to come to Jesus. You may remember the disciples' response: "They rebuked them." The disciples thought they were pretty clear about the kind of people Jesus did and did not have time for. They knew who was in the Inner Ring, and they didn't want to let anyone else in. They had erected their own Berlin Wall to separate first-class passengers from coach; and they weren't about to allow an enemy to crawl over. They didn't dream that the wall's days were numbered.

"Something there is that doesn't love a wall, that wants it down." This is the central line from a poem by Robert Frost called "The Mending Wall." In the poem, a farmer comes out in the spring with his neighbor to walk their property line. Every spring they find the same thing: The stone wall that had stood erect last year has crumbled a bit; rocks keep falling down; the fence keeps coming down. Maybe it's the wind and weather. Maybe it's a mystery. But every year they build up the wall that separates them, and over the next year it keeps falling into disrepair. "Something there is that doesn't love a wall, that wants it down." The other farmer likes having the wall there: "Good fences make good neighbors," he says.

"Spring is the mischief in me," Frost writes, and he allows himself to begin to wonder if it's really true that good fences make good neighbors. Maybe life isn't about walls and fences and keeping people out.

> Before I built a wall I'd ask to know
> What I was walling in or walling out,
> And to whom I was like to give offence.

The only man-made object visible from the moon is a wall—the Great Wall of China.

Since Cain and Abel, the human race has been building walls. It happens in the backseat of crowded cars between quarreling siblings: "You'd better not cross this line." Walls go up between husbands and wives, between coworkers, between denominations and cultures and races and countries. There was a wall between a desperate Gentile woman and twelve self-important disciples. The apostle Paul called that particular wall "the dividing wall of hostility." It had been around as long as anybody could remember. Everybody figured it would last forever.

But something there is that doesn't love a wall, that wants it down.

One of God's deepest but most often-misunderstood characteristics is his desire to include in his community anybody who will have him. Philip Yancey writes in *What's So Amazing About Grace?* that if he had to summarize all the Old Testament teachings about what foods could be eaten and who was unclean he would do it under this phrase: "No oddballs allowed." No lobsters in their diet; no blemished lambs at the altar, no menstruating women in the camp. There was an important principle behind this; but over time it was turned into grounds for exclusion of oddball people. Communities always have a way of becoming exclusive over time. This was the rule that made the disciples sure that the woman bothering Jesus was to be excluded: "No oddballs allowed."

When Jesus came, Yancey writes, he replaced the old law with a new rule of grace: "We're all oddballs, but God loves us anyway."

The desire to make it into the Inner Ring is by its nature insatiable. You will never succeed. However, when it comes to the choice to *include* people, you can hardly fail. They may refuse you, of course. But the mere effort will expand your heart and bring joy to God.

I was talking with an old friend recently about what regrets we had in life. The first one that came to his mind was striking to me. When we were in high school, he had been asked to Turnabout (the traditional girls-ask-the-boys dance) by a girl who was not in the inner ring or the next couple of rings close to it. She was bright, gifted, and artistic, but for some unknown reason she was positioned on the outer fringes of high school social castes. She was different somehow. My friend said no, as gently as he could, but firmly. The truth was, he told me, he was kind of afraid of what people might think. It might make him look as if he was farther away from the inner ring than he wanted to be.

There are always people around you who feel left out, like a mouse without a hole.

"I could have gone, and made it a great night," my friend said. "I should have just ignored the whole stupid system of who's 'in' and who's 'out' instead of letting it have any power over my life. If I could do high school all over again, I would have gone to the dance."

There are always people around you who feel left out, like a mouse without a hole. Maybe it's somebody at work whom not many people pay attention to. Maybe it's a widow in your neighborhood who doesn't get visited much. Maybe there is a wall between you and persons of another color. You don't mean for it to be there, but you haven't taken any steps to knock it down. You could begin to cultivate a friendship with someone who is different from you. You could say yes to the dance.

The Test: Part Two

Jesus goes on to part two of the exam. His next words are addressed to the disciples in response to their question. Jesus says, "I was sent only to the lost sheep of Israel."

Why does Jesus say this? On many other occasions he makes it very clear that he has come for the whole world; he is not willing that *any* should perish.

Earlier, Matthew records Jesus as saying that "many will enter the kingdom from the east and west." This was code for "Gentiles."

So why does Jesus tell the disciples he's not going to respond to this woman, when in fact later on that is precisely what he does?

Jesus is testing. Great teachers don't just give lectures and hand out information. They know that experience is more powerful than just presentation. So Jesus doesn't give his disciples a lecture about their smug, exclusive attitudes. He tried that after his disciples shooed the children away, and the lecture approach did not work very well.

The disciples need some remedial help.

When I was in first grade, teachers would assign students to reading groups based on how well they could read. They would name all the groups after birds so everyone would feel equal, but you could always tell how you were doing by what bird your group was named after. There were the Eagles, the Robins, and the Pigeons. The Pigeons were not reading *War and Peace*.

The disciples don't know it, of course, but they are in the Pigeon group. They need something stronger than a lecture.

So Jesus appears to agree with them: "Of course, I'll get rid of her. I'm sent to Israel—God's favorites! We have no time for gentile female second-rate riffraff. Good call, guys! I'll send her away."

But Jesus doesn't send the woman away.

Jesus watches to see how the disciples will respond. Will anybody disagree? Will anyone get it?

No.

They all nod their heads: "That's right. Send her away."

Simultaneously, the woman goes through part two of the test.

Although Jesus is talking to and facing his disciples, the woman hears all that is said. Jesus' words say to her in effect: "You are an outsider. I am the Son of David. You are not my mission. Why should I serve you?"

Is her concern for her child so deep, her confidence in Jesus' compassion and power so strong, that she will persevere in her petition despite the obstacles? Even when he seems unwilling to help her?

In her mind she can hear her daughter's screams. She has no one else to turn to, nowhere else to go. She is a little mouse without a hole.

The woman kneels on the ground, in a posture of reverence and humility, and utters a single phrase, a cry of the human soul: "Lord, help me!"

She doesn't understand it all. But still she calls him "Lord."

The disciples watch this. Now the tension starts to build very strong inside them, as Jesus knew it would. Their theology tells them this woman is to be shunned, rejected, ignored, turned away. They themselves would say just the same thing Jesus said.

And yet . . .

Something inside them is deeply moved. This is the cry of a desperate mother for a beloved daughter who is in physical and spiritual agony. Could it possibly be that God is better than their theology?

This is striking at their sense of identity, at prejudices and beliefs about their own superiority and who it is God really loves, at an exclusiveness that is so much at their core, it will not get rooted out all at once.

A seed is being planted here that won't be fully harvested until Peter sees the Holy Spirit fall on a Gentile named Cornelius and says, "I now realize how true it is that God does not show favoritism but accepts men from every nation who fear him and do what is right."

Robert Putnam writes that sociologists distinguish between two kinds of connections: bonding and bridging. Bonding happens when people who perceive themselves to be similar develop deeper connections; but bridging activities involve people who have been separated. Bonding activities might involve people in the same ethnic group or economic status. Bridging connections, by definition, are "outward looking and encompass people across diverse social cleavages."

Jesus is the greatest bridger the world has ever seen. When the church understood his heart, it became a community like nothing else the world has ever seen.

Jesus is the greatest bridger the world has ever seen. When the church understood his heart, it became a community like nothing else the world has ever seen.

The disciples don't get it yet, so Jesus speaks again. He has been speaking to his disciples, and we are not told that he turns around. Picture Jesus saying this next line—as I think he did—still looking at his disciples, still watching their faces, still testing:

> "It is not right to take the children's bread and toss it to their dogs."

The meaning is clear. The word *children* stands for Israel. *Dogs* would be Gentiles—including this woman.

Dogs in the Middle East are despised animals at this time. They are scavengers and garbage eaters, considered almost as unclean as pigs. Jesus is forcing his disciples to face themselves.

In effect, Jesus says to them, "You want me to get rid of this woman? Limit my ministry to Israel? Okay, I will do what you ask. But before I do, take a moment to watch her. Listen to her daughter's screams."

Then Jesus gives voice to their theology. It is one thing to have contempt for someone behind their back. It is another thing to hear the ugliness of our thoughts and feelings expressed out loud to a real human being.

The test is, will any of them speak up for this woman? Will one of them love her?

No. Not one. Not today.

This is the end of the disciples' test. There will be other tests in days to come, and they will do better. They are still learning.

But not today.

Why does it take so long? Thinking of sin as *exclusion* helps us get to the core of Jesus' teaching. Volf says Jesus "names as sin what often passes for virtue, especially in religious circles." The religious leaders in Jesus' day believed that their refusal to associate with people who did not live up to their religious standards was the highest proof of their devotion to God. The righteous had to separate themselves from the outcasts. The more spiritual you tried to be, the bigger the category of outcasts got: people were excluded based on ethnicity (Gentiles), gender (women), physical problems (lepers), or practicing what were called "despised trades" (the rabbis' list included tax collectors, dung collectors, and pigeon keepers). The outcasts were considered defiled, and to associate with them would defile the righteous. The righteous believed that the essence of spiritual maturity lay in *excluding* people.

Jesus, who was sinless and innocent, nevertheless embraced the outcasts. He did not condone sin, but he clarified where unfair labels had made people outcasts, and he offered the possibility of redemption for those who had truly fallen. He associated with the outcasts; he spoke with them, touched them, ate with them, loved them. "By embracing the outcast," Volf writes, "Jesus underscored the sinfulness of the persons and systems that cast them out."

When people truly begin to follow Jesus, they find themselves becoming Embracers.

The Greatest Gift

In a town called Paradise, California, lived a young man named John Gilbert. I like to think of him as a friend of mine, though we never met; I have traded letters with his family. When he was five years old, John was diagnosed with Duchenne's Muscular Dystrophy. It is a genetic, progressive, and cruel disease. He was told it would eventually destroy every muscle and finally, in a space of ten more years or so, take his life.

John passed away a short while ago at the age of twenty-five. Toward the end of his life, he needed the help of machines even to breathe. He had only enough strength to move a computer mouse with his right hand. But he did that brilliantly. He sent me a manuscript of the story of his life that is one of the most moving pieces I have ever read.

Each year John lost something. One year it was the ability to run; he couldn't play sports with other kids. Another year he could no longer walk straight, so all he could do was watch others play. Eventually he lost the ability to speak.

John knew something about the pain of exclusion. He wrote that junior high—not surprisingly—was perhaps the hardest era of his life. Junior high is difficult for almost everyone, I suppose. Tony Campolo once said that the old Roman Catholic theology is right, that there really is such a thing as purgatory. It's junior high, a place between heaven and hell where you are made to go suffer for your sins.

But what John experienced was far worse than most of us could imagine. Certain groups of students used to humiliate him because of his condition and because he had to bring a trained dog to school with him. He attended one dance in junior high; it was a disaster, and he never went to another. A bully used to torture him in the lunch room, where there were no supervising teachers, until he was afraid to go to school. No one ever stood up for him; maybe because they were afraid for themselves. "What a silly species we are!" John writes. "We all need to feel accepted ourselves, but we constantly reject others."

But there were other moments in John's life. At one point he was named the representative for everyone with his condition in the state of California. He was flown to Sacramento and was ushered with his mother into the governor's office for a private meeting. The governor took a large glass jar filled with candy and told John to dig in. John looked at his mother, who said it was okay to take one, but the governor said *he* was the *governor* and John should do what *he* said. John stuffed his pockets.

That night the National Football League sponsored a fund-raising auction and dinner at which John was a guest. The players let him hold their huge Super Bowl rings, which almost extended to John's wrist.

When the auction began, one item particularly caught John's attention: a basketball signed by the players of the Sacramento Kings professional team. John got a little carried away, because when the ball was up for bids, he raised his hand. As soon as the hand went up, John's mother flagged it down. In John's words, "Astronauts never felt as many G's as my wrist did that night."

The bidding for the basketball rose to an astounding amount for an item that was not the most valuable treasure on the docket. Eventually, one man named a figure that shocked the room and that no one else could match.

The man went to the front and collected his prize. But instead of returning to his seat, the man walked across the room and placed it in the thin, small hands of the boy who had admired it so intently. The man placed the ball in hands that would never dribble it down a court, never throw it to a teammate on a fast break, never fire it from three-point range. But those hands would cherish it.

John writes, "It took me a moment to realize what he had done. I remember hearing gasps all over the room, then thunderous applause, and seeing weepy eyes. To this day I'm amazed. . . . Have you ever been given a gift you could never have gotten for yourself? Has anyone ever sacrificed a huge amount for you without getting anything in return except . . . the joy of giving?"

It was as simple as this: Somebody noticed. Somebody cared. Somebody acted. Somebody gave.

Have you bought a basketball for anybody lately? When was the last time you noticed—really *noticed*—that someone felt left out, all alone, excluded?

I hope you are doing well on this test. I hope you are living as Jesus' student devoted to learning from him how to love.

The Woman Who Wouldn't Give Up

Let's return to the story. Jesus uses very harsh language about dogs to force the disciples to face themselves. At the same time, he softens it slightly for the woman. There are two main words available for dogs, and Jesus uses the word that means a little dog—a doggy.

The scene has a flavor like this. A wimpy little guy comes into a coffee shop, leaving his wimpy little dog outside, a miniature poodle. A huge, heavily tattoed biker comes in—eyes the guy, and tells him, "You might want to go check on that little excuse for a dog. I left my German shepherd out there, and I doubt that you'll have much of a dog left."

The little man goes out, comes back in, and says to the biker, "I don't know how to tell you this, but my dog just killed your dog."

"No way. How?"

"He got stuck in your dog's throat."

Jesus is talking here about a little puppy, not an attack dog. A "doggette." He uses the word *dogs* for the disciples' sake. "You want me to treat all Gentiles like dogs? Here's what it looks like." Making them "little dogs" softens it for the woman.

This is the hardest part of the test for the woman. Will she run away? She could. She could decide it's not worth the effort, this strange tug-of-war, and give up.

Will she insult Jesus back? He and his people have been enemies to her and hers for a long time. She might think, *Who do you think you are? Where do you get off talking to me like this?*

Or—is her love for her daughter so intense, is her trust in Jesus' power to heal so deep, is her faith in Jesus' compassion so strong, is her commitment to him as "Lord/Master/*kurios*" so unwavering that she will keep going?

The woman's response is unbelievable. "Yes, Lord," she says, calling him "Lord" for the third time. Then she says, "But even the dogs eat the crumbs that fall from their masters' table."

She picks up on the diminutive form of the word *dogs* and uses the same diminutive form for the word *crumbs*. "Even the little doggettes get the little crumbs from their masters' tables."

She comes back at Jesus with grit, grace, and even wit. There is an element of something like playfulness here, as if she is sparring with Jesus.

She's got a little attitude going: "You are still my lord and master. Go ahead and make it look like you're pushing me away—I know your heart. I'm not going anywhere. By all means, feed the kids. But I think you have a crumb for even me. I bet you do."

The woman just won't give up.

I think of this woman when I watch our neighbors across the street. The husband in that family has always been something like glue in our cul-de-sac. He has never met a stranger. He is a home improvement guy; from the time we moved into our house eight years ago he has never been without a project. He would bring us over to see every new renovation—when he finished the basement, when he redid the floors and knocked out a wall, when he added a gazebo. Each time my wife would look at me, saying with a single silent glance, *What have you been doing with all* your *time?*

One Monday morning very early last May, the paramedics came to our cul-de-sac. We watched as they carried our neighbor away in the ambulance. I drove to the hospital and sat in the waiting room with his wife when they came from the operating room and said he didn't make it. He was in his early forties. They have two children, both teenagers, both at home. Now, for that little house, life is an endurance test. I marvel at her determination as I see her care for her home, raising her children, holding on to hope. I marvel at how the embrace of a family brings strength.

Why does something like that happen? I don't know.

I only know that ultimately, the choice everyone faces is the choice between hope and despair. Jesus says, "Choose hope."

Will you keep going when you don't know why? When you can't get any answers that would make the pain go away, will you still say, "My Lord," even though his ways are not clear to you? Will you keep going—with all the grace and grit and faith you can muster—and live in hope that one day God will set everything right. Will you trust that God is good?

Ultimately, the choice everyone faces is the choice between hope and despair. Jesus says, "Choose hope."

I think of Jacob, who wrestled with a man throughout one night and realized afterward that it was God. The man crippled Jacob's hip and told him to let go, and Jacob said, "I will not let you go unless you bless me."

When the man saw Jacob would not quit, he blessed him and gave him a new name: Israel. "You have struggled with God and with men and have overcome."

Why does God wrestle with Jacob? Why not just give him a blessing outright?

I don't know the whole answer to those questions. I think it has something to do with the fact that God prizes that quality in the human spirit that will not give up.

God wants greatness of soul—people who will endure, wrestle, persevere, refuse to quit, and cling to his goodness even when there is much they can't see clearly.

The woman is a foreigner, a pagan, an enemy—but to Jesus her name is "Israel": one who wrestles with God. Jesus' disciples look on with open mouths. They have never seen someone show such confidence with Jesus or demonstrate such risk-taking love.

When this woman approached, they thought they were watching their inferior. They thought initially that it would have been an act of remarkable condescension on their part merely to listen to her. The thought that *she* might have something to teach *them* would not have occurred to them in their wildest dreams.

But she does. It turns out she is their master in every respect. She is relating to Jesus on a level of understanding, humility, and trust that puts them to shame!

This is the irony of the spirit of exclusion. It causes us to think that merely to associate with those we consider outsiders is doing them a favor. We forget that wherever the spirit of exclusion reigns, it marks those farthest from the Fellowship of the Trinity. When we exclude, we don't just hurt those we keep outside; we damage our own souls far more. And when we embrace, we ourselves are the ones who receive the greatest gift. The spirit of exclusion places us in the outermost ring of all. Ultimately, the only ones the Excluders can keep away from God's community are themselves.

The disciples look at Jesus. Now, finally, he turns away from them to face the Canaanite woman. Now, finally, the mask is off.

For a moment Jesus concealed the great goodness of his heart because he had a purpose. Now that purpose is fulfilled. The woman sees his face; she feels his love. Now the test is over.

It is time for the grades to be given out.

Jesus says, "Woman," but in the Greek text a single letter comes first: "O woman."

Jesus' heart is full. Maybe his eyes are as well. He turns to the woman and expresses his admiration:

"Wow! O woman—great is your faith."

Jesus' word *great* comes from a form of the word we use today: mega-malls and mega-churches. Jesus says this gentile woman has mega-faith.

He doesn't use that word for his disciples. When they flunked an earlier test during a storm on the Sea of Galilee, Jesus said to them, "You of little faith."

But the woman's faith—the faith of one who they thought was their enemy, their inferior—is instead given one of the greatest commendations ever offered by the One they try so haltingly to follow.

It turns out they—who thought they were in the exclusive Inner Ring—are in the Pigeon group. And she—a pagan gentile woman—is one of the Eagles.

The woman understands what they do not. That the most desirable society in the universe turns out also to be the humblest and the least exclusive. The Father, Son, and Holy Spirit are determined that the circle of love they share from all eternity should be ceaselessly, shamelessly inclusive. It is not full yet. They invite all who will to join them. No one is left out except those who refuse to enter.

Learning to Dance

1. When was a time in your life when you felt most on the outside?
2. When did you first notice the existence of an "inner ring"' in your school or place of work?
3. Do you have any regrets about people in the past whom you may have excluded? What would you like to do differently?
4. When you tend to exclude people, what lies behind that action: fear, pride, ignorance, the desire to feel superior?
5. Robert Putnam speaks of the difference between "bonding" and "bridging." Are you involved in any "bridging" activities or relationships? What do you think you might like to try?
6. Misguided people in Jesus' day thought that the essence of spiritual maturity meant excluding people. Where might such an idea come from?
7. How can you disagree with someone without excluding them?
8. Look for people who feel left out. Watch for ways to include them.

THE SECRET OF A LOVING HEART: GRATITUDE

What is the use of the most sublime enlightenment and divine revelation if we do not love?

Jean Pierre de Caussade

A man wanders into a small antique shop in San Francisco. Mostly it's cluttered with knickknacks and junk. On the floor, however, he notices what looks like an ancient Chinese vase. On closer inspection it turns out to be a priceless relic from the Ming dynasty whose value is beyond calculating. It is worth everything else in the store put together. The owner clearly has no idea about the value of this possession, because it's filled with milk and the cat's drinking out of it.

The man sees an opportunity for the deal of a lifetime. He cleverly strategizes a method to obtain the vase for a fraction of its worth. "That's an extraordinary cat you have," he says to the owner. "How much would you sell her for?"

"Oh, the cat's not really for sale," said the owner. "She keeps the store free of mice."

"I really must have her," the man countered. "Tell you what—I'll give you a hundred dollars for her."

"She's not really worth it," laughed the owner, "but if you want her that badly, she's yours."

"I need something to feed her from as well," continued the man. "Let me throw in another ten dollars for that saucer she's drinking out of."

"Oh, I could never do that. That saucer is actually an ancient Chinese vase from the Ming dynasty. It is my prized possession, whose worth is beyond calculation. Funny thing, though; since we've had it, I've sold seventeen cats."

The ability to assign value is one of the rarest and most precious gifts in the world.

The ability to assign value is one of the rarest and most precious gifts in the world. People who live deeply in community learn to discern and express the value of other human beings. They are masters of expressing love in word and gesture. They assign high worth, value, and importance to others by viewing them as priceless gifts. They see that in addition to the "as-is" tag, every human being carries another sticker from God: "Made in my image. Worth the life of my Son. My prized possession whose value is beyond calculation."

In a word, what they give is called "honor."

Every subculture has rules that govern how it honors people. For children, it may be a shy question: "Can you come out and play?" For junior high school boys, in a kind of reverse sociological experiment, the language of affection generally involves hitting, wrestling, and the search for the ultimate insult. As we grow older, the modes of expression get a little more sophisticated, but the dynamic stays the same.

Every society adopts ways to welcome and host people, to honor and value people whom we treasure, or to ignore and hurt those we choose to demean. Understanding this is central to one of the great encounters between Jesus and an "as-is" character in the New Testament.

Etiquette: Then and Now

Let us see where we are with etiquette in this century, then we'll work our way back to biblical times. See how well you do with this quick etiquette assessment tool.

1. At a formal dinner, when should one start eating the main course?
   a. After the hostess is served
   b. After the hostess lifts her fork
   c. After three or four people have their food
   d. ASAP, with urgency and passion
2. What does one do at a formal dinner if one is still hungry after the main course?
   a. Request a second helping
   b. Ask in a plaintive voice, "Is that all there is?"
   c. Yell, "Look out the window!" and take food from your neighbor's plate while he's distracted
   d. Surreptitiously call Domino's Pizza
3. What is the correct response if one's cell phone goes off in church?
   a. Quickly slide it forward and point disgustedly at the person in front of you
   b. Shout "hallelujah" until it stops ringing (charismatics only)
   c. Give a larger than usual offering
   d. Answer the phone, yell, "My baby!" and run out of the room. (This only works well if you have small children.)

In Jesus' day, the rules were different, but the dynamics were the same. Kenneth Bailey writes about them in *Through Peasant Eyes*, a commentary on the gospel of Luke.

One day Jesus arrives at the home of a religious leader for dinner. Luke makes a point of telling us that Jesus had been invited, because as a visiting rabbi he would be regarded as a guest of honor. Certain rules of etiquette would be taken for granted.

The customary greeting was a kiss. This was not necessarily an expression of affection; it was simply a polite acknowledgment of the guest's arrival. The kiss could take different forms, depending on the status of the parties involved. If the guest was a person of equal social rank, the host would kiss him on the cheek. If a child were greeting a parent or a student his rabbi, a kiss on the hand was in order. (In the Garden of Gethsemane, Judas would have kissed Jesus, his rabbi, on the hand. This is one reason why the scene of Judas' treachery is so painful. To kiss the hand was a profession of loyalty from disciple to master; Judas twisted it into an act of mockery and betrayal.)

To neglect this ritual was equivalent to ignoring someone. To put it in our cultural terms, imagine arriving at the home of someone who invited you for dinner. The door is open, so you assume they intend for you to come in, but the family members are busy watching television and never rise from the La-Z-Boy, look you in the eye, or say hello. To do this to a casual guest is rude; to do it to a guest of honor is a deliberate insult.

The washing of feet was mandatory before a meal. If the guest was of high status, the host would perform this duty himself. If not, he might have a servant do it. A particularly lazy or arrogant host might simply give the guests some water and expect them to bathe their own feet, but this would be borderline offensive—a little like telling your guests they will have to wash their own dishes after dinner.

A thoughtful host would give his guests some olive oil for anointing, though this was somewhat optional. In a world that had a surplus of heat and a scarcity of deodorant, such a gesture was particularly refreshing.

In this story, Jesus arrives at the home and receives nothing. He is no longer an obscure carpenter. He has become a renowned teacher, attracting multitudes of people not only from his own country but all the way from places like Tyre and Sidon. He has an international following. Yet, at the home of Simon he is given no greeting, no water for his feet, and no anointing for his head.

These are not subtle omissions, easily overlooked. This is a deliberate slap in the face. Everybody present knows it. Bailey observes, "The insult to Jesus has to be intentional and electrifies the assembled guests. War has been declared and everyone waits to see Jesus' response." The tension in the room is so thick you can cut it with a knife.

Overwhelmed by Love

Banquets like this one are public affairs. In the courtyard of the well-to-do, anybody may walk up and watch and listen.

A woman is present. She is a prostitute and is known as such in the village.

She had heard Jesus teaching, maybe earlier that day. Something about him struck very deep in her heart. She began to wonder, perhaps, "How in the world did I come to this?" No one grows up thinking they will become a prostitute.

Once this woman had been someone's little baby—the object of a mother's hopes and dreams. Maybe her husband had rejected her, and this was the only way she could survive economically. Maybe her heart had hardened, and this was simply the easiest way she could get the most money. One thing is certain: This woman knows what it means to be despised, unwelcome. Prostitutes were usually slaves who had either been captured in war or abandoned as infants and then raised to be part of the sex trade. It is possible that this woman had been sold into slavery by her parents. She carries in her heart the enormous wound of rejection—perhaps even rejection at the hands of her parents. She certainly knows rejection as an adult. No decent person will speak to her, welcome her, or acknowledge her. Doors open for her only at night, in secret and in shame.

When the woman hears Jesus teach, the thought occurs to her that she—right there in her life, her sin—is loved by God. He thinks of her and longs for her as if she were his daughter. She is valued. It's not too late—even for her.

She hears Jesus will be attending this dinner. Of course, she would not be invited in a million years. She gathers all her courage and comes into the courtyard. She is overwhelmed by the idea of God's love.

She sees how Jesus is treated by Simon. She watches as the one who has given her new life is ignored and insulted. The watching crowd waits for Jesus to make a few strained remarks about being unwelcome and then leave in a huff. He does not. He accepts his humiliation without protest. No one comes to his side; no one stands up for him.

The woman can't stand it. Her love and devotion and anger all well up to the surface.

What can she do?

She can't be the one to give Jesus a kiss of greeting. It would be presumptuous. Think of how those around the table would interpret that.

Then she has an impulse: She could kiss Jesus' feet. To wash someone's feet was an act of abasement; to kiss them would be an act of utter humility. She decides to act—quickly, before losing her nerve.

Imagine the drama. Jesus reclines on a cushion, with his feet facing away from the table. Suddenly a woman who had been watching from the courtyard, who clearly was not invited, stands at his feet. Everyone is watching.

She kneels down to kiss his feet so that someone might greet him, someone might give him honor. She crouches there for—how long?—and then, in a moment of desperate courage, dares to look up at his face. She stopped looking into peoples' eyes many years ago, for all she ever saw was either lust or condemnation. But she looks into Jesus' face. And instead of judgment or ridicule or embarrassment, she sees love.

She has not seen that look in a man's eyes in a long time. If ever. Here she sees it in the eyes of the best man she has ever known. He loves her. Not as an object, but as a daughter. Not as a commodity, but as a friend. Not in the shadows, but in the light.

Tears come to her eyes—a few at first, then more. Then they are pouring down her face.

Tears of sadness for what she has done.

Tears of gratitude because Jesus offers forgiveness.

Tears of joy because now a whole new life lies in front of her. Jesus' eyes become a kind of mirror in which she sees the possibility of becoming a new woman. She could get a do-over.

Jesus' feet, unwashed by Simon, are wet from her tears.

The woman wonders, *How can I dry these feet?* There's no use asking for a towel, because Simon would never give her one. On impulse she lets down her hair.

This is another shocking breach of etiquette. A woman always wears her hair up in public. She never allows it to hang loose in mixed company; it is considered too provocative a situation for men to handle. If a married woman lets her hair down in front of any man other than her husband, it is grounds for divorce.

Everyone watching knows her profession. The woman has let down her hair many times before, with many men. But now she is doing it one final time. This time she is getting it right. With her hair she wipes Jesus' feet.

She has an alabaster jar of ointment—most likely a flask worn around the neck as a kind of perfume. Again, because of her profession, this flask is quite important. In an era not known for its hygiene; the use of perfume helped make her work less unpleasant for her.

But now she empties the flask. This is an act of great significance. She will not need it any more. She is pouring out her old way of life. She knows she cannot anoint Jesus' head because it would be unseemly; she is a sinful woman, he a holy man. So she pours it on Jesus' feet.

She kisses them over and over.

She has been so broken and undone by his sheer goodness that it is as if she has forgotten who she is and where she is, and she unashamedly pours herself out in adoration and gratitude.

The Story of a Loan Shark and Two Bookies

Simon is watching. This dinner is not turning out at all the way he planned. Interestingly, Luke does not tell us why Simon treats Jesus so shabbily. Maybe Simon had planned to snub him all along. Maybe he really wanted Jesus to come to his home, but with all those people present cannot bring himself to publicly align himself with the rabbi. Perhaps he is afraid his reputation might take a hit. Whatever the reason, he is distancing himself from this rabbi. What is striking is the difference between Simon's and the woman's responses to Jesus' situation.

As Simon watches the drama with the woman, he says to himself, *Jesus must not be "it" after all. If he were a prophet, he would know who this woman is. He wouldn't let her touch him with a ten-foot pole.*

But Jesus knows who the woman is and who Simon is. Jesus wonders if there is any way to get Simon to see the value of the apparently worthless object on his floor. So he tells Simon a little story.

"Two men owed money to a moneylender." This is the only time the word *moneylender* appears in the New Testament, and it refers to one who lends money at interest. Those who allowed themselves to get into debt were not highly thought of in those days, and moneylenders were an even worse class. In our day the story might run like this: "Let me tell you about two gamblers in over their heads to a bookie named Fast Eddie."

Both men owed money, and neither could pay it back. Both faced the same fate. The only apparent difference between them is that one owed a great deal more than the other. The real difference is that the bookie with the larger debt *knew* he was desperate.

When they could not pay, Jesus says, and expected to lose all they had and face prison at best, Fast Eddie calls them in and makes them an offer they can't refuse. Both debts are forgiven.

Now, Jesus asks Simon, which one is going to have his world turned upside down? Which one will be filled with relief and gratitude and joy, seized with love for one who would graciously set him free? Little-debt or Big-debt?

Simon begins his answer: "I suppose. . . ." The answer is obvious, but Simon doesn't want to admit it. He is headed toward the end of a very short cul-de-sac, and he doesn't like it at all, so he pretends that it's a tough call. "I suppose it would be Big-debt."

Jesus says with some humor, "You have judged rightly." Give the boy a cigar!

This teaching of Jesus stands in striking contrast with thoughts of our day. We think of people having the capacity to love who have mostly gotten life right—healthy people with high self-esteem and low regret factors. Normal people.

There is no such thing, dear. Jesus says the great lovers are those who have come face-to-face with their own great brokenness and have been undone by great grace.

Then comes one of the greatest conversations in Scripture. The text says that Jesus turns toward the woman, but continues to speak to Simon. The dynamic of this encounter depends on visualizing the scene that Luke has deftly sketched, so let's take a moment to get a clear picture of what Jesus is doing.

Up to now, the conversation has been between Jesus and Simon. Now Jesus keeps speaking to Simon, but his eyes are locked on the woman, and her eyes are fixed on him. Usually, in conversation you face the person you're speaking to. (Unless, like me, you're Swedish. Then you look at your shoes. If you're a Swedish extravert, you look at the other person's shoes.) It is an irresistible impulse to gaze at what somebody speaking to you is gazing at. By facing one person while addressing another, Jesus is compelling Simon to look where he looks, see what he sees. He is inviting Simon to see that lying there on his floor is a prized possession of God whose value is beyond all calculation.

By turning toward the woman, Jesus is also sending a message to her. He is telling her, in effect, that though his words are addressed to

Simon, they are intended for her as well. She becomes a third member of the conversation; the one with whom Jesus aligns himself. She has boldly loved Jesus; now he boldly loves her.

Imagine her: Beaming under Jesus' gaze, her tears flowing, her heart pounding because it is filled with shyness and fear and shame and hope and unspeakable love.

Everyone in the courtyard turns to look at her. Jesus is now not just her forgiver. He has become her protector and advocate and friend. She was going to be his champion; now he is hers.

"Do you see this woman?"

Simon doesn't. He sees a theological object lesson. He sees a discard, a vessel so unclean he wouldn't use it to feed his cat. He doesn't see what Jesus sees at all.

"You did not give me any water for my feet." Jesus is humble and restrained here. He doesn't even note that since he's a rabbi, Simon should have personally washed his feet. He doesn't point out that he wasn't treated as an honored guest. He just observes that Simon should have at least provided water, which would have been done for the lowest-status guest.

"She wet my feet with tears and wiped them with her hair." She transformed a common courtesy into an expression of the heart.

"You did not give me a kiss." Again, Jesus' modesty is striking. He does *not* say, "You didn't kiss my hand," which is the gesture of honor a disciple would pay to a teacher. Someone who considered himself Jesus' equal would have kissed his cheek. Jesus merely notes that the kiss was omitted altogether.

The one who is forgiven much loves much. The one who is forgiven little loves little.

"This woman ... has not stopped kissing my feet." The woman is still on the floor, kissing Jesus' feet as her tears flow. I picture him whispering to her, "You can stop now." In that dusty, unswept, unwashed, dung-filled world, feet were considered the nastiest part of the body. The ultimate insult in defeat is to "make the enemy a footstool" for the feet of the victor. To have one's nose in their general vicinity is not done. To kiss them is unthinkable.

"You did not put oil on my head," Jesus notes, referring to common olive oil, "but she has poured perfume on my feet." She didn't use a cheap substance, but poured out the best she had. It has cost her everything—her money and her way of making a living. It is the promise of new life.

"Therefore, I tell you, her many sins—[a big debt]—have been forgiven." Can you imagine how the woman's heart explodes as Jesus looks her in the eye and pronounces before this of all groups: "Your many sins are forgiven!"

That is why the woman loves so lavishly. The one who is forgiven much loves much. The one who is forgiven little loves little.

The Greatest Sin of All

It is worth noting what Jesus is *not* saying in this parable. He is not saying, "Simon, you are a righteous man. You have hardly sinned at all. You don't need much grace."

The difficulty is, Simon perceives himself to have little sin. That is what makes it so hard for him to be overwhelmed by grace. He really does think God is getting a pretty good deal in him. He thinks of himself as a small debtor. He looks at large-debt people and wonders why they can't be more righteous, like him.

Question: Who is really the big debtor?

There is a great sin defiling this room. But it is not the sin Simon thinks.

It is the sin of

Lips that won't kiss
Knees that won't bend
Eyes that will not weep
Hands that will not serve
Perfume that will never leave the jar

It is the sin of a heart that will not break, a life that will not change, a soul that will not love.

The greatest command is the command to love. The greatest sin is refusal to obey the greatest command. Jesus says, in effect, "Simon, don't you see? You have the biggest debt of all."

If only Simon could see it!

If only he would fall to the ground beside this sinful woman.

If only he could see and feel pain over his sin as she does over hers.

If only he could be overwhelmed by the realization that Jesus loves him anyway in the midst of his lovelessness.

If only his tears would begin to flow and mingle with this woman's, and they would bathe the feet of Jesus together.

Then Simon would realize that he and this prostitute are just a couple of bookies in the family of forgiven debtors. Two more members in the Fellowship of the Mat.

She needs grace for a heart that is broken.

He needs grace for a heart that is hard.

Richard Mouw tells of an occasion when Mother Teresa was teaching a young member of her community who came from a well-to-do family how to care for the poor and dying on the streets of Calcutta. She said that when you see people on the streets, filled with disease, disfigured by sores, covered with maggots, touch them very gently with great love and delicate care, the way a priest handles the elements of holy mass, for Jesus is there in the distressing disguise.

We complicate our faith and lives in many ways, but at the core, our purpose is simple: We are called to love.

Who is the big debtor? You are. I am.

We complicate our faith and lives in many ways, but at the core, our purpose is simple: We are called to love.

"I Love You This Much"

I was washing my car, and one of my daughters was helping me. Usually she makes a lot of noise, but she had been ominously silent for some minutes. I looked at her. She had emptied the trunk of the car and was washing the contents: books, a dress for her mother, a tennis racquet. Ruined! I realized that there was a sinner in my midst. Defiled. Four years old. I looked down to pronounce judgment, and she looked up at me with big brown eyes, stretched her hands as far as she could, and said the words I would say when I tucked her in at night.

"I love you this much."

What can you do?

A woman comes before Jesus whose whole life is warped by sin. She kneels before him and offers a contrite heart. But this time it is Jesus, the offended party, the blameless one, who stretches out his hands and says, "I love you this much."

Jesus says it to crooked tax collectors, unfaithful friends, prodigal sons, and a thief on a cross. He'd say it to Simon, if only Simon would let him. He'll say it to you right now.

In that Jewish society, there are strict rules forbidding what is taking place. Jesus is not supposed to allow this woman to touch him. Because she does so, he will be regarded as defiled. So he is sharing in her uncleanness. He is willing to take on himself the pain of her sin and suffer the humiliation.

He is suffering for her. His reputation is being damaged. He is mocked.

But he is willing. In fact, he is not just willing but *wants* to do this for her. It brings him joy. He is genuinely happy to take on this woman's pain to bring her healing.

So he is for you and me. This is the Jesus of the cross.

Jesus is willing to take on her defilement.

Because he does this, this woman's life will never be the same.

The one who is forgiven much loves much.

Jesus has been looking at the woman the whole time he is talking to Simon, and now does he address her directly: "Your faith has saved you; go in peace."

The prostitute has known many emotions, many states of heart: fear, guilt, hurt, anger, desire, shame, maybe joy sometimes, certainly loneliness.

But peace? Never.

Jesus says, in effect, "Go in peace that all these people judging and condemning you cannot touch. Hold your head up. Don't walk out of here as a despised, unclean thing shamed by the righteous. Walk out of here as a daughter of the king."

Such is the power of love.

You and I have this power.

Dale Galloway tells the story of a young boy named Teddy Stollard. He was not the kind of kid who got invited to parties. He slouched in his chair and looked bored most of the time; he only spoke when called upon, and then in monosyllables. He never dressed right; he had smelly clothes; he was a rather unattractive boy.

Whenever his teacher would mark Teddy's papers, she got a certain perverse pleasure out of marking all the wrong answers. She would put the "F" on top with a little flair. She might have known better, because his history was on record:

First grade: Teddy is a good boy and shows promise, but has a poor home situation.

Second grade: Teddy is quiet and withdrawn. His mother is terminally ill.

Third grade: Teddy is falling behind. His mother died this year; his father is uninvolved.

Fourth grade: Teddy is hopelessly backward. His father has moved away; Teddy's living with an aunt. He is deeply troubled.

Christmas came, and all the children brought presents to school. They were carefully wrapped, except for Teddy's, which was packaged in brown paper and held together with tape and marked, "For Miss Thompson. From Teddy."

The teacher would open the gifts one by one for the class to admire. When she opened Teddy's, it was a rhinestone bracelet with most of the stones missing, and a bottle of perfume that was mostly gone. The other children started to laugh, but Miss Thompson caught herself. Snapping on the bracelet, she said: "Isn't it lovely, class? And doesn't the perfume smell good?"

At the end of the class, Teddy approached her shyly. "I'm glad you liked my gifts, Miss Thompson," he whispered. "All day long you smelled like my mother. And her bracelet looked nice on you, too."

After he left, Miss Thompson put her head down on the desk and cried. She asked God to forgive her. She prayed that God would help her to see what he sees when she looks at a motherless boy.

When the children came back to school the next day, Miss Thompson was a new teacher. She tutored the children who needed extra help, Teddy most of all. By the end of the year he had caught up with most of his classmates and was ahead of some. After that, she didn't hear from him for quite a while. Then one day she received a note:

> *Dear Miss Thompson,*
>
> *I wanted you to be the first to know I am graduating from high school, and I am second in my class.*
>
> *Love, Teddy Stollard*

Four years later came another note:

> *Dear Miss Thompson,*
>
> *I wanted you to be the first to know I am graduating first in my class. The university has not been easy, but I liked it.*
>
> *Love, Teddy Stollard*

Four years later, another note:

> *Dear Miss Thompson,*
>
> *I wanted to you be the first to know that as of today I am Theodore J. Stollard, M.D. How about that? I want you to come sit where my mother would have sat, because you're the nearest thing to family that I've had.*
>
> *Love, Teddy Stollard*

The ability to assign value is one of the rarest and greatest gifts in the world.

So value what God values. There is an ancient story about a poor traveler who is amazed by the welcome he receives at a monastery. He is served a lavish meal, escorted to their finest room, and given a new set of clothes to replace the rags he arrived in. Before leaving, he commented to the abbot on how well he was treated. Yes, the abbot said, we always treat our guests as if they are angels—just to be on the safe side.

Learning to Dance

1. Why do you think Simon's heart toward this woman was so different from Jesus'?
2. As you relived Jesus' encounter with the woman, what most impacted your heart? Why?
3. How is your heart doing these days? Is it growing in the ways you use to pay honor to people?
4. What are some ways that you are sometimes treated that make you feel dishonored?
5. When is the last time you were overwhelmed by a sense of God's grace for you?
6. What practices or activities help you stay in touch with your need for God's forgiveness?
7. "We always treat our guests as if they are angels—just to be on the safe side." Take one day to attempt to treat someone this way. What are the primary barriers that make it hard to carry this out?

CHAPTER 12

NORMAL AT LAST: HEAVEN

All their life in this world . . . had only been the cover and title page: now at last they were beginning Chapter One of the Great Story which no one on earth has read: which goes on for ever: in which every chapter is better than the one before.

C. S. LEWIS, *THE LAST BATTLE*

My people aren't paradise people. We've lived in Minnesota all our lives and it took a lot out of us. My people aren't sure if we'll even like paradise: not sure that perfection is all it's cracked up to be.

GARRISON KEILLOR

What were the most exciting five minutes of your life? What were the most breath-taking, exhilarating, emotion-producing three hundred seconds you ever experienced?

There is a good chance that, if we were able to remember them, the most exciting five minutes of life would be the very first five.

After nine months of darkness and isolation, you discover through a traumatic experience that there is a whole world out there, full of colors, tastes, sounds, sensations, and other people.

You have entered a realm beyond your wildest imaginings.

If you could talk then, you might have said, "Mom, I had no idea. I actually had reservations about leaving the womb. Now I see: This is a much better arrangement. I wouldn't have missed this for anything."

If those first minutes after birth were indeed the most exciting five minutes of your life, it has been all downhill from there. But even that is nothing compared with what's to come.

I believe that the most amazing five minutes you will ever experience will be the first five minutes after you die. Think about that!

For centuries, the brightest minds on earth have devoted whole lifetimes to try to penetrate that veil and learn what lies on the other side of death. Five minutes after you die, you will know. You will experience whatever lies beyond this world. You will have the foretaste of your destiny for all eternity.

Those five minutes really are coming. Whatever lies beyond them, they are inevitable. They will happen for every one of us. This is reality.

Think about the sights that you will see, the voices you will hear, the experiences you will have. The writers of Scripture say that for every human being those five minutes will indicate an eternal destiny of either indescribable joy or unspeakable loss. So let's spend some time thinking about the most exciting five minutes of human existence.

What Is Heaven Like?

Mrs. Olson directed a choir for fifth and sixth graders in the church where I grew up. When she grew frustrated with the boys—which happened often and for good reason—she would clap her hands and say, "You children better start singing the way I'm telling you to sing, because when we get to heaven, that's what we'll be doing—singing all the time; singing, singing, singing."

For an eleven-year-old boy, the idea of five or ten billion years under the enthusiastic direction of Mrs. Olson was not my idea of eternal bliss.

Along the same line, I had lunch one time with a friend who said, "I believe in God, but frankly, I'm afraid heaven seems boring. I don't know what I'd do after a while."

For some people, heaven is like the ultimate retirement village. You finish up your work down here, have a few years of adventure and risk, then pass on to something like an eternal weekend in Palm Springs.

One man asked me in all seriousness, "Will there be golf in heaven?" He had a little syllogism worked out: "I can't be happy unless I'm golfing; heaven is supposed to make me perfectly happy; therefore there must be golf in heaven."

I tried to explain to the man that heaven is the place of ultimate joy, but I may need to be changed so that I rejoice in whatever heaven offers. Is it really possible that God made us for nothing more significant than an eternal game of golf? Besides, we know in heaven that there will be no lying, no swearing, no cheating—so how can there be any golf? In the other place, we're told, there will be "weeping and wailing and gnashing of teeth." That sounds a lot more like a golf course to me. There will be no golf in heaven. Tennis, yes, but no golf.

I was at a funeral sometime ago where the pastor said that heaven will be like a worship service that never ends. I have to confess to feeling a little ambivalent about that idea as well.

Mark Buchanan writes,

> I assume you're like me: I can get itchy-skinned and scratchy-throated after an hour or so of church. I can get distracted and cranky when it goes too long. My feet ache, my backside numbs, my eyes glaze, my mind fogs, my belly growls. I find myself fighting back yawns, and then not fighting them back, letting them gape and roar, a signal to my oppressors: **Let my people go.**
>
> And I'm the pastor.

Max DePree tells a wonderful story about his father. His dad had reached the age of ninety-nine. He was having some problems and had to go to the hospital. He and Max had some serious conversations, and he assured his son that he was ready to die. At one point during his stay, Max's father was quite uncomfortable and refused to get into the bed; he insisted on sitting up in his chair. The nurses tried to get him to lie down so he could sleep, but he refused. They eventually asked Max to talk to him.

Max sat in a chair next to his father, and the two of them spoke quietly together for some time. Then Max asked his father if he would like to get into bed. No.

They talked some more. Max asked him about the bed again. No. Four times this liturgy was repeated. Finally Max asked his dad why he didn't want to lie down. "Because if I lie down, I'm going to die," his dad said.

"But, Dad!" Max told him. "You told me you were ready to die."

"I am," his dad replied, "*but not today*." Ninety-nine years old, and he's ready to die—but not today. Heaven is something to look forward to, but I'll take a rain check just now.

Neil Plantinga notes that although Jesus asked us to pray for the kingdom to come, many of us whisper our prayers so God can't quite hear them. "'Your kingdom come,' we pray, and hope it won't. 'Your kingdom come,' we pray, 'but not right away.' When our earthly kingdoms have had a good year, we don't necessarily long for the kingdom of God to break in. We like our own setup just fine."

One of the reasons many people don't look forward to heaven is that we badly misunderstand what the Bible is saying about it.

I believe one of the reasons many people don't look forward to heaven is that we badly misunderstand what the Bible is saying about it. Lewis Smedes, an ethics teacher of mine in grad school, used to ask students if they wanted to go to heaven when they died. Everyone raised a hand. Then he asked, "Be honest, now—who would like to go right now, today, before the sun goes down?"

A few raised their hands slowly, giving what they thought must be the correct answer, looking around to see if they were the only ones. They were. Most people wanted a rain check. They were ready to die, but not today.

Then Professor Smedes asked who would like to see the world we live in set straight on its hinges once for all, tomorrow: "No more common colds, no more uncommon cancers. Everyone would have his day; there would be no second-class citizens. Prisoners and slaves would be free; hungry people would have plenty; no one would lift a finger to harm another; and we would all be at peace with everyone, even with ourselves. Anybody interested in that?"

There was a frenzy of hand-lifting. Smedes said that if a new world tomorrow is what you really want, you want to go to heaven.

Redemption is always the redemption of creation. God never creates something in order to destroy it; and if it goes wrong, he intends to redeem it. Smedes notes that sometime ago there was a book written about "the *late* great planet earth," as if we were to look forward to God's destroying what he had made. But Paul says that creation itself "waits in eager expectation for the sons of God to be revealed." Far from being burned up or destroyed, Paul says that creation "will be liberated from its bondage to decay and brought into the glorious freedom of the children of God." God loves this world that he has made, and, as Smedes says, "he has no plans to preside over its demise. His plan is to make it right again." If in your heart you want that, you want heaven.

Most of all, of course, it is people who need to be made right again. So most of what heaven offers comes under the category of what life among redeemed people—people who are finally "normal" in God's eyes—will look like. But they express this in ways that take some patience and study for us to understand.

Many people have an image of heaven that is like something from a cartoon. In speaking of heaven, the writers of Scripture were attempting to express what defies description. If, for example, you had to describe a jet to someone who lived a thousand years ago, how would you do it? You would have to use symbols: "It's something like a giant metal bird. . . ." You would have to use images of what they know to convey what they do not know.

This is precisely what the writers of Scripture do when it comes to heaven.

C. S. Lewis writes,

> There is no need to be worried by facetious people who try to make the Christian hope of heaven ridiculous by saying that they do not want to spend eternity playing harps. The answer to such people is that if they cannot understand books written for grown-ups, they should not talk about them at all. All the scriptural imagery—harps, crowns, gold, and so on—is of

> course a symbolical attempt to express the inexpressible.... People who take these symbols literally might as well think that when Christ told us to be like doves, he meant that we were to lay eggs.

Images of Heaven

So let's take a look at some of the images used in Scripture to describe the indescribable reality of heaven. Most of these are from the pen of John, the disciple whom Jesus loved. John wrote the book of Revelation, which contains many of the Bible's most unforgettable pictures of heaven, when he was an old man—perhaps ninety—imprisoned on a little island called Patmos, far from all the people he loved. When you're ninety years old and living in exile, you start thinking about heaven a lot.

"Blessed are the dead who die in the Lord from now on," John wrote. We generally think of those who have died as being most unfortunate. We rarely hear a news account of someone who died or read an obituary in the newspaper that begins, "Blessed...."

But for John, the one word to describe those who have died in Christ is *blessed:* fortunate, happy, lucky. Because now they are really alive.

Let's look at some of his images. John says heaven is like a city with streets made of extremely expensive material. He doesn't mean by this that when we get to heaven we should expect to see curbs and gutters and traffic signs and a really nice mall.

John's point is that we will finally live in community. No more pit bulls or fences to divide us. No more suicide bombers. No broken homes. We will experience deep, open, intimate, joy-producing, trusting relationships.

According to John's gospel, Jesus is working on accommodations: "In my Father's house are many mansions." You may be wondering, "Will I get an English Tudor or Victorian? What if it's a split-level when I wanted more of a ranch-style home?" Garrison Keillor writes that when the men from Lake Wobegon arrive in heaven, they will look at the Father's mansions and talk about siding: aluminum versus cedar shakes. Jesus isn't saying that we will get our dream house; he is saying that we will finally find home.

For John, the one word to describe those who have died in Christ is *blessed:* fortunate, happy, lucky. Because now they are really alive.

When people buy a house, they generally put a fair amount of time into it. If they are married, one of them usually makes decisions that require taste and judgment; the other just moves heavy things and puts together heavy things.

But over time, something happens. After we have lived in the house awhile, after we have brought a baby or two home from the hospital, after we have celebrated a few Christmases, after we have stayed up all night rocking a sick child, after we have wept over a death or two, after we have laughed and cried and fought and made up and watched the seasons come and go and seen raven-colored hair turn gray and then white—after all this, we wake up one day and find that what was once just a house has become a home.

My grandmother lived with us for many years when I was a boy, and when she cooked she used every pot and pan in the kitchen. One of her specialties was banana bread, which she would bake, slice, butter heavily, then cut into little squares for us to eat. She died thirty years ago, but to this day I can't smell banana bread without hearing her voice and recalling my childhood home.

No word in the English language moves the human heart in quite the same way as the word *home*. Jesus recognizes that the deepest yearnings of the human heart—to belong, to be safe, to be prized—are really a yearning for heaven. When we get there, it will not seem strange to us. When we get there, we will say, "This is home."

Everybody knows that the apparel department in heaven is quite simple: no T-shirts or leisure suits. It will be all robes, all the time; and only white robes at that. You may be concerned about this because you've had your colors analyzed and you're an autumn; you would prefer something in a shade of sienna or forest green.

This one John spells out for us: "Fine linen stands for the righteous acts of the saints." In this state of blessedness, we will simply be incapable of being unfaithful to God. Our hands will naturally do acts of service; our mouths will speak words of truth and beauty. As John writes, "In their mouth no lie was found; they are blameless." Our hearts will be full of affection and courage.

I have a little book that I write confessions in. When I have been insensitive or dishonest or have acted out of pride and ego, I make note of it. Every once in a while I read the book, and it's depressing. I will never have anyone else read that book.

In heaven, I won't need the book any more. No remorse. No regret. No shame.

John says that when he saw his vision of the heaven and earth, "there was no longer any sea." What does this mean? What does God have against the sea? What about people who like to sail?

The sea, in John's day, was primarily a place of danger. He speaks of the sea one day having to give up the dead that are in it. John himself was imprisoned on an island, so the sea is what separated him from those he loved. Every day John had to look out on the water and see beyond it those whom he would give anything to be able to embrace and converse with and love. John was a prisoner of the sea.

Therefore, when John says the sea will be no more, he is saying that the day is coming when we will no longer be separated from one another. We will be delivered, not just from the physical barriers that separate us, but from the spiritual ones as well. No more abandoned children, no more broken homes, no more lonely hearts clubs. The sense of oneness that now characterizes the Trinity will finally be ours as well.

John says that every tear will be wiped from every eye. There will be no more death or mourning or crying or pain, for the old order will have passed away. Love will triumph.

After many years as a college president, Robert McQuilken resigned his position to care for his wife, Muriel, who had developed Alzheimer's disease. He writes of how much she taught him, even with the disease. She always loved to pick flowers; when her memory began to erode, she would pick them inside the house, too. Someone had given them an Easter lily—two stems with four or five flowers on each. She cut off one of the stems. Robert did the irrational thing, told her how disappointed he was, and asked her please not to cut the other stem. The next day he was telling this story to his son, explaining how badly he felt for rebuking Muriel when she could neither understand nor remember. While they were talking, Muriel came out with the other stem—which she had just cut—and placed it at Robert's feet. "Thank you," he said simply.

"You're doing better, Dad," his son said.

Robert describes how Muriel became increasingly confused and would say yes when she meant no. The time came when she could no longer make sentences—except for one. There was only one sentence left, and she said it often: "I love you."

When Robert left for work, although he had hired a companion to stay home with her, Muriel would often go after him. The walk to school was a mile roundtrip; she would sometimes make it ten times a day. Sometimes at night, when he helped Muriel get ready for bed, Robert would find her feet bruised and bloodied. When he told their family doctor, the doctor choked up. "Such love" was all he could say.

Robert read a newspaper columnist's response to a letter writer who had ended a relationship because "it wasn't meeting my needs." The columnist responded, "Do you still have the same needs? What would he have to do to fulfill them: needs for communication, common interests, sexual fulfillment. If the needs are not met. . . ."

Robert reflected on the eerie irrelevance of every one of those criteria for him.

> Eventually he decided that he could not remain president of his college and care for Muriel. When the time came, the decision was firm. It took no great calculation. . . . "Had I not promised, forty-two years before, 'in sickness and in health . . . till death do us part'?
>
> "I have been startled by the response to the announcement of my resignation," he writes. Husbands and wives renew marriage vows, pastors tell the story to their congregations. It was a mystery to me, until a distinguished oncologist, who lives constantly with dying people, told me, 'Almost all women stand by their men; very few men stand by their women.'
>
> "It is more than keeping promises and being fair, though. As I watch her brave descent into oblivion, Muriel is the joy of my life."

Such love is the heart of community. God's promise is that one day this love will be redeemed. There will be no more anguish, no more "brave descent into oblivion." Alzheimer's and death will not have the last word. There will be only joy.

The End of Community

Note one more thing about heaven: It is the only place where community is fully available. John uses much different images to speak of the reality of hell. For instance, he says hell is a place where the smoke of their torment "goes up for ever and ever."

Smoke is one of John's recurring images of spiritual reality. This expression appears a number of times in the Old Testament. It was the image of a conquered city that has been burned; from a distance we can see the smoke of the wreckage rising into the sky.

When we see this, we may think, *Once there were homes and shops and schools. Children played, people fell in love, neighbors cared for each other. Now all that is gone.*

The rising smoke is an image of the utter loss of community. I mention this because sometimes people say, "I wouldn't mind hell—all my buddies will be there. At least we'll be together." They picture hell like a giant bowling alley where it's always "Miller time."

Huckleberry Finn said that he was taught heaven would be a place where "all a body would have to do was go around all day long with a harp and sing, forever and ever." He knew he wasn't interested in such an arrangement. So when he was told that Tom Sawyer was not headed for heaven either, Huck responded, "I was glad about that, because I wanted him and me to be together."

But this is not the picture of John's vision. For John, all the things that make community possible—humility, servanthood, civility, honesty, generosity—are gifts of God.

To reject God is to reject everything that makes community possible.

Just as heaven involves images like streets of gold and pearly gates to reflect the perfect community, perfect oneness, so the image of hell is the exact opposite, the image of a destroyed city, the end of all community.

Imagine being so locked up in your own pride and self-centeredness that you become incapable of relationship. You never know the joy of friendship, the goodness of serving and being served, the embrace of a loving heart.

In *The Great Divorce*, C. S. Lewis pictures hell as a lonely, gray town trapped in twilight, where the houses are built at a huge distance from one another, yet people are continually moving farther away from each other.

And the smoke of their torment goes up forever and ever.

Heaven Is a Person

The loss of community is not God's intent. He is building a community of blessed life, and he will be its primary sustainer and most glorious inhabitant.

And we will see him.

Trapped on the island of Patmos, John has a vision of the throne room of heaven. It is a strange vision of one "like a son of man," with hair that is white like wool, eyes that blaze like fire, a double-edged sword coming out of his mouth, and hands holding the stars of the churches and the keys to death and Hades.

John falls down before the person's feet as though dead, and the "son of man"—who is, indeed, the Son of Man—touches him with his right hand and says, "Do not be afraid. I am the First and the Last. I am the Living One; I was dead, and behold I am alive for ever and ever!"

John says that the figure has white hair. In our day, white hair is something to be avoided as a sign of aging and infirmity. The only thing worse than having white hair is having no hair at all!

But the Bible has a different view. The writer of Proverbs says that "gray hair is a crown of splendor; it is attained by a righteous life."

(That proverb is becoming one of my personal favorites as the years go by.)

The loss of community is not God's intent. He is building a community of blessed life, and he will be its primary sustainer and most glorious inhabitant.

God has all the wisdom we associate with age, except that he is eternal. Yet, one day all the wisdom he has will be put at our disposal. We will never again say a foolish word or make a wrong decision. We will be guided by pure wisdom.

The Son of Man also holds seven stars in his hand. His *right* hand. This means the figure is ready for action. The right side was considered most noble. That is why a powerful man was called the right-hand man of a king and why a soldier with a sword in his right hand was ready to fight.

You may be left-handed, and you don't like that. Too bad! Jesus was right-handed.

The stars are associated with the messengers, or angels, of the churches to whom John is writing: John is saying that the churches are perfectly safe in the hand of God.

The Son of Man also has eyes like a flame of fire. Certain pairs of eyes cause us to behave differently when they are focused on us. Where does a mother have eyes? In the back of her head. She seems to see and know everything we do. The eyes of God are constantly watching. They miss nothing.

The man has a sword sticking out of his mouth. This is a strange image to us. It does not mean that when we see Jesus one day, he will have a blade between his lips. In John's day, a sword was the symbol of power. To have a sword coming from the mouth is a way of saying that the word of the Son of Man carries unopposable authority. He speaks, and it is so.

This is why John gives this person that great title "the ruler of the kings of the earth." In our day, we experience separate spheres of power: political, economic, cultural, and so on. In Jesus' day, kings held all the power. And Jesus is the ruler over the kings.

To put it in our terms, think of all the holders of power in every sphere in our day—all the movers and shakers and opinion molders. Jesus is ruler over them all, whether they know it or not. Jesus is ruler over presidents and prime ministers, over statesmen and party hacks. He is ruler over Democrats and Republicans. But he is also ruler over Bill Gates and Donald Trump, over Dan Rather and Peter Jennings, over Oprah and Big Bird.

Jesus is ruler over Harvard and Oxford and Texas A & M. He is ruler over Bruce Springsteen, Steven Speilberg, and Madonna. He is ruler over Madison Avenue and Wall Street, over 1600 Pennsylvania Avenue and Hollywood Boulevard.

These people and powers may not realize now that Jesus is ruler, but the day is coming when they will—maybe today, maybe tomorrow—but it is coming. On that day, "every knee will bow"—even the most proud and stubborn. Every tongue will "confess that Jesus Christ is Lord"—Lord of Lords and ruler of the kings of the earth.

This is the holy, transcendent, awe-inspiring figure John sees in his vision. And then things get very serious.

John says that when he saw this figure, he "fell at his feet as though dead." No wonder! He is overcome by the distance that separates a sinful human being from a holy God. John falls at Jesus' feet in awe, wonder, fear, and utter surrender. He is undone.

Then comes one of the most wonderful moments in Scripture.

John says, "He placed his right hand on me."

Imagine falling as if dead at Jesus' feet and having him take that all-powerful right hand, empty now, and place it on your shoulder.

"Don't be afraid," he says. "I'm the one you saw who died, yet lives."

Richard Mouw, the president of Fuller Seminary and a professor of philosophy, gave an unforgettable parable about this scene. It took place when he was in kindergarten, long before he became a philosopher.

One day in December a visitor came to kindergarten. He was wearing a big red suit with a splendid sash. His head and his hair were as white as snow, and on his feet were boots as black as coal. His voice was "like the sound of rushing waters": Ho! Ho! Ho!

"I'm here to see who's been naughty and who's been nice, how you've behaved. Who will come tell me what they want?"

These five-year-old kids were terrified. Santa stood in the midst of them, the glory of Santa shown round about them, and they were sore afraid. No one moved.

The teacher was a little embarrassed. She did not understand why no one was volunteering for the great white throne judgment.

Finally Santa looked at five-year-old Rich Mouw. "Come sit in Santa's lap," he ordered. Rich didn't know why he was chosen, but he walked as slowly as he could to the front of the room.

What Rich didn't know was that Santa was actually a man from Rich's church, a man named Mr. Cooper. Rich already knew him and, in fact, liked him a lot.

Santa felt Rich's fear. Santa pulled back his beard. He put his other hand on Rich's shoulder. Quietly, so no one else could hear, he said: "Hey, Richard, don't be afraid. It's me—Mr. Cooper. You already know me. I'm your old friend. It's okay. Don't be afraid."

It is no wonder that the apostle John said he fell at Jesus' feet as if he were a dead man. No human being in his right mind could do anything else. And then John feels a hand on his shoulder.

"Hey, John, don't be afraid. It's me! Jesus! The one you loved. You already know me. I'm your old friend. Don't be afraid." The Son of Man, the Ancient of Days, the Alpha and the Omega, the First and the Last, the ruler of the kings of the earth, the one who went to the cross. It's me! It's Jesus!

"By the way, do you remember death and Hades? The ultimate enemy of humankind that have kept them locked in a prison of fear and aloneness from their birth? Here are the keys. Got'em from my dad. No one who follows me is going to be trapped by death—not one of my friends. I've got the keys. Death? It's no big deal. I've been dead, and it hasn't slowed me down at all."

The Ultimate Wedding

There is one more image from John we want to look at. Not only will we see God, John says, but we will also experience the joy of a wedding. The pleasure we enjoy on earth in the wedding of a bride and groom who are ecstatically in love is but a dim echo of the joy we will know in heaven when Jesus and his church finally know perfect community. "Blessed are those who are invited to the wedding supper of the Lamb!"

Our first two children were girls. When they were very young, they were quite sure they wanted to live in our home forever. Leaving sounded awful. They would sometimes ask, "When I grow up, can I still live here with you and Mommy?" It was no use trying to tell them that the day would come when they would want to leave. Not that home isn't wonderful, but the day would come when they would be grown-up.

Perhaps they would fall in love and want to have their own home and family. It wasn't any use telling them such things, because they simply could not believe that there would ever be a man in their life whom they would think of as bigger or smarter or more handsome (they were *very* small) or whom they could love as much as they loved their daddy. They just couldn't believe it. And frankly, it sounded a little far-fetched to me.

The One whom we glimpse now only through a glass darkly we will experience face-to-face, and we will gasp at his beauty, and we will know that this is our destiny. We were meant for him.

In spite of that, *I* knew that the day would come—not today, not tomorrow, but someday—when they would be all grown-up. Somewhere, somehow, the day would come when they would see ... him. Then they would understand. What they saw "through a glass, darkly," they would then see "face to face." And my little girl would come to me and say in the way grown-up girls do, "Daddy, he is my destiny. I was meant for him. And I must be with him. I can't imagine life without him." Being a very wise daddy, then, if the man is good enough and kind enough, and if my daughter is old enough (say, forty-five), I would say, "This is the moment! This is the union about which I prayed since before you were born. Enter into life, love, and joy."

The Bible says that the kingdom of heaven is the story of a groom who awaits his bride. Right now you may not want to leave this place. But the day will come—maybe not today, maybe not tomorrow, but the day will come—when we will be fully grown. And we will see him. And then we will understand. Then the One whom we glimpse now only through a glass darkly we will experience face-to-face, and we will gasp at his beauty, and we will know that this is our destiny. We were meant for him.

You will know, as surely as you sit there reading this now, that you must be with him, that life would be nothing without him. Being a very wise groom he will say, "This is the moment. This is the union I have longed for since before you were born. Enter into eternal life, love, and joy."

Then no one will be lonely. No one will be alone. No one will be foolish or fallen or do anything they regret.

Then, finally, the human race will no longer be the "as-is" department of the universe. Then, for the first time since Eden, everyone will be the person God intended them to be. Then we will discover that what we call the end of our lives is not the end at all; it is only the beginning of Chapter One of the Great Story, which no one on earth has read, which goes on forever, in which every chapter is better than the one before.

And we will all be normal at last.

Learning to Dance

1. What have been "the most exciting five minutes of your life" so far?
2. Where did you get your earliest ideas about heaven?
3. Has the thought of eternity in heaven ever seemed as if it might get a little boring for you? Why or why not?
4. If you were able to go to heaven right now, would you? Should a person desire that?
5. How does thinking about the reality of heaven affect the way you live this day?
6. In past centuries, people used to sometimes meditate on the reality of death. One way to do that is to think about what will be said at your funeral or written in your obituary. Take some time to reflect or write on this. What is the legacy you would like to leave?
7. What changes are you most looking forward to about the kind of person you will be in heaven? Why not ask God to start making those changes in you now?

SOURCES

Chapter 1: The Porcupine's Dilemma

13: Dallas Willard, *The Renovation of the Heart*. Colorado Springs: NavPress, 2002, 189.

13: Henri Nouwen, "Moving from Solitude to Community to Ministry," *Leadership Journal*, Spring 1995, 83.

14–15: Dietrich Bonhoeffer, *Life Together.* Trans. Daniel Bloesch and James Burtness. Minneapolis: Fortress Press, 1996, 9.

15: "All we like sheep": Isaiah 53:6 KJV.

15: "For all have sinned": Romans 3:23.

17: "There is almost no one": Martin Seligman and David Rosenham, *Abnormality*. New York: W. W. Norton, 1998, 17.

17–18: Neil Plantinga, *Engaging God's World*. Grand Rapids: Eerdmans, 2001, 52.

19: Jane Howard: Quoted in the *Franklin-Covey Day Planner* for February 1, 2002.

19: Willard, *Renovation of the Heart*, 179.

19: Edward Hallowell, *Connect*. New York: Simon & Schuster, 1999.

19: Neil Plantinga, *Not the Way It's Supposed to Be*. Grand Rapids: Eerdmans, 1995, 10.

21: Bonhoeffer, *Life Together*, 82.

21: Ibid., 83.

21: Rene Spitz: Cited in Hallowell, *Connect*, 133.

21: "Irritable back": See entry on porcupines in J. O. Whitaker, *National Audubon Society Field Guide to North American Mammals*. New York: Alfred E. Knopf, 1996.

23: Miroslav Volf, *Exclusion and Embrace*. Nashville: Abingdon Press, 1996, 111.
23: "While they were in the field": Genesis 4:8.
23: Newspaper account: *Chicago Tribune*, Sunday, 28 April 20002, section 1, 1.
23: "I heard you in the garden": Genesis 3:10.
24: Willard, *Renovation of the Heart*, 182.
25: David Costello, *The World of the Porcupine*. New York: J. B. Lippincott, 1966.

Chapter 2: The Wonder of Oneness

27: Dallas Willard: Unpublished study guide quoted in Richard Foster, *The Celebration of Discipline*. San Francisco: Harper & Row, 1979, 162.
27: Martin Buber, *I and Thou:* Quoted in James Edwards, *The Divine Intruder*. Colorado Springs: NavPress, 2000, 14.
27: Suzy Becker, *The All Better Book*. New York: Workman, 1992, 42.
28: Jean Elshtain, "Everything for Sale," in *Books & Culture* (May/June 1998): 9.
29: Marla Paul: Cited in Lee Strobel, *God's Outrageous Claims*. Grand Rapids: Zondervan, 1997, 118–20.
29: 90 percent: Alan Loy McGinnis, *The Friendship Factor*. Minneapolis: Augsburg Press, 1979, 11.
29: Jacqueline Olds: Cited in Alice Kelly, "Are You Lonely?" *Shape* (April 2001): 108–12.
30: Jean Vanier, *Community and Growth*. New York: Paulist Press, 1989, 140.
30: Albert Schweitzer: Quoted in Leo Buscaglia, *Love*. New York: Ballantine Books, 1994, 17.
30: Edward Hallowell, *Connect*. New York: Simon & Schuster, 1999, xii.
31: "And God said": Various verses of Genesis 1, in various translations.
32: Vanier, *Community and Growth*, 58.

33: Robert Putnam, *Bowling Alone*. New York: Simon & Schuster, 2000, 331.
33: Study on the common cold: For more information on these and other studies, see Hallowell, *Connect*, chapter 1, and especially Putnam, *Bowling Alone*, 492–94.
34: Willard: Quoted in Foster, *The Celebration of Discipline*, 162.
35: Miroslav Volf, *Exclusion and Embrace*. Nashville: Abingdon Press, 1996, 127.
35: "The Father is in me": John 10:38 NRSV.
36: Larry Crabb, *Connecting: Healing for Ourselves and Our Relationships*. Dallas: Word, 1997, xi.
37: Dallas Willard, *The Renovation of the Heart*. Colorado Springs: NavPress, 2002, 180.
37: "The Spirit comes in the Son's name": See John 14:26–16:13.
37: Frederick Dale Bruner, *Holy Spirit: Shy Member of the Trinity*. Eugene, OR: Wipf & Stock, 2001, 10.
38: "If I glorify myself": John 8:54.
38: He came not to be served: See Mark 10:45.
38: He submitted to the Spirit: See Mark 1:10–12.
38: "Not my will, but yours": Luke 22:42.
38: "This is my priceless son": See Matthew 3:17; 17:5.
38: Bruner, *Holy Spirit*, 12.
38: Dallas Willard, *The Divine Conspiracy*. San Francisco: HarperSanFrancisco, 1998, 318.
39: Neil Plantinga, *Engaging God's World*. Grand Rapids: Eerdmans, 2001, 20.
39: "In the image of God": Genesis 1:27 NRSV.
40: "My prayer is not for them alone": John 17:20–21.
40: "Where two or three are gathered": Matthew 18:20 KJV.
41: Brennan Manning, *The Wisdom of Tenderness*. San Francisco: HarperSanFrancisco, 2002, 25–26.
42: "Make every effort": Ephesians 4:3.
42: Markus Barth, Ephesians 4–6, Anchor Bible, vol. 34A (New York: Doubleday, 1974), 67.
42: What John wrote: See 1 John 4:20 for example.

42: Anne Lamott, *Bird by Bird: Some Instructions on Writing and Life*. New York: Doubleday/Anchor, 1994, 121.

Chapter 3: The Fellowship of the Mat: True Friendship

44: Aristotle, *Nichomaceian Ethics*. Trans. Martin Ostwald. Indianapolis: Bobbs-Merrill, 1962, 1155a5.

44: Yogi Berra: Quoted in Robert Putnam, *Bowling Alone*. New York: Simon & Schuster, 2000, 20.

45: Quickly kill: See Robert Gundry, *Mark: A Commentary on His Apology for the Cross*. Grand Rapids: Eerdmans, 1993, 110ff.

45: "Rabbi, who sinned": John 9:2.

46: Alan Loy McGinnis, *The Friendship Factor*. Minneapolis: Augsburg Press, 1979.

46: "They met together daily": Paraphrase of Acts 2:46.

48: Jean Vanier, *Community and Growth*. New York: Paulist Press, 1989, 47.

49: "There was no room left": Mark 2:2.

51: Dolores Curren, *Traits of a Healthy Family*. New York: Ballantine, 1983, 41.

51: Robert Putnam, *Bowling Alone*. New York: Simon & Schuster, 2000, 231, emphasis his.

51: Lewis Smedes: Personal communication.

52: Urie Bronfenbrenner: Quoted in Curren, *Traits of a Healthy Family*, 71.

52: Henry Cloud: Henry Cloud and John Townsend, *How People Grow*. Grand Rapids: Zondervan, 2001, 129–30.

53: "Child, your sins are forgiven": Paraphrase of Mark 2:5.

54: Harry Stack Sullivan: Personal communication from psychologist David Brokaw.

54: Vanier, *Community and Growth*, 102.

56: "Son, your sins are forgiven": Mark 2:5.

56: Fyodor Dostoyevsky, *The Brothers Karamazov*. Trans. David Magarshack. New York, Penguin Books, 1958, 63.

56: Vanier, *Community and Growth*, 26.

56: Paul Wadell, *Becoming Friends*. Grand Rapids: Brazos Press, 2002, 106.

59: Dallas Willard, *The Divine Conspiracy*. San Francisco: HarperSanFrancisco, 1998, 243.
59: "Do not judge": Matthew 7:1.
59: "If you forgive others": Matthew 6:14–15 TNIV.
59: "Those who do not love their brother": 1 John 4:20 TNIV.
61: "Where two or three are gathered": Matthew 18:20 KJV.

Chapter 4: Unveiled Faces: Authenticity

65: Dietrich Bonhoeffer, *Life Together*. New York: Harper & Row, 1954, 112.
66: Robert Karen, *Becoming Attached*. New York: Oxford University Press, 1998, 5ff.
66: Paul Tournier, *The Meaning of Persons*. New York: Harper & Row, 1957, 138.
66: Jan Yager, *Friendshifts*. Stamford, CT: Hannacroix Creek Books, 1999, 192.
66: "In the cool of the day": Genesis 3:8.
67: Tim Alan Gardner, *Sacred Sex: A Spiritual Celebration of Oneness in Marriage*. Colorado Springs: Waterbrook Press, 2002, 56.
67: "They were both naked": Genesis 2:25 KJV.
69: "Did God really say": Genesis 3:1.
69: "God did say": Genesis 3:3.
70: "She also gave some": Genesis 3:6.
70: "The eyes of both were opened." Genesis 3:7 NRSV.
70: Fig leaves: See Genesis 3:7.
72: Rainer Marie Rilke in a letter to Paula Modersohn-Becker, 12 February 2002: Quoted in McGinnis, *The Friendship Factor*. Minneapolis: Augsburg Press, 1979.
72: "If I make my bed in Sheol": Psalm 139:8 NRSV.
73: Dallas Willard, *The Divine Conspiracy*. San Francisco: HarperSanFrancisco, 1998, 323.
73: "I heard you": Genesis 3:10.
73: "The woman you put here": Genesis 3:12.
73: "Bone of my bones": Genesis 2:23.
74: "Glad and sincere hearts": Acts 2:46.

75: Neil Plantinga: For a helpful discussion about ethical dilemmas, see Neil Plantinga, *Not the Way It's Supposed to Be*. Grand Rapids: Eerdmans, 1995, 14.
75: "A gossip can never keep a secret": Paraphrase of Proverbs 20:19.
77: Moses' meeting with God: 2 Corinthians 3:12–18 based on Exodus 33:18–23; 34:29–35.
77: "Put a veil over his face": 2 Corinthians 3:13.
78: Richard Foster, *The Celebration of Discipline*. San Francisco: Harper & Row, 1979, 126.
79: Tournier, *The Meaning of Persons*, 142.
80: McGinnis, *The Friendship Factor*, 28.
80: Sidney Jourard, *The Transparent Self*. New York: Litton Educational Publishing, 1971, 18.
81: Aelred of Rievaulx: *Spiritual Friendship*, Book 1. Cranbury, NJ: Associated University Presses, 1994.
81: McGinnis, *The Friendship Factor*, 37.
81: "My soul is overwhelmed": Mark 14:34.
81: "No longer do I call you": John 15:15 NKJV.
82: Timothy Jones, *Finding a Spiritual Friend*. Nashville: Upper Room, 1998.
82: James Pennebaker: Quoted by Jones, *Finding a Spiritual Friend*, 33–34.
82: "Confess your faults": James 5:16 KJV.
83: Bonhoeffer, *Life Together*, 113.
83: *Ibid. See the chapter entitled "Confession" for a broader discussion.*
85: Ibid., 112.

Chapter 5: Put Down Your Stones: Acceptance

88: Dorothy Day: Quoted in Philip Yancey, *What's So Amazing About Grace?* Grand Rapids: Zondervan, 1997, 158.
88: Anne Lamott, *Bird by Bird: Some Instructions on Writing and Life*. New York: Doubleday/Anchor, New York, 1994, 22.
89: "Accept one another": Romans 15:7.
90: "My great-aunt": Deborah Tannen, *You Just Don't Understand*. Harlingen, TX: Quill, 2001, 172.
93: "One witness is not enough": Deuteronomy 19:15.

94–95:C. S. Lewis, *Mere Christianity*. 1952; reprint, New York: HarperCollins/Signature Classics Edition, 2002, 94–95.

97: Yancey, *What's So Amazing About Grace?* Grand Rapids: Zondervan, 1997, 11.

98: "Go ahead and throw your stone": Based on John 8:7.

99: Philip Yancey, *The Jesus I Never Knew*. Grand Rapids: Zondervan, 1995, see chapter 8.

99: Dallas Willard, *The Divine Conspiracy*. San Francisco: HarperSanFrancisco, 1998, 226–27.

99: "No condemnation": Romans 8:1.

99: "If God is for us": Romans 8:31.

100: C. S. Lewis, *The Four Loves*. 1958; reprint, New York: HarperCollins/Signature Classics Edition, 2002, 42–43.

100: Dorothy Bass and Craig Dykstra, eds., *Practicing Our Faith*. San Francisco: Jossey-Bass, 1997. See the chapter on keeping the Sabbath.

100: Paul Tournier: Quoted in Alan Loy McGinnis, *The Friendship Factor*. Minneapolis: Augsburg Press, 1979, 72.

101: Bertrand Russell: Quoted in the *Franklin-Covey Day Planner* for February 3, 2002.

102: "Where are all the stone throwers?": Paraphrase of John 8:10.

102: "Go, and sin no more": John 8:11 KJV.

102: Jean Vanier, *Community and Growth*. New York: Paulist Press, 1989, 47.

103: Willard, *The Divine Conspiracy*, 225.

103: Kenneth Bailey, "The Lady's Not for Stoning," *Presbyterian Outlook* (April 1999): 17.

Chapter 6: The Art of Reading People: Empathy

105: Robert Frost, "How hard it is to keep from being king when it's in you and in the situation," in *The Poetry of Robert Frost*. New York: Holt, Rinehart and Winston, 1969, 456.

106: Ken Davis, *Lighten Up!: Great Stories from One of America's Greatest Storytellers*. Grand Rapids: Zondervan, 2000, 96.

107: "The lamp of the LORD": Proverbs 20:27, U.K. edition of the NIV.

107: "You have searched me": Psalm 139:1–3.
108: "His face was downcast": Genesis 4:5.
108: Dallas Willard, *Renovation of the Heart*. Colorado Springs: NavPress, 2002, 162.
108: Daniel Stern: Cited in Daniel Goleman, *Emotional Intelligence*. New York: Bantam Books, 1995, chapter 6.
109: David Givens, *The Nonverbal Dictionary of Gestures, Signs, and Body Language Cues*. Spokane, WA: Center for Nonverbal Studies Press, 2001.
111: "When words are many": Proverbs 10:19.
111: Bill Hybels, *Making Life Work*. Downers Grove, IL: InterVarsity Press, 1998, chapter entitled "Speak Truth."
111: William Backus and Marie Chapian, *Telling Yourself the Truth*. Minneapolis: Bethany House, 2000, 6.
112: Henri Nouwen, *The Way of the Heart: Desert Spirituality and Contemporary Ministry*. New York: HarperCollins, 1991, 43.
112: "A word aptly spoken": Proverbs 25:11.
112: "Quick to listen": James 1:19.
112: Daniel Goleman, *Working with Emotional Intelligence*. New York: Bantam Books, 1995, 176.
113: Zacchaeus: Luke 19:1–10.
113: Paralytic at the pool: John 5:1–15.
113: "A cheerful look brings joy": Proverbs 15:30.
113: W. H. Auden: Sources on the Internet.
115: "Praise the LORD!": Psalm 150:1 NRSV.
116: "The Effect of a Pratfall on Increasing Interpersonal Attractiveness": Article by E. Aaronson, B. Willerman, and J. Floyd in *Psychometric Science* 4 (1966).
117: Goleman, *Working with Emotional Intelligence*, 165.
118: Anne Lamott, *Bird by Bird: Some Instructions on Writing and Life*. New York: Doubleday/Anchor, 1994, 50.
119: "I stand at the door": Revelation 3:20 TNIV.
120: "What were you arguing about?": See Mark 9:16, 33.
121: "A word aptly spoken": Proverbs 25:11.

Chapter 7: Community Is Worth Fighting For: Conflict

125: Jean Vanier, *Community and Growth*. New York: Paulist Press, 1989, 120–21.
127: "Greater love hath no man": John 13:15 KJV.
127: "During the war in Vietnam": See Neil Warren, *Make Anger Your Ally*. New York: Doubleday, 1985.
128: "As you, Father, are in me": John 17:21 NRSV.
128: "You are still worldly": 1 Corinthians 3:3.
129: Causes of anger: Carol Tavris, *Anger: The Misunderstood Emotion*. New York: Simon & Schuster, 1982.
129: Robert V. Levine, *A Geography of Time:* New York: Basic Books, 1998.
129: "If your brother or sister sins": Matthew 18:15, U.K. edition of the NIV.
131: Take the first step: See Matthew 5:23–24.
133: The Jim Carrey effect: Based on the movie *Dumb and Dumber*.
133: Warren, *Make Anger Your Ally*, 168.
133: "People with a hot temper": Proverbs 14:17 GNB.
134: Ken Davis: In a talk at Willow Creek Church.
135: "Be angry but do not sin": Ephesians 4:26 NRSV.
136: "Finally, brothers and sisters, whatever": Philippians 4:8 TNIV.
137: The Greek-speaking members: Acts 6:1.
137: Ananias and Sapphira: Acts 5:1–11.
137: Paul and Barnabas: Acts 15:37–40.
138: "I plead . . .": Philippians 4:2.
138: "Contended at my side": Philippians 4:3.
138: Tavris, *Anger*, 132–33.
139: 33,000 denominations: *Newsweek*, April 16, 2001, 49.
139: "Be brought to complete unity": John 17:23.
140: "Both the observation of": Howard Kassinove, ed., *Anger Disorders*. Washington, DC: Taylor & Francis, 1992.
141: Tavris, *Anger*, 121.
141: Research on anger: Kassinove, *Anger Disorders*.
142: "Show him his fault": Matthew 18:15.
143: "If he listens to you": Matthew 18:15.

Chapter 8: Spiritual Surgery: Forgiveness

149: Lewis Smedes, *How Can It Be All Right When Everything's All Wrong?* San Francisco: HarperSanFrancisco, 1992, 43.

149: Beth Kephart, *Into the Tangle of Friendship*. Boston: Houghton Mifflin, 2000, 6–7.

151: Lamech: Genesis 4:23–24.

151: "The LORD was grieved": Genesis 6:6.

152: Peter: See Matthew 18:21.

152: "I tell you, not seven times": Matthew 18:22.

153: The CEO and the Embezzler: See Matthew 18:21–27.

157: Lewis Smedes, *Forgive and Forget*. San Francisco: Harper & Row, 1984.

158: "Those who write about ethics": See L. Gregory Jones, *Embodying Forgiveness: A Theological Analysis*. Grand Rapids: Eerdmans, 1995, for an opposing view on forgiveness.

158: C. S. Lewis on forgiveness: C. S. Lewis, *Letters to Malcolm, Chiefly on Prayer*. 1964; reprint, New York: HarperCollins/Signature Classics Edition, 2002, 137–38.

159: "Will the Bloods ever?": Lewis Smedes, *The Art of Forgiving*. Nashville: Moorings, 1996, p. 57.

161: "The ministry of reconciliation": 2 Corinthians 5:18.

161: Garrison Keillor, *Leaving Home*. New York: Viking, 1987, 155–57.

161: "Cup of Cold Water" debate: See Matthew 10:42.

164: Act II: See Matthew 18:28–30.

165: Charles Williams, *The Forgiveness of Sins*. Grand Rapids: Eerdmans, 1984, 66.

165: Study in *Journal of Adult Development:* Cited in *Christian Century* (January 2–9, 2002): 15.

165: Frederich Buechner, *Wishful Thinking*. New York: Harper & Row, 1973, 2.

166: Anne Lamott, *Traveling Mercies*. New York: Doubleday/Anchor, 2000, 128, 134.

167: Epilogue: See Matthew 18:31–35.

167: "This is how my heavenly father": Matthew 18:35.

Chapter 9: The Gift Nobody Wants: Confrontation

169: Dietrich Bonhoeffer, *Life Together*. Trans. Daniel Bloesch and James Burtness. Minneapolis: Fortress Press, 1996, 105.

170: Ken Davis, *Lighten Up!: Great Stories from One of America's Greatest Storytellers*. Grand Rapids: Zondervan, 2000, 43.

171: Neil Plantinga, *Not the Way It's Supposed to Be*. Grand Rapids: Eerdmans, 1995, 105.

172: "You will know the truth": John 8:32.

172: Bonhoeffer, *Life Together*, 105, emphasis mine.

172: William Paulson: quoted in Marjorie Thompson, *Soul Feast*. Louisville: Westminster John Knox Press, 1995, 137.

173: David Watson, *Covenant Discipleship*. Nashville: Discipleship Resources, 1996, 17.

173: Ibid., 55–56.

174: M. Scott Peck, *The Road Less Traveled*. New York: Simon & Schuster, 1978, 52–53.

174: David: A Story of Life: See 2 Samuel 11.

175: "Isn't this Bathsheba": 2 Samuel 11:3.

176: "The woman conceived": 2 Samuel 11:5.

176: Gary Richmond, A View from the Zoo Series. Nashville: W Publishing Group.

178: "The LORD sent Nathan": 2 Samuel 12:1.

178: Jean Vanier, *Community and Growth*. New York: Paulist Press, 1989, 260.

179: "The man ... deserves to die!": 2 Samuel 12:5.

180: M. Scott Peck, *The Different Drum*. New York: Simon & Schuster, 1987, 87ff.

181: "Whitewashed tombs": Matthew 23:27.

182: "I have sinned against the LORD": 2 Samuel 12:13.

182: "A man after God's own heart": See 1 Samuel 13:14.

183: Patrick Morley, *The Man in the Mirror*. Grand Rapids: Zondervan, 1999, 337.

Chapter 10: Breaking Down Barriers: Inclusion

185: C. S. Lewis, "The Inner Ring" in *The Weight of Glory and Other Addresses*. New York: Macmillan, 1980, 103.

186: Miroslav Volf, *Exclusion and Embrace*. Nashville: Abingdon Press, 1996.
187: Lewis, "The Inner Ring," 996–97.
188: Groucho Marx, *Groucho and Me: The Autobiography of Groucho Marx*. New York: Simon & Schuster, 1959, chapter 26.
188: "Could we have the two seats": Paraphrase of Mark 10:37.
189: "Jesus withdrew to the region": Matthew 15:21–28.
189–190: Kenneth Bailey, "The Lady's Not for Stoning," *Presbyterian Outlook* (April 1999).
190: "Tyre and Sidon will be better off": See Matthew 11:20–24.
191: "They rebuked them.": Luke 18:15.
192: "The dividing wall of hostility": Ephesians 2:14.
192: Philip Yancey, *What's So Amazing About Grace?* Grand Rapids: Zondervan, 1997, 153.
193: "I was sent only": Matthew 15:24.
193: "He is not willing that any": See 2 Peter 3:9.
195: "I now realize how true it is": Acts 10:34–35.
195: Robert Putnam, *Bowling Alone*. New York: Simon & Schuster, 2000, 22.
196: Volf, *Exclusion and Embrace*, 72.
197: Ibid, 163.
201: "I will not let you go": Genesis 32:26.
202: "You of little faith": Matthew 14:31.

Chapter 11: The Secret of a Loving Heart: Gratitude

204: Jean Pierre de Caussade, *The Sacrament of the Present Moment*. New York: Harper & Row, 1982, 89.
206: Kenneth Bailey, *Through Peasant Eyes*. Grand Rapids: Eerdmans, 1983.
206: One day Jesus arrives at the home: See Luke 7:36–50.
207: Bailey, *Through Peasant Eyes*, 8.
208: "It is possible": Craig Evans and Stanley Porter, eds., *Dictionary of New Testament Background*. Downers Grove, IL: InterVarsity Press, 2000, 11.
210: "Two men owed money": Luke 7:41.
212: "Do you see this woman?": Luke 7:44.

212: "Make the enemy a footstool": See Hebrews 1:13; 10:13.
214: Mother Teresa: Richard Mouw, *Uncommon Decency*. Downers Grove, IL: InterVarsity Press, 1992, 153.
216: Dale Galloway: In a sermon.
217: An ancient story: Adapted from Richard Meyer, *One Anothering*, vol. 2. Philadelphia: Innisfree Press, 1999, 131.

Chapter 12: Normal at Last: Heaven

219: C. S. Lewis, *The Last Battle*. 1956; reprint, New York: HarperCollins/Signature Classics Edition, 1998, 165.
219: Garrison Keillor, *Leaving Home*. New York: Viking Press, 1987, 217.
221: "Weeping and wailing and gnashing of teeth": See Matthew 13:42, 50 KJV.
221: Mark Buchanan, *Heaven-Bent*. Unpublished manuscript, 50.
222: Neil Plantinga, *Engaging God's World*. Grand Rapids: Eerdmans, 2001, 104.
222: Smedes on heaven: He writes about this exercise in *How Can It Be All Right When Everything's All Wrong?* San Francisco: HarperSanFrancisco, 1992, 151–52.
223: "The *late* great planet earth": Hal Lindsey, *The Late Great Planet Earth*. Grand Rapids: Zondervan, 1970.
223: "Waits in eager expectation": Romans 8:19.
223: "Will be liberated from its bondage": Romans 8:20.
223: Smedes, *How Can It Be All Right*, 151.
223–224: C. S. Lewis, *The Problem of Pain*. 1940; reprint, New York: HarperCollins/Signature Classics Edition, 2002. See chapter 10, "Heaven."
224: "Blessed are the dead": Revelation 14:13.
224: "A city with streets": Revelation 21:21.
224: "In my Father's house": John 14:2 KJV.
224: Keillor, *Leaving Home*, 218.
225: "Fine linen stands for": Revelation 19:8.
226: "In their mouth no lie": Revelation 14:5 NRSV.
226: "There was no longer any sea": Revelation 21:1.
226: Every tear will be wiped: See Revelation 21:4.

226–227: "Ministry or Family," *Leadership Journal* (Spring 1991): 39–41.

228: "Goes up for ever and ever": Revelation 19:3.

228: Image of a conquered city: See Isaiah 34:10, for example.

228: Huckleberry Finn: Mark Twain, *The Adventures of Huckleberry Finn*. New York: Fawcett Columbine, 1996, 5–6.

229: C. S. Lewis, *The Great Divorce*. 1946; reprint, New York: HarperCollins/Signature Classics Edition, 2002.

229: "Like a son of man": Revelation 1:13ff.

229: "Do not be afraid": Revelation 1:17–18.

229: "Gray hair is a crown": Proverbs 16:31.

230: "The ruler of the kings": Revelation 1:5.

231: "Every knee will bow": Romans 14:11.

231: "Confess that Jesus Christ": Philippians 2:11.

231: "Fell at his feet": Revelation 1:17.

231: Richard Mouw: Personal communication.

232: "Blessed are those who are invited": Revelation 19:9.

233: "Through a glass, darkly": 1 Corinthians 13:12 KJV.

Willow Creek Association

Vision, Training, Resources for Prevailing Churches

This resource was created to serve you and to help you build a local church that prevails. It is just one of many ministry tools that are part of the Willow Creek Resources® line, published by the Willow Creek Association together with Zondervan.

The Willow Creek Association (WCA) was created in 1992 to serve a rapidly growing number of churches from across the denominational spectrum that are committed to helping unchurched people become fully devoted followers of Christ. Membership in the WCA now numbers over 10,000 Member Churches worldwide from more than ninety denominations.

The Willow Creek Association links like-minded Christian leaders with each other and with strategic vision, training, and resources in order to help them build prevailing churches designed to reach their redemptive potential. Here are some of the ways the WCA does that.

- **Prevailing Church Conference**—an annual two-and-a-half day event, held at Willow Creek Community Church in South Barrington, Illinois, to help pioneering church leaders raise up a volunteer core while discovering new and innovative ways to build prevailing churches that reach unchurched people.

- **Leadership Summit**—a once-a-year, two-and-a-half-day conference to envision and equip Christians with leadership gifts and responsibilities. Presented live at Willow Creek as well as via satellite broadcast to over sixty locations across North America, this event is designed to increase the leadership effectiveness of pastors, ministry staff, volunteer church leaders, and Christians in the marketplace.

- **Ministry-Specific Conferences**—throughout each year the WCA hosts a variety of conferences and training events—both at Willow Creek's main campus and offsite, across the U.S. and around the world—targeting church leaders in ministry-specific areas such as: evangelism, the arts, children, students, small groups, preaching and teaching, spiritual formation, spiritual gifts, raising up resources, etc.

- **Willow Creek Resources®**—to provide churches with trusted and field-tested ministry resources in such areas as leadership, evangelism, spiritual formation, spiritual gifts, small groups, stewardship, student ministry, children's ministry, the use of the arts—drama, media, contemporary music—and more. For additional information about Willow Creek Resources® call the Customer Service Center at 800-570-9812. Outside the U.S. call 847-765-0070.
- ***WillowNet***—the WCA's Internet resource service, which provides access to hundreds of transcripts of Willow Creek messages, drama scripts, songs, videos, and multimedia tools. The system allows users to sort through these elements and download them for a fee. Visit us online at www.willowcreek.com.
- ***WCA News***—a quarterly publication to inform you of the latest trends, resources, and information on WCA events from around the world.
- ***Defining Moments***—a monthly audio journal for church leaders featuring Bill Hybels and other Christian leaders discussing probing issues to help you discover biblical principles and transferable strategies to maximize your church's redemptive potential.
- ***The Exchange***—our online classified ads service to assist churches in recruiting key staff for ministry positions.
- **Member Benefits**—includes substantial discounts to WCA training events, a 20 percent discount on all Willow Creek Resources®, access to a Members-Only section on WillowNet, monthly communications, and more. Member Churches also receive special discounts and premier services through WCA's growing number of ministry partners—Select Service Providers.

For specific information about WCA membership, upcoming conferences, and other ministry services contact:

Willow Creek Association

P.O. Box 3188, Barrington, IL 60011-3188

Phone: 847-570-9812

Fax: 847-765-5046

www.willowcreek.com

The Life You've Always Wanted

Spiritual Disciplines for Ordinary People

EXPANDED EDITION

John Ortberg

What does true spiritual life really look like? What keeps you from living such a life? What can you do to pursue it? If you're tired of the status quo—if you suspect that there is more to Christianity than what you've experienced—John Ortberg points to a road of transformation and spiritual vigor that anyone can take. It is the road that leads to *The Life You've Always Wanted*.

The Christian life is about more than being forgiven, more even than making it to heaven. John Ortberg calls us back to the dynamic heart of Christianity—God's power to bring change and growth—and shows us how we can attain it ... and why we should attain it. *The Life You've Always Wanted* offers modern perspectives on the ancient path of the spiritual disciplines. Ortberg shows us that Christianity isn't a matter of externals, of outer form that gets the church stamp of approval, but of Christ's character becoming etched with ever-increasing depth into our own character.

As with a marathon runner, the secret lies not in trying harder, but in training consistently. Hence the spiritual disciplines. They're neither taskmasters nor an end in themselves. They're exercises that strengthen our endurance race down the road of growth. As we continue down that road, we'll see the signposts of joy, peace, and kindness, and all the hallmarks of a faith that's vital, real, and growing.

Paved with humor and sparkling anecdotes, *The Life You've Always Wanted* is an encouraging and challenging approach to a Christian life that's worth living. Life on the edge that fills our ordinary world with new meaning, hope, change, and a joyous, growing closeness to Christ.

Pick up a copy today at your favorite bookstore!

Hardcover 0-310-24695-4
Unabridged Audio Pages® CD 0-310-24805-1
Unabridged Audio Pages® Cassette 0-310-24806-X

Love Beyond Reason

Moving God's Love from Your Head to Your Heart

John Ortberg

"Pandy" was only a child's rag doll—one arm missing, the stuffing pulled out of her. But in the eyes of the small girl who loved her, she was priceless.

In *Love Beyond Reason*, John Ortberg reveals the God you've longed to encounter—a Father head-over-heels in love with you, his child, and intensely committed to your highest joy. Ortberg takes you to the very core of God's being to discover a burning, passionate love that gives, and gives, and gives. He explores the life-changing ways this love has expressed itself through Jesus. And he shows how you, like Jesus, can love your mate, your family, your friends, and the world around you with the same practical transforming love.

Using powerful and moving illustrations Ortberg demonstrates the different characteristics of love—how it ...

- hears the heart
- delights in giving second chances
- balances gentleness and firmness
- chooses the beloved
- touches the untouchable
- teaches with wisdom
- walks in grace
- searches for those in hiding

... and walks in the kind of humility that, in the person of Jesus, willingly descended from the heights to don the rags of our rag-doll humanity.

John Ortberg pulls back the curtains of misconception to reveal what you've always hoped and always known had to be true; God's love really is a *Love Beyond Reason*. And it's waiting to flood your life with a grace that can transform you and those around you.

Pick up a copy today at your favorite bookstore!

Hardcover 0-310-21215-4
Softcover 0-310-23449-2

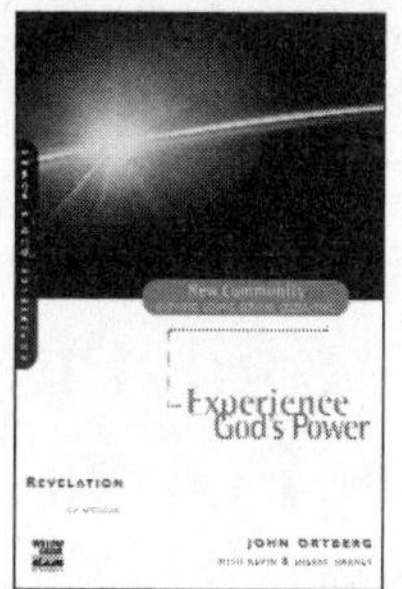

Continue building your new community!

New Community Series

Bill Hybels and John Ortberg with Kevin and Sherry Harney

If you appreciate not having to choose between Bible study and building community, then you'll want to explore all eight ***New Community*** Bible study guides. Delve deeply into Scripture in a way that strengthens relationships. Challenging questions will encourage your group members to reflect not only on Scripture but also on the old idea of community done in a new, culturally relevant way.

Each guide contains six transforming sessions—filled with prayer, insight, intimacy, and action—to help your small group members line up their lives and relationships more closely with the Bible's model for the church.

Exodus: *Journey Toward God* 0-310-22771-2
Parables: *Imagine Life God's Way* 0-310-22881-6
Sermon on the Mount[1]: *Connect with God* 0-310-22884-0
Sermon on the Mount[2]: *Connect with Others* 0-310-22883-2
Acts: *Build Community* 0-310-22770-4
Romans: *Find Freedom* 0-310-22765-8
Philippians: *Run the Race* 0-310-22766-6
Colossians: *Discover the New You* 0-310-22769-0
James: *Live Wisely* 0-310-22767-4
1 Peter: *Stand Strong* 0-310-22773-9
1 John: *Love Each Other* 0-310-22768-2
Revelation: *Experience God's Power* 0-310-22882-4

Look for New Community at your local Christian bookstore.

GRAND RAPIDS, MICHIGAN 49530 USA
WWW.ZONDERVAN.COM

www.willowcreek.com

www.biblestudyguides.com